AF605336

GREEN and GOLD COOKERY BOOK

Containing tried and tested recipes, contributed by experienced housewives and cookery experts

Preface

In 1999, we celebrate the 75th Anniversary of King's College. By chance, it is also the 25th Anniversary of the foundation of Pembroke School, the product of King's happy marriage with Girton Girls' School. What better time, therefore, to re-publish the famous *Green and Gold Cookery Book*, a mainstay on kitchen shelves since 1923.

This wonderful cookbook still fulfils its two original purposes: that is, to provide funds for a worthy school (now Pembroke), and to provide splendid and established recipes, tried and true, for its many purchasers. The book is a trusted friend and can be found in kitchens all over Australia.

This new edition has a metric conversion table, but otherwise, it is essentially untouched in other ways. Its original authors and the main contributors of recipes would be proud, and perhaps surprised, to see that their book still has such valued currency!

Malcolm Lamb
Principal, Pembroke School

• • •

Preface to 31st Edition

When in 1923 I suggest to the late Mesdames C.R. Morris and G. McRitchie the compiling of a recipe book to help raise funds for King's College (now King's Campus, Pembroke School), little did I think that such a book would reach its 31st edition.

These two ladies gave time and energy to collecting advertisements for the first two editions to help defray the cost of publication. I had the interesting job of receiving, checking and sorting the recipes, most of which were accompanied by a small donation.

The *Green and Gold* recipe books are known in all Australian states, and many have found their way to England, Canada, and the U.S.A. The sales of these books have been a big financial aid to the College and I hope from the resetting in an Australia-wide publication that even greater sums will be realised for the benefit of the College.

Annie L. Sharman
1960

General Index

TABLE OF MEASURES

By a spoon is meant a rounded spoon; that is, as much above the rim of the spoon as under it.

Half a teaspoon is a level spoon.

A quarter of a spoon is a level spoon divided lengthways.

One-eighth of a spoon is half a quarter of a spoon.

One tablespoon of flour equals 1 oz.

One scant tablespoon of sugar equals 1 oz.

One dessertspoon of butter or fat equals 1 oz.

Six tablespoons of liquor equal one gill.

Four gills equal one pint.

One heaped teacup of flour equals 4 oz.

One scant teacup of sugar equals 4 oz.

One heaped large teacup of flour equals 6 oz.

One heaped breakfast cup of flour equals 8 oz.

One scant breakfast cup of sugar equals 8 oz.

Eight to ten eggs equal 1 lb.

A FEW CATERING HINTS

One 2 lb. sandwich loaf will cut approximately 60 small sandwiches.

A ½ lb. butter is sufficient to spread a 2 lb. loaf for sandwiches.

One lb. sugar is sufficient for 100 people.

Three pints of milk is sufficient for tea for 50 people.

A gallon of milk is sufficient for 50 cups of coffee.

HOW TO USE AN ELECTRIC RANGE

In the preparation of food the objective of all good cooks is to render the food more easily digestible, and to make it more palatable. Electric Cooking attains these objects economically and with maximum efficiency. From a practical point of view one of the greatest advantages of Electric Cooking is that the temperature can be regulated to any degree required. Thus the unskilled cook is assured of good results by paying careful attention to time and temperatures.

An Electric Range used regularly for cooking food in an average household of, say, five persons, will use one unit of electricity per person per day. For a larger family, the cost will not increase proportionately, seven persons requiring, perhaps, six units per day. The actual cost varies, naturally, with the class of cooking practised.

Roasting and baking of meat, poultry, pies, cakes or pastry in an electric oven give perfect results without excessive attention or anxiety. In a definite time after switching on, the oven will be at the desired heat.

Electricity is clean, simple, healthy, and economical. It is easily regulated, and produces perfectly reliable results.

To obtain the best results from any electrical appliance it should be kept clean. It is very easy to do this with an electric range. After the range has been used, wipe it over with a damp cloth. A little cleansing powder, steel wool or olive oil will remove any obstinate marks. Clean the range while it is still warm, but not while the current is on. Make a habit of doing this thoroughly each time it is used, and you will be surprised how well it maintains its original finish and lustre.

USE OF BOILING PLATES

The boiling plates are used for frying, boiling, stewing, simmering, etc. To obtain the quickest and most economical results, saucepans and other utensils with good flat bottoms are recommended, as these make good contact over the whole of the element. Aluminium or enamel saucepans give satisfactory results, but heavy cast iron utensils take longer to heat.

Whenever possible use a saucepan that covers the element to prevent the escape of heat. Twin and triple saucepans are economical because two or three saucepans can be heated together over the same element. Pressure Cookers and Steamers with several tiers are also economical.

The switches controlling the heat of the boiling plates are all plainly marked, either numbered or "high", "medium" or "low". Use the highest number or "high" heat to bring liquids to the boil, switching afterwards to a lower number or "medium" or "low" as required. Liquids will boil for several minutes after the switch has been turned "off".

Never use an asbestos mat on any boiling plate as it is harmful to the element. Avoid "boilovers" as the sudden change of temperature caused by liquid coming in contact with hot metal is the direct cause of element failures.

Care should be taken to see that all switches are turned to "off" when the range is not in use.

USE OF GRILLER

Grilling is done either just under the top oven element on a rack close to the top of the oven, or in a separate compartment depending upon the type of range. Heat the top oven element by turning the switch to the grill position, or the element in the grilling compartment for 4 or 5 minutes until it glows. Place the grilling pan as close to the element as possible and leave door open if grilling in oven until the grilling is completed. Sear the meat quickly on both sides to keep in the juices which prevents the meat becoming dry. Turn meat frequently to cook it evenly.

Toasting can be done under the heated top element, but it is cheaper to use an electric toaster.

USE OF THE OVEN

To heat the oven set the thermostat to the required temperature, when the pilot light will come on. When the temperature is reached the pilot light will automatically cease to glow, and food should then be placed in the oven. The temperature will remain constant and no notice should be taken of any intermittent glowing of the pilot light, as this means that the heat of the oven is being maintained.

For an oven fitted with side elements or side and bottom elements the food is usually placed towards the top and bottom for two trays and towards the centre for one tray.

For an oven fitted with top and bottom elements or just a bottom element food is usually placed towards the centre of the oven for one or two trays. When cooking two trays of food they should be reversed half-way through the cooking.

Should you have completed the cooking of dishes requiring a high temperature and desire to continue immediately with the other dishes requiring a lower temperature, set the thermostat at the lower temperature and place the dishes in the oven. On completion of cooking turn the dial or dials to "off".

In heating certain ovens where there is a separate switch marked Preheat, Bake, and Grill, it is necessary to set the thermostat dial to the desired temperature and the oven control switch to Preheat. The pilot light will glow until the oven reaches the set temperature and then go out.

Place food in the oven, then turn the control switch to Bake, which immediately switches off the top oven element when the oven heat will automatically remain at the set temperature by means of the bottom element only.

TEMPERATURE GUIDE FOR THERMOSTATICALLY CONTROLLED OVENS

VERY HOT OVEN	500°-550°	Scones, Pastry
HOT OVEN	450°-500°	Cream Puffs, Small Cakes
MODERATE OVEN	400°-450°	Biscuits, Buns
SLOW OVEN	350°-400°	Log Cakes, Block Cakes, Sponges, Custards, etc.
VERY SLOW OVEN	250°-350°	Rich Fruit Cakes, Meringues, Macaroons

NOTE.—THE TEMPERATURES IN THIS BOOK ARE FOR THERMOSTATICALLY CONTROLLED STOVES ONLY.

TIME AND MONEY SAVERS TO REMEMBER WHEN USING ELECTRIC RANGES

BOILING PLATES

1. Regulate the switches to give just the heat required. Remember that "MEDIUM" or "LOW" use less current than "HIGH." Use a simmerstat where ever possible for long cooking.
2. The saucepan should completely cover the Boiling Plate. Heat is wasted if a small saucepan is used on a large boiling plate.
3. Saucepans boil more quickly with the lid on.
4. **Never use an asbestos mat on any boiling plate.**

OVEN

1. Open the Oven door as little as possible. Resist the temtation to look at the food to see if it is cooking. This wastes electricity and slows up the cooking.
2. Clean the Range after you have finished baking while it is still warm. If dirty marks and grease are left on they will be harder to remove, and spoil the enamel surface.

OVEN DINNERS IN ELECTRIC RANGES

It is economical when using the oven to cook the whole dinner in it. Suggested menus are as follows:—

MENU 1

Roast Rolled Lamb.

Roast Potatoes and Carrots.

Cabbage (in covered basin with salt and little boiling water).

Elizabeth Apple Pudding.

Arrange oven racks, one on the lowest oven rung curved downwards, and the other curved upwards on the third rung from the bottom. Place prepared carrots and potatoes with about two tablespoons dripping in baking dish on lower rack. Turn both switches high until oven reaches 450°. Place meat in dish with vegetables and leave switches "high" for 5 to 10 minutes. Lift out meat and vegetables, turn and replace on higher rack. Place shredded cabbage and Elizabeth Apple Pudding on lower rack and turn both switches "low" for half an hour. Then turn top oven switch "off" and leave bottom "low" until quarter hour before meat is cooked, then turn "off." Elizabeth Apple Pudding will be cooked in ½ to ¾ hour. Vegetables will be cooked in same time as meat.

MENU 2

A Casserole of Meat and Vegetables.

A Green Vegetable in a covered basin with salt and a very little boiling water.

Baked Apples and Creamed Rice or Barley Kernel Pudding.

Arrange the two oven racks as in menu 1. Place scrubbed and pricked potatoes on lower rack at back, then heat oven to 450°. Put in casserole on lower rack covered with plate, not its lid, if pyrex ware. Leave both switches "high" ten minutes. Raise casserole to higher rack and put its lid on securely. Place basin of green vegetables also on higher rack, then apples and pudding on lower rack. Turn top switch "off," bottom "medium," 15 minutes, then "low" till last quarter hour of cooking, then it can be turned "off". All food will be cooked 1½-2 hours from time casserole was put in.

HOW TO GET THE BEST SERVICE FROM AN AUTOMATIC GAS COOKER

The automatically controlled gas oven has the following characteristics:—

1. One burner only.
2. The flue outlet at the bottom.
3. The base closed with a detachable plate referred to as the "bottom plate."
4. It provides two regions at different temperatures. By making use of these two regions, foods requiring different temperatures can be cooked simultaneously, the main portion above the flue outlet being used for the high temperature cooking (e.g., joints, bread, etc.) while the bottom portion of the oven is used for low temperature operations (e.g., custards, milk puddings, etc.).
5. A "thermostat," which controls the temperature of the oven accurately and without attention. This instrument enables the housewife not only to cook automatically, but also to reproduce from day to day any cooking conditions which she has found particularly suitable for her requirements.

OVEN COOKING: To Use the Thermostat

Turn the head until the required number is seen on the dial, turn the oven tap on full, light the gas, and allow 15 minutes to heat the oven. The oven tap should remain untouched throughout the cooking period. The thermostat will gradually cut down the gas as the oven heats up, and will automatically control the temperature so that it does not rise above that required for the cooking operation in hand. It is, therefore, unnecessary to make any adjustments during the cooking process.

If later the oven is required at a higher or lower temperature, for a further cooking operation, the thermostat can be turned up or down for the appropriate number, and a few minutes be allowed for the temperature to rise or fall as needed.

It is not necessary to open the oven door to examine the food during the cooking. In fact, it is undesirable to do so for the following reasons: Opening the door causes the oven to cool, with the result that the thermostat automatically increases the gas supply until after the door has been closed, and the oven has again reached its correct temperature. There follows a waste of gas, and for a short time after closing the door, cooking proceeds with a high flame in the oven. This may lead to uneven baking or burning of smalls, e.g., trays full of cakes, biscuits, etc., which normally are quickly finished.

Solid trays should be used to hold all foods requiring a support, and three trays of small foods may be baked at once. When two or three trays of small things are to be baked simultaneously, it will be found that the cooking is more even when a good space is left between shelves than when they are placed close together.

Choice of Utensils for the Oven

Most housewives acquire an assortment of cooking utensils. When arranging to cook a whole dinner menu which will necessitate making full use of available space, it is advisable first to collect the utensils intended to hold the food and to see that they fit together on the correct runners. All types of casseroles and pie-dishes may be used, but for plate tarts, thin tin, aluminium or enamelled-ware is the most satisfactory. Fierce bottom heat has been eliminated in the automatically-controlled oven by the use of the single burner and bottom flue outlet. Therefore, double bottomed tins, thick earthenware or china plates, necessary with some ovens to avoid burning, should not be employed.

Need for Closing the Oven Door Tightly

If the door of a thermostatically-controlled oven is not tightly closed, heat will escape through the opening and the thermostat will increase the gas supply to compensate. It is important, therefore, in the joint interests of good cooking and gas economy, not only to push the oven door into the closed position, but also to turn the handle until the door is securely latched.

Use of Hotplate

Boiling.—Do not allow the flames to extend beyond the base of the utensils as this is a waste. The heat of the flame is in the tips.

Simmering.—Use the smallest burner turned low. If more heat is required, use a large burner low, in preference to the simmer turned high. When the large burner is used, the heat is more evenly distributed over the bottom of the pan and consequently is less likely to burn.

Steaming.—Only a small quantity of gas is required. Use only sufficient gas to give a gentle volume of steam.

Grilling and Toasting.—Make frets red hot before attempting to grill or toast. Place a saucepan or kettle over burner to deflect the heat as it rises. This saves gas and heats the frets more quickly. When frets are red, place bread under to toast, and meat under to grill. When grilling, apply great heat to both sides of the meat to harden the outside and seal in the red juices, then lessen the heat until the meat is cooked. The best results are obtained if the meat is turned from side to side every two or three minutes.

MANAGEMENT OF NON-AUTOMATIC COOKERS

Use of Oven

Do not use solid sheet (browner or deflector) to cook on; this should be used for browning purposes only. Food requiring a support should be placed on round trays. A space of two inches should be allowed around baking dishes and tray to enable the heat to rise to the deflector. The greatest heat is at the top of the oven.

A full flame is one giving a distinct blue cone of ½ inch length in centre of flame.

Scones, Puff and Flaky Pastry and Baked Suet Crust

Cook on two shelves in upper portion of oven under browning sheet, gas full flame for 15 minutes to heat oven, reduce slightly before putting in food.

Short Pastry

should be cooked on two shelves in upper portion of oven under browning sheet with gas full flame for 10 minutes to heat oven; reduce to half flame and put food in oven.

Small Cakes and Buns

should be cooked on two shelves in upper portion of oven under browning sheet, gas half flame for 15 minutes to heat oven; reduce to quarter flame and place cakes in oven.

Sponges, Layer Cakes and Biscuits

should be cooked on two shelves in upper portion of oven under browning sheet, gas half flame for 10 to 15 minutes to heat oven; reduce to quarter flame and place in cakes.

Large Fruit Cakes (Rich and Plain)

should be cooked in centre of oven, gas half flame for 10 minutes to heat oven; reduce to quarter flame and place cakes in oven. Cook rich cakes without the deflector.

Baked Meat

Gas at full flame for 10 minutes; reduce slightly and place meat in baking dish, near the bottom of the oven. After 5 to 10 minutes, turn gas to between half and quarter flame.

Milk Puddings and Baked Custards

may be cooked on top of deflector when baking meat, or placed in a dish of water and cooked under deflector; gas at quarter flame.

PRESSURE COOKING

Pressure cooking means high temperature cooking, whereby heat is driven through the food at a much faster rate than any ordinary cooking method. Hundreds of meal preparation hours will be saved yearly, and in addition less fuel will be used, which is extremely important in these days of fuel shortages.

Because the food is cooked in a steam tight cooker, less steam, heat and food odours pervade the kitchen. The colours of foods are retained, particularly with vegetables.

Probably the most important factor with pressure cooking is the retention of food values. Oxidation (exposure to air) and soaking in water are minimized.

Some important points are given :

1. Correct amount of water to be used as per instruction book.
2. Time cooking period from the movement of vent weight (when correct steam pressure is indicated).
3. At above point reduce heat so that correct pressure is maintained.
4. When time is up reduce pressure. This is done according to instruction book issued with all cookers.

In addition it is necessary to refrain from overloading the cooker, and remember, that a cooker is more than a saucepan—it saves time, labour and fuel, therefore it deserves your best attention in keeping it clean, which is in fact an easy matter owing to the steam created within the cooker.

To give some indication of times required, a fresh vegetable chart is given below:—

Food.	Amount of Water.	Time Mins.	Comment.
Beans	¼ Cup	1¾ - 2¼	
Cabbage (quartered)		2 - 2½	
Carrots		2 - 2½	
Cauliflower	½ Cup	3 - 4	
Marrow	½ Cup	2 - 4	
Peas	¼ Cup	½ - 1	definitely no longer
Potatoes	½ Cup	9 - 14	than time given.

It is worthy of mention that soups are a speciality in pressure cooking mainly because the gelatine is extracted from meat bones, and the soup is cooked in minutes instead of hours, giving an extra high nutritive content.

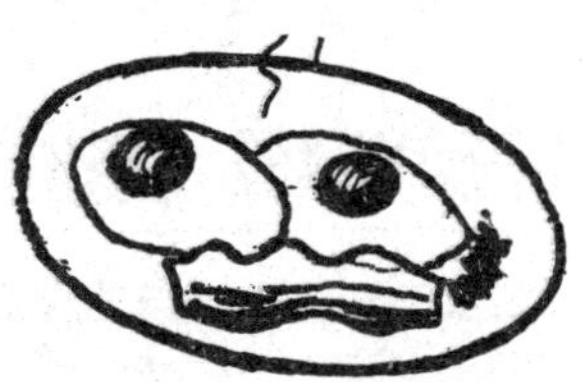

BREAKFAST DISHES

BREAKFAST DISHES

BRAINS IN BATTER

Soak brains in salt and water, take off skin and any dark pieces, wash well, boil for 10 to 15 minutes, and drain. Dust salt and pepper over, cut in pieces, and fry each piece in a light batter made as follows:—One egg (beaten), a little salt, quarter cup of milk, enough S.R. flour to thicken—about two tablespoons. Have fat boiling, and drop spoonfuls of batter in with some brains in each. Fry a light brown. Do not turn until it bubbles.

Tripe may be cooked in the same way. An onion in the batter is an improvement, and gives it a flavour. — Mrs. Lloyd Prince.

BREAKFAST WONDERS

Cut small or mince any cold meat. Make a paste with cold potatoes, 1 egg, salt, and S.R. flour to bind; roll out and cut with scone cutter. Place meat between two rounds of paste, and press edges together. Fry a golden brown. —C. J. McRitchie.

EXCELLENT RECIPE FOR CRUMPETS

Break two eggs into a basin. Beat slightly and add two teaspoons sugar. Sift ½ lb. self-raising flour in another basin and pour in eggs to make a light dough (a little milk may be needed). Work quickly, roll to ½ in. thick, cut into rounds. Prick with a fork. Bake in hot oven for about 10 minutes. Tear open and butter while hot. Serve at once.

In an Electric Cooker bake at 525°.

Bake in Gas Cooker at 450° F.

DEVILLED MEAT

Put in a small frying pan one good dessertspoon butter, one teaspoon curry powder, one dessertspoon vinegar, pepper, salt, a little cayenne to taste, pinch of nutmeg, also a little tomato sauce if liked. Cut slices of cold meat and simmer very gently in the mixture, turning once. The meat should only heat, not cook or brown, or it becomes tough. Serve on hot buttered toast. (A good breakfast or luncheon dish for a small family.)

EGGS A LA TRIPE

Three onions, half a pint milk, little butter, three eggs, one tablespoon flour, pepper and salt.

Peel the onions and cut in quarters. Boil with salt in cup of water. When soft, drain off the water. Mix flour to a smooth paste with milk; add butter and pepper. Add this to the onions, and stirring, boil till it thickens. Have the eggs boiled hard; shell and slice. Lift the onions with sauce into hot dish, and place egg on top. Garnish with toast.

—Miss B. Skewes, Victor Harbor.

BAKED EGGS

Break six eggs into a very well buttered pie-dish. Bake in oven until eggs are nearly hard, and then cover with bread crumbs well mixed with pepper, salt and grated cheese to taste. Put small pieces of butter on top, and brown. The eggs should be quite hard before serving.

In an Electric Cooker bake at 425°
Bake in Gas Cooker at 350° F.

BOILED EGGS

1. Place eggs in boiling water and cook for three minutes.
2. Place eggs in cold water, bring to the boil, and boil for one minute.
3. Have ready a saucepan of boiling water, place in it the eggs, lift off the fire, and leave in saucepan for six minutes.

CURRIED EGGS

Four hard-boiled eggs, 1 oz. butter, one onion, one dessertspoon curry powder, one teaspoon flour, salt, pepper, one teaspoon chutney, one gill stock, two tablespoons cream, a squeeze lemon juice, boiled rice.

Melt the butter in a saucepan and add the onion sliced thinly.

Cook slowly till onion begins to colour. Add curry powder, flour, chutney, salt and pepper, and brown. Stir in gradually the stock, cook slowly for 20 minutes. Add two eggs cut in small pieces, the cream and lemon juice. Pour mixture on to a hot dish, put round a border of boiled rice. Cut the other two eggs into six pieces; cut a small piece from end of each. Place between the curry and rice. —A. Sharman, Black Forest.

NEST EGGS

One pound and a half mashed potatoes, two tablespoons milk, 2 oz. butter, salt and pepper, and eggs.

Make the potatoes very hot. Add butter, milk and seasoning. Form in round shape with spoon on hot baking dish. Break an egg into each and bake in a hot oven till set. Serve hot.

—Mrs. Proctor, Victor Harbor.

POACHED EGGS

Half fill a shallow saucepan or frying pan with boiling water. Add vinegar or lemon juice in the proportion of one teaspoon to one pint, and a good pinch of salt. Break the egg in a saucer and gently slip into the pan. Gather up the white, and gently pour over the water. Cook till set—three to five minutes. Lift out with an egg slice, trim off rough edges, and serve on hot buttered toast. The eggs may be garnished with chopped parsley.

POACHED EGGS A LA MAITRE D'HOTEL

Poach the eggs carefully and serve on rounds of buttered toast. Place a pat of maitre d'hotel butter about the size of a shilling on the top of each egg. Serve at once.

SCRAMBLED EGGS

One egg, quarter teaspoon chopped parsley, one teaspoon butter, one-eighth teaspoon salt, pepper, one tablespoon milk.

Boil milk and butter. Add beaten egg and flavourings. Stir over a slow fire till mixture thickens. Serve on hot buttered toast.

SCOTCH EGGS

Four hard boiled eggs, ½ lb. sausage meat, egg and bread crumbs.

Remove shells from eggs, brush with a little white of egg, and cover with sausage meat. Coat with egg and bread crumbs. Deep fry; drain well. Cut a small slice off each end of egg. Cut in halves; place each half on a round of fried bread. Serve on a hot dish with brown sauce. Garnish with sprigs of parsley. If liked, the sauce may be omitted and the eggs served on a lettuce leaf.

TOMATO NEST EGGS

Four large firm tomatoes, four eggs, a little grated cheese, salt, butter, pinch cayenne (optional).

Wipe the tomatoes and cut a large slice off the top. Scoop out the pulp, season inside with cheese, salt and cayenne. Place tomatoes on a greased slide, and carefully break an egg into each one. Place a little butter and cheese on top and replace lid. Bake in a quick oven till eggs set. Serve on rounds of buttered toast.

In an Electric Cooker bake at 375° for 15 minutes.

Bake in Gas Cooker at 400° F.

HARD BOILED EGGS

Place eggs in boiling water, boil for 10 minutes. Put into cold water to remove shell easily.

Note.—If overcooked, a circle of green forms round yolk.

Putting in boiling water prevents the yolk inclining to one side.

Place eggs in cold water, bring to boil. Boil for 6 minutes current low. Put into cold water to remove shell easily.

FRIED EGGS AND BACON

Remove the rind from the bacon and soak in boiling water to draw out some of the salt. Warm the frying pan and cook the bacon slowly in its own fat till clear. Place on a hot dish. Add more dripping if necessary. Heat, but do not make smoking hot. Break the eggs into a saucer, and slip into the pan. Cook slowly, pouring teaspoonful of fat over egg. Drain on an egg slice, and serve with the bacon.

KIDNEY SAVOURY

Remove all fat and skin from three kidneys. Chop them fine. Put small pieces of butter in saucepan. When hot, put in a teaspoon of chopped shallots and cook for three minutes, taking care not to let shallots brown. Then add the chopped kidneys and cook five minutes. Sprinkle in about half a teaspoon of flour. Season them. Moisten it with two tablespoons of good gravy. Cook for two minutes longer. Serve on buttered toast. Sprinkle with chopped parsley. —Mrs. Proctor, Victor Harbor.

LIVER AND BACON

One lamb's fry, ½ lb. bacon, 1 oz. flour, 1 teaspoon salt, quarter teaspoon pepper.

Soak the fry in cold salted water for half an hour. Cut in pieces one inch thick, wash well and dry thoroughly. Coat with seasoned flour. Remove rind from bacon and scald if necessary. Heat frying pan and cook bacon in its own fat. If necessary add more fat and cook liver 10 to 12 minutes. Place liver in centre of dish, bacon round edge. Pour over gravy and garnish with chopped parsley.

To Make Gravy.—Carefully drain off fat, stir in the remainder of seasoned flour, and brown well. Add gradually half pint stock or water and boil for three minutes. — A.L.S.

MOON BALLS

Half lb. flour, 1 teaspoon baking powder (or ½ lb. S.R. flour), good half cup milk (or milk and water), little salt.

Make light dough, knead very little, and roll out ½ inch thick. Cut as for scones, put into very hot deep fat; fry till golden brown. These are delicious served with bacon, and may also be served with golden syrup, honey, or jam.

— Mrs. K. W. Smith, King's College.

OATMEAL PORRIDGE

One ounce oatmeal, one pint boiling water, one good pinch salt.

Sprinkle oatmeal into boiling water and stir till it boils. Add the salt and simmer for three-quarters of an hour. For best results use a double-boiler saucepan.

One ounce oatmeal, three-quarters of a pint water, salt.

Put the oatmeal and water in a basin and let it stand overnight. Put in a saucepan and stir till it boils. Add salt, and simmer for half an hour, stirring occasionally.

OMELETTE

Separate the yolks of two or three eggs from the whites, beat the yolks with a little salt and pepper. Add a tablespoon S.R. flour, two tablespoons cream or milk and a little chopped parsley. Beat whites separately, and mix all together. Have frying pan ready with boiling butter, pour in the mixture. Cook over a slow fire. When set and a light brown, roll over like a pancake and serve hot.

— Mrs. Lloyd Prince.

Before cooking milk or eggs (omelettes and pancakes in particular) scour your pan with salt and rinse with hot water to prevent burning. See that the omelette pan is thoroughly dry before putting in the butter.

— Miss L. Grey, Railway Town, Broken Hill.

CREAMED SAUSAGES

Partly boil the sausages for 10 minutes, i.e., put into cold water and bring to boil and boil for 10 minutes. Then skin the sausages. Bring half pint of milk (with ½ oz. butter dissolved in it) to boil and thicken with cornflour. Remove from fire and season to taste with tomato sauce. Cut sausages into dice and add to this mixture. Pour over buttered toast and serve hot.

— V. A. Lushey.

CRUMB SAUSAGES

Prick sausages, roll in flour, and coat with beaten egg and bread crumbs. Fry in smoking hot fat. Serve on a hot dish and pour over the gravy.

FRIED SAUSAGES

One pound sausages, half oz. flour, half teaspoon salt, one-eighth teaspoon pepper, half pint water or stock, 1 oz. dripping, two slices fried bread, one tablespoon tomato sauce.

Prick sausages with a fork and cover well with seasoned flour. Cook in smoking hot fat for 15 to 20 minutes. Lift on to a hot dish. Cut bread into neat pieces, dip in milk or water, and fry a golden brown. Drain carefully on white paper. Make a gravy with the remainder of flour, sauce and stock. Strain over the sausages and garnish with fried bread and chopped parsley.

SAVOURY POTATO OMELETTE

Two ozs. mashed potato, 2 ozs. cold chopped or minced meat, teaspoon chopped onion and ½ teaspoon herbs. Add one egg, well beaten. Melt 2 ozs. butter in frying pan; when hot add it to the mixture. Spread mixture smoothly in pan and let it brown.

— Mrs. T. W. Neill, McLaren Vale.

TO USE STALE BREAD

Cut four fairly thick slices of bread, dip lightly into mixture, made up of one egg well beaten, half a cup of milk, pinch of salt, pinch of pepper. Fry in dripping till nicely browned; serve with fried bacon. —Mrs. Noble, Brighton.

TASTY DISH MADE FROM COLD MEAT

Cut the cold meat very small, add one onion also cut small, pepper and salt to taste, just cover with water and stew gently for about three-quarters of an hour. Thicken with a little flour. Have ready some slices of toast well buttered and heap on top of toast. —Mrs. J. Sheppard, Railway Town, Broken Hill.

TOMATO CHEESE

Two large tomatoes, two or three small pieces of cheese (that are too dry for table use), two tablespoonfuls of milk, a little pepper and salt. Cook in small saucepan two or three minutes and serve on toast.

—Mrs. J. E. McGrath, St. Peters.

TOMATO TOAST

Chop up a little bacon and put into a small saucepan to cook with a small piece of butter for a few minutes, then add two or three tomatoes, which have been skinned and cut up, and a little pepper. When tomatoes are well cooked break in two eggs and stir well. When thick enough, put on the pieces of buttered toast. —F. Laughton.

VEAL CROQUETTES

Cold veal or ham or tongue, stock, bread crumbs, season. Mince meats not too fat, a few chopped mushrooms if available. Moisten with stock, dip in eggs and bread crumbs. Fry in boiling fat. Sweetbreads and mushrooms done this way are very tasty.

—M. Higginbottom.

LUNCHEON DISHES

SALADS AND DRESSINGS

LUNCHEON DISHES

BAKED EGGS WITH HAM

Butter a fireproof dish and spread slices of ham on it. Put in a hot oven for two or three minutes until the ham is very hot, then break an egg on each slice of ham. Set in the oven. Serve with a green salad or a dish of green vegetables.

— Miss Gwen Scammell.

BEEF OMELETTE

A pound and a half fresh beefsteak put through mincer, two eggs, teacupful of bread crumbs. Add pepper, salt and sage. Mix well and form in the shape of a tongue. Bake for one hour in casserole. Serve cold. — Mrs. David Williams.

In an Electric Cooker bake at 400°.
Bake in Gas Cooker at 375° F.

CAMBRIDGE SAUSAGE

One pound steak, ½ lb. fat bacon, two cups bread crumbs, two eggs, teacupful of bread crumbs. Add pepper, salt and sage. Mix Worcestershire sauce, one pinch salt.

Mince steak and bacon, add crumbs, sauce, salt, and beaten eggs. Form into a roll, tie in a floured cloth, boil two and a half hours. Remove cloth when cold, sprinkle thickly with brown bread crumbs. — "K.K." — M. Higginbottom.

— Mrs. Godson, Woodville.

Use one cup bread crumbs and a half teaspoon dried herbs or one teaspoon allspice instead of the sauce.

— Mrs. C. J. Elfenbein.

HOME-MADE CAMP PIE

One pound steak, one cup bread crumbs, nutmeg to taste, half cup water, pepper and salt.

Mince steak well. Mix all together, put in mould, and steam for two hours. To be eaten cold.

DRESDEN PATTIES

Cold fowl or any meat, stock or milk, slices of stale bread, half cup cream, one tablespoon flour, one of butter.

Cut bread 2 in. thick into rounds 2 in. Remove centre of each round half-way through. Dip in cream, brush with egg, when drained, sprinkle with crumbs. Fry in hot fat. Drain and fill centres with the meat mixture, that has been stewed for five or ten minutes. — M. Higginbottom.

EGG AND BACON PIE

Take $\frac{1}{4}$ lb. bacon scalded and cut into small pieces, removing the rind. Beat up three eggs, adding one tablespoon of milk. Season with pepper and salt and a little chopped parsley. Then mix in the bacon and pour into a sandwich tin or deep plate lined with short pastry. Cover this with a layer of short pastry and bake in hot oven for half an hour. — J.C.C.

In an Electric Cooker bake at 450°.
Bake in Gas Cooker at 400° F.

EGG AND POTATO PIE

Four or five hard-boiled eggs, 1 lb. well-mashed potatoes, one dessertspoon chopped parsley, one teacup white sauce, salt and pepper.

Slice eggs, mix parsley with potato. Grease a pie-dish and put in it a layer of potato. Lay egg slices on this. Pour over the sauce. Stand a little while, then add remainder of potato. Smooth over and mark the top with knife or fork. Add small pieces of butter on top. Brown and heat in moderate oven.

— W.G.T.

In an Electric Cooker bake at 450°.
Bake in Gas Cooker at 400° F.

EGG AND TOMATO SAVOURY

Five or six tomatoes, three or four eggs, pepper, salt, sugar. bread crumbs, butter.

Grease a pie-dish. Place in it a bed of peeled and sliced tomatoes. Season with salt, pepper and sugar. Place on the raw eggs. Cover with more slices of tomato and seasoning. Cover with bread crumbs. Bake in moderate oven. — W.G.T.

In an Electric Cooker bake at 400°.
Bake in Gas Cooker at 375° F.

EGGS AND SPINACH

Two cups cooked spinach, two eggs, two tablespoons milk, two tablespoons butter, two tablespoons cheese (cut fine), half teaspoon salt, little pepper.

Chop spinach, beat egg yolk, add milk, melted butter and seasoning. Mix with spinach and fold in stiffly beaten whites. Fill buttered moulds with mixture and place in pan of hot water and bake in moderate oven until firm. Turn out and garnish with slices of hard-boiled egg. Pour cheese sauce around.

— Miss J. Colliver.

In an Electric Cooker bake at 400°.
Bake in Gas Cooker at 350° F.

FRICASSEE OF SHEEP'S TONGUES

Cook the tongues and cut off the roots, then split in halves lengthwise. Boil desired ingredients together, then strain and thicken. Put in the tongues and make hot, adding yolk of egg and a little cream.

FRITZ SAUSAGE

One and a half pounds of chuck steak, ¼ lb. bacon, 1½ cups (large) of bread crumbs, one teaspoonful of salt, one small teaspoonful of pepper, one dessertspoonful of Worcester sauce, pinch of thyme and one egg.

Mince the steak and bacon very finely, add bread crumbs and the well-beaten egg; mix well together; make into a roll and tie in a floured cloth. Put into boiling water and boil 1¼ hours. Turn out and roll in bread crumbs and serve cold.

— Edith F. Rutt.

GALANTINE OF BEEF

One pound beefsteak minced, ½ lb. bread crumbs, 1 lb. ham or bacon, mixed mace and nutmeg, salt and pepper to taste, two eggs.

Put all ingredients in a basin and mix thoroughly. Form into the shape of a roll and tie up in a greased pudding cloth. Put into a saucepan of boiling water; boil gently for three hours. Then undo cloth, re-roll very tightly, place on flat dish or board with another dish on top of the roll. Press with a weight. When cold brush with melted glaze.

LUNCHEON DISH

Take some warm mashed potatoes; add a little flour, milk. Make into paste. Roll out, not too thick. Cut into squares. Put a little finely-cut meat on, and roll. Fry in boiling fat. Serve hot, with sauce.

— M. Higginbottom.

POTATO PUFFS

One pound cold mashed potatoes, 1 lb. flour, ¼ lb. butter, a little salt, and sufficient water to make stiff paste. Half lb. cold minced meat, pepper and salt.

Mix potatoes and flour together. Then add water. Turn out on board and work well. Roll out thinly and cut with cutter. Take meat and place a little in each one. Fold over and press edges tightly together. Fry in pan half full of boiling fat. Cook on each side till light brown—about five minutes.

— Mrs. J. E. McGrath.

PORK AND BEANS

Half lb. haricot beans, ½ lb. pickled pork, 1 tablespoon golden syrup, 1 level teaspoon salt, a good pinch cayenne.

Wash the beans in plenty of cold water; well cover with cold water and leave soaking overnight. Next morning throw away any beans that are floating on the top, then pour off the water. Put the beans into a saucepan with plenty of cold water, bring to the boil and boil for 20 minutes, removing the scum as it rises. Strain and put into casserole. Cut the pork into small pieces, add it with the salt, cayenne, golden syrup, and ¾ pint of the water in which the beans were cooking. Cover and cook in a very slow oven for 5-6 hours.

— A. L. Sharman, Black Forest.

Bake in Gas Cooker at 325° F.
In an Electric Cooker bake at 400°.

POTTED MUTTON

Four lbs. leg of mutton (knuckle end), 2½ cups cold water, quarter teaspoonful of cayenne pepper, and salt to taste; place mutton in saucepan with water, simmer gently till meat falls off bones (about 5 hours), remove from saucepan, cut meat finely, return to saucepan, bring it to boil; place it in wet mould. Leave overnight to set.

LUNCHEON SAVOURY PIE

Take ½ cup of minced meat, 2 medium-sized tomatoes, one small finely chopped onion, one cup of bread crumbs, soaked in 1½ cups of stock, salt and pepper to taste; grease pie-dish, put layer of minced meat, thinly sliced tomato, chopped onion, soaked bread crumbs alternately till pie-dish is full; lastly, a layer of dry bread crumbs and grated cheese. Place small pieces of butter on top, bake till light brown.

In an Electric Cooker bake at 400°.

TOMATO AND CHEESE SAVOURY

Cut some fairly thick slices of cheese and cover the bottom of a small flat dish with them; take six small tomatoes, skin and halve them, then arrange over the cheese; season with pepper and salt; set tiny dots of butter on top of each tomato; sprinkle lightly with bread crumbs.
Bake in a hot oven till lightly brown and serve very hot.

— Miss M. Treasure, Black Forest.

TOMATOES AND EGGS

This is an appetising luncheon dish:—Take six large tomatoes, six small eggs, pepper and salt, two and a half tablespoonfuls of grated cheese, six pieces of fried bread. Wipe the tomatoes, remove the stalks, cut off a slice from the top of each (opposite end to the stalk end), and scoop out some of the pulp. Season the inside with pepper and salt, and sprinkle in half teaspoon of grated cheese. Stand them on a greased baking dish in a hot oven until the tomatoes are almost cooked, being careful not to break them. Remove from oven and cool slightly. Break each egg in a cup, pour one in each tomato. Return to oven, and leave until eggs are just set. Cut six rounds of bread about ¾ in. thick, fry till a golden brown on both sides, drain on paper. Place one tomato on each piece of fried bread. Arrange on a lace paper, and serve hot. Pulp of tomatoes can be used in a salad or cooked separately, and served with tomato eggs.

TOAD IN THE HOLE

Arrange 1 lb. of lamb chops in a greased pie-dish; sprinkle with pepper and salt. Then pour over them a batter made with a cup of S.R. flour, two or three eggs, and enough milk to make it a nice consistency. Bake for about an hour; cover with a piece of greased paper when about half done.

—Mrs. R. F. Slattery, Welland.

In an Electric Cooker bake at 450°

SALADS AND DRESSINGS

BEETROOT MOULD

Ingredients.—Two bunches beetroot, one small lettuce, two dessertspoons gelatine, two cups hot water, pepper, salt and vinegar.

Directions.—Cook beetroot till tender, peel and cut in slices. Line a fluted mould with the slices, then fill centre with small dice-shaped pieces of beetroot. Dissolve gelatine in hot water. Pour over beetroot, and allow to set. Garnish with shredded lettuce and sliced tomato. Serve with mayonnaise dressing or vinegar. — Miss B. Colliver.

BEETROOT SALAD

One bunch cooked beetroot, half pint vinegar, three cloves, six peppercorns, one blade mace, one teaspoon salt, one dessertspoon sugar.

Put the vinegar and flavourings in a saucepan and boil five minutes. Strain, and when cold pour over the beetroot, which has been peeled and thinly sliced.

JELLIED BEETROOT

Cook beet tender, slice and sprinkle with sugar, pour over one tablespoonful unflavoured powdered gelatine mixed in half a cup of boiling water and half a cup of vinegar. When set, cut in squares for table use. —Mrs. Crosby.

HARICOT BEAN SALAD

Beat the yolk of an egg and add oil by degrees as for a mayonnaise dressing (if oil is not available, melted margarine may be substituted for it). When the mixture is of the consistency of beaten butter, season it with salt, pepper and a little curry powder, and add sufficient vinegar to bring it to the proper consistency. Drain some small white haricot beans, which have been boiled until tender, on a soft cloth, and let them get cold; then put them into a suitable dish, scatter over them some finely-chopped chives and parsley, and dress them with the egg mixture. Garnish the top of the salad with beetroot cut into small squares, and surround with some carefully washed watercress.

HERRING SALAD

Get a tin of herrings preserved in tomato sauce, open it, remove the fish carefully on to a flat dish, and divide each into two pieces. Put a little heap of cold cooked white haricot beans into the middle of a salad bowl, and dress them with oil and vinegar; then arrange the pieces of herrings on the beans. Fill in the space between with small leaves taken from the heart of a large lettuce, and scatter a little chopped parsley over the fish.

POTATO AND BEETROOT SALAD

Cold potatoes and beetroot, chopped parsley, salad dressing, chopped shallot (if liked).

Cut the potatoes and beetroot into thin slices and place in a salad bowl in alternate layers. Sprinkle finely chopped parsley and shallot between every other layer. Garnish with beetroot and hard-boiled egg, and serve with a salad dressing.

TOMATO JELLY SALAD

One can tomatoes, three stalks celery, small cup of cold water, one small onion, small bay leaf, three cloves, salt and paprika, ¾ oz. gelatine.

Soak gelatine in water. Cook other ingredients together for half an hour. Add, when boiling, quarter teaspoon carbonate soda. Pass through sieve to remove seeds. Add gelatine and stir till dissolved. Put in mould or small moulds, and serve with salad dressing. — Miss D. Cochrane, Auburn, Victoria.

SALAD DRESSING

One yolk hard-boiled egg, quarter teaspoon mustard, half teaspoon salt, two teaspoons sugar, one teaspoon oil, half teacup milk or cream, half teacup vinegar.

Pound the yolk of the egg with the back of a wooden spoon; add the salt, sugar and mustard. Work in gradually the oil, then the milk and cream, and lastly the vinegar. The liquids must be added slowly, and the mixture must be kept well stirred. If liked, the oil and egg may be omitted.

POTATO SALAD

Boil some potatoes and mash to a cream with milk, butter, pepper and salt. Chop one onion finely, and mix together with about two tablespoons vinegar. Place in a glass dish and sprinkle with chopped parsley. Garnish with hard-boiled egg cut in slices.

— B.A.S.

BOILED SALAD DRESSING

Melt one heaped dessertspoon of butter, and add one heaped dessertspoon of flour. Stir until smooth. Add half a cup milk. Cook for a minute, stirring all the time. Add salt to taste and one well-beaten egg. Heat over fire to almost boiling point, stirring all the time. Add mustard, sugar and vinegar to taste.

— Mrs. A. W. Piper.

One dessertspoon flour, one teaspoon mustard, one-half teaspoon salt, one tablespoon butter, 1½ tablespoons sugar, one-half cup white wine vinegar.

Method: Melt butter in saucepan, add dry ingredients, then vinegar. Mix well and stir until it comes to the boil; add a little tarragon vinegar. When required, thin down with a little milk.

Four times these quantities can be used as it will keep indefinitely.

One egg, two tablespoons sugar, three tablespoons milk, four tablespoons vinegar, one teaspoon mustard, pepper and salt to taste, butter size of walnut.

Beat egg and sugar well, add milk and mustard, salt and pepper. Pour out gradually the vinegar, stirring all the time. Melt butter in a saucepan, add the above mixture, and stir till it thickens.

— Mrs. A. V. Gent.

Six tablespoons sugar, four dessertspoons flour, two teaspoons salt, four teaspoons mustard, four tablespoons butter, two teacups vinegar.

Mix dry ingredients to smooth paste with part of vinegar. Add remainder and butter, and stir all constantly until it thickens. Boil one minute. Bottle, and use as required by adding milk to right consistency.

— Mrs. Crosby.

SOUPS

FISH

SOUPS

STOCK

One pound shin beef or beef bones, one carrot, half turnip, one onion, one piece celery, six peppercorns, one teaspoon salt, one quart water, one blade mace, a bouquet garni (a bunch of herbs, three sprigs of parsley, two sprigs of thyme, one sprig of marjoram, one bay leaf).

Wash meat and bones and cut meat in small pieces. Put in a stock pot or saucepan with water and salt. Bring to boil, remove the scum and add vegetables, cut in rough pieces, add the flavouring. Simmer for four or five hours. Strain, remove fat when cold.

Use for making soups, stews, gravies and sauces.

A RICH BROWN STOCK

Four pounds knuckle veal, 4 lb. shin beef, three onions, ½ lb. lean bacon, one bunch parsley, herbs, six cloves, mushrooms, tomatoes, two carrots, three turnips, one head celery, 1½ oz. salt, four quarts water, four blades mace, six peppercorns.

For 1 lb. meat and bones allow one pint water and one pint extra to allow for evaporation; to be added gradually, to prevent stock boiling too quickly.

Cut the meat and chop bones and put into a large saucepan with the vegetables cut up roughly, the herbs (tied up) and the mace, peppercorns and cloves (in a muslin bag), the salt and water. Simmer slowly four or five hours. Remove scum as it rises. Strain through a colander and remove fat when cold. If a very brown stock is required, the meat and onion may be first browned in two tablespoons of hot fat.

— M. Higginbottom.

TO CLEAR STOCK

If a clear stock is wanted, do not brown meat or vegetables. Use the white and shell of an egg. Whisk over the fire. Boil for half an hour. This removes any impurities. Always clear stock the day it is to be used. — M. Higginbottom.

BROWN SOUP

Cut up 2 lb. shin of beef or any raw meat, two small onions, one turnip, one carrot. Fry in fat, drain, add three quarts water, bring slowly to boil. Add one head celery, pepper, salt, herbs. Boil three hours, skim well.

— M. Higginbottom.

CLEAR SOUP

Clear soup is made from good brown stock which has been cleared. Vegetables cut in matches, fancy shapes or small dice, macaroni, vermicelli, may be added. These are best cooked before adding to stock.

— M. Higginbottom.

LENTIL SOUP

Melt 1 oz. dripping in a saucepan, and add ½ lb. lentils (which have been washed and soaked overnight), one small onion, one small carrot, one small turnip; cut into dice and stir until fat is absorbed. Do not allow to brown. Add one quart water or stock and seasoning, one dessertspoonful salt, one teaspoon pepper. Boil until vegetables are soft, rub through a sieve, return to saucepan, add 1 oz. flour mixed to a paste with a little milk, and boil for a few minutes. Add half pint milk and reheat. Serve with croutons of toast.

— Mrs. W. H. Colliver.

OX TAIL SOUP

One ox tail washed. Cut in pieces, brown in boiling fat, drain, put in pot with one carrot, turnip cut up, three small onions, four cloves, one dessertspoon salt, remove tail, strain stock and thicken with flour. Some of the vegetables may be added cut in small pieces just before serving. This is better prepared the day before, as the fat is more easily removed when cold.

— M. Higginbottom.

PEA SOUP

Three quarts stock, one carrot cut up, one onion, one stick celery, one pint split peas (soaked), one teaspoon salt, half teaspoon pepper. Simmer an hour and a half, strain, press through a wire sieve. Serve with sippets of toast.

— M. Higginbottom.

POTATO SOUP

One pound potatoes, ½ oz. butter or dripping, one onion, one piece celery, one quart boiling water, 1 oz. sago, half pint milk, one teaspoon salt, six peppercorns.

Cut the onion, celery and the potatoes into thin slices and cook in the fat till the fat is absorbed. Add the water, salt and peppercorns (tied in a muslin bag), and cook slowly till soft. Rub through a sieve, return to saucepan, add sago, and cook till clear. Add milk, but do not boil.

—D. Besanko, Clarence Park.

POTATO CHOWDER

Six potatoes (sliced), ¼ lb. bacon, one tablespoon of chopped onion, butter and flour, one pint milk, one pint water, one teaspoon salt.

Fry potatoes and onions till a pale brown. Put in a saucepan with the bacon (cut up finely), the water and the salt. Simmer till tender—about 20 minutes. Mix the flour to a smooth paste and add. Boil for three minutes. Add the milk, and serve hot.

SCOTCH BROTH

One pound neck mutton, one carrot, one onion, one small turnip, one quart water, one teaspoon salt, one-eighth teaspoon pepper, 1 oz. pearl barley, one piece celery.

Wipe and trim the meat and cut into chops. Put into a saucepan with the water and salt and bring slowly to the boil. Remove the scum, add the vegetables, cut in small dice, and the washed barley. Simmer for two hours. Take out chops, remove meat from bones, and cut in small pieces. Remove fat from broth, add the meat and one dessertspoon of chopped parsley.

— Miss D. Chenoweth, Willaston.

TOMATO SOUP

Twelve tomatoes, two onions, small piece mace, one quart hot water; boil for one hour in a covered saucepan, then strain through colander and put liquor back in saucepan and add one heaped teaspoonful carbonate soda and stir until it stops fizzing. Add as much milk as you have liquor, one tablespoon butter, pepper and salt to taste. Thicken with three tablespoons cornflour.

— Mrs. James Hurst, Paracombe.

Six large tomatoes, one quart stock, one small blade of mace, one carrot, one onion, six cloves, half teaspoon sugar, quarter teaspoon pepper and salt, 1 oz. butter, 1 oz. flour, half cup milk.

Place all in a saucepan. Simmer for one hour. Rub all through colander. Melt butter in saucepan, add flour, and mix well together, then add soup gradually. Let it boil, and then add sugar and pour on to milk.

— Mrs. H. R. Adamson, Malvern.

One pound tomatoes, 1 oz. butter or dripping, one onion, one blade mace, six peppercorns, 1 oz. bacon, one quart water, 1 oz. cornflour, half pint milk, one teaspoon salt.

Heat the fat in a saucepan and add the tomatoes, onion and bacon cut up roughly and cook till fat is absorbed. Add the mace and peppercorns (in a bag) and the salt and water. Cook till soft. Rub through a sieve. Return to saucepan and add the cornflour mixed to a smooth paste. Boil three minutes. Add the milk, but do not boil.

— E.K.B.

Soup may be thickened with 1 oz. sago instead of cornflour.

— J.C.C.

Two pounds tomatoes stewed for 15 minutes in one gill of water. Strain through flour sieve. The more pulp forced through the better and richer will be the soup. Return pulp to saucepan. Add an equal quantity of milk, butter size of walnut, pepper and salt to taste, and, when heated, a thickening of flour. Boil gently for five minutes.

— Mrs. E. Haselgrove, Unley Park.

One pound tomatoes, 1 onion, 1½ cups water (or stock), 1 cup milk, 1 dessertspoon butter, 1 small slice of bacon, 1 teaspoon cornflour, pepper and salt to taste, and a little grated nutmeg.

Cut tomatoes and onion small, and put into a stewpan with the butter, bacon, and water. When tender, beat through strainer and return to stewpan; then mix the cornflour with the milk, and add pepper and salt and a little grated nutmeg.

Let it simmer for a little while, and serve very hot.

— Mrs. R. F. Slattery, Welland.

FISH

BOILED FISH

Wash the fish, dry well and rub with lemon. Place in a saucepan of almost boiling water with one teaspoon salt and a slice of lemon or a little vinegar. Simmer till done (the flesh is white and leaves the bone). Lift out on a fish slice and drain. Serve with parsley or egg sauce, and garnish with lemon and parsley.

PARSLEY AND LEMON SAUCE FOR BOILED FISH

Wash handful of parsley, dry and mince finely, add pulp and rind of lemon. Melt ½ oz. butter in a saucepan with ½ oz. flour. Add parsley and lemon to sufficient stock to make the sauce, with a little mace and a few capers.

Stir over fire, and when cooked add, off the fire, yolks of two beaten eggs. Then return all to the fire and stir until sauce thickens, but it must not boil.

—Miss B. Skewes, Victor Harbour.

TO FRY FISH

In frying fish of any kind sprinkle a little salt on the bottom of the pan when the fat is boiling; the fish can be easily turned without breaking in the least. —Mrs. F. J. Wright.

FRIED FISH (Cutlets or Fillets)

Wash and dry the fish, roll in seasoned flour (half tablespoon flour, half teaspoon salt, one-eighth teaspoon pepper) and coat with egg and bread crumbs. Heat three or four tablespoons of dripping in a frying pan. Cook the fish for seven to ten minutes, according to size, and turn once. Drain on kitchen paper. Serve on paper doyley on a hot dish and garnish with lemon and parsley.

The fish may be deep-fried, three to five minutes being long enough to cook it.

A DAINTY FISH DISH

Boned garfish dipped in batter or egg and bread crumbs. Fry until a light brown.

FRIED FISH IN BATTER

For the Batter.—Four ounces flour, one yolk of egg, one gill milk, one pinch salt.

Sift the flour and salt. Mix with the yolk of the egg and milk. Beat well till smooth and light. Allow to stand for half an hour before using. Coat the fish with the batter. Deep fry for three to five minutes. Drain well. Serve on a paper doyley on a hot dish and garnish with lemon and parsley.

GRILLED FISH

Clean, skin and fillet a whiting. Sprinkle with salt and rub with lemon juice. Grill gently for eight to ten minutes, turning frequently. Serve on a hot dish with a little butter. Garnish with lemon and parsley.

KEDGEREE

One small tin salmon, ¼ lb. rice, 2 oz. butter, salt, hard-boiled egg, half pint milk, cayenne and nutmeg to flavour.

Cook rice in boiling water for 10 minutes, strain and cook in milk till soft. Flake the fish, chop white of egg finely, and add with other ingredients and mix well. Serve on a hot dish, sprinkle with yolk of egg and chopped parsley.

MOULDED SALMON

One pound salmon, two eggs beaten, two tablespoonfuls butter melted, half a cup fine bread crumbs, pepper, salt, and mixed parsley. Make all into a smooth paste, put in buttered basin and steam one hour.

Sauce: Melt one large tablespoonful butter, add one of flour, then liquor of salmon; if too thick add milk and one tablespoonful tomato sauce. Stir until thickened and pour over moulded salmon.

SALMON IN JELLY

Ingredients.—One small tin salmon, two dessertspoons gelatine, two cups hot water, juice of one lemon, one hard-boiled egg, pepper and salt.

Directions.—Take the tin of salmon and open into a basin. Break up with a fork finely, then dissolve the gelatine in the hot water, adding the juice of one lemon, also pepper and salt. Mix all thoroughly together. Wet a round cake tin or mould and place slices of hard-boiled egg at the bottom, then pour mixture in very gently, and allow to set. Garnish with shredded lettuce, slices of tomato and lemon. Serve with vinegar.

—Mrs. W. H. Colliver.

STUFFED TOMATOES

Two or 3 Fresh Herrings, 2 tablespoonfuls mayonnaise sauce, 6 firm tomatoes, pepper and salt.

For this dish it is essential to use firm tomatoes. Cut them in half, scoop out a little of the pulp, put it into a basin, add to the flaked flesh of the herrings. Add seasoning, and the mayonnaise sauce. Return the mixture to the tomatoes, sprinkle the top with a little chopped parsley, if available. Serve alone or on a bed of crisp lettuce leaves, placing any of the surplus mixture in the centre of the dish.

HERRING SNACKS

One small tin Fresh Herrings, 2 tablespoonfuls stiff mayonnaise sauce, 1 or 2 gherkins, toast.

Remove the skin and bones from two or three herrings, and flake and pound well in a basin. Add the stiff mayonnaise sauce, add pepper and salt and spread on fingers of buttered toast. Garnish the top with finely-chopped gherkins.

KIPPER CANAPES

One small tin Kippered Herrings, 1 oz. butter, 3 eggs, salt, cayenne pepper, slices of buttered toast.

Drain the kippers, flake the flesh finely, and add to the beaten egg. Season with cayenne and salt. Melt the butter in a small saucepan and cook lightly, as for scrambled eggs. When the mixture has lightly set, pile it on fingers or rounds of buttered toast, and garnish with parsley.

DEVILLED HERRINGS

One small tin Fresh Herrings, 1 oz. butter, 1½ oz. flour, ½ teaspoon made mustard, 1 saltspoonful curry powder, sprinkling of cayenne pepper, 1 small onion, 1 teaspoonful Worcestershire sauce, salt to season, ½ pint milk, bread crumbs and grated cheese.

Chop the onion finely and cook it in the butter a few minutes without browning. Stir in the flour, mustard, curry powder and Worcestershire sauce. When blended, add the milk, and stir over a low heat until it cooks and thickens. Remove the skin and bones from the herrings, break them up, and add to the sauce. Taste, and, if necessary, add more seasoning. Place in a pie-dish. Sprinkle the top with a mixture of bread crumbs and grated cheese, put a few small pieces of butter on top and bake in a very hot oven or under a grill until the top is well browned.

SAVOURY SALMON

Soak three sheets gelatine in cold water till soft. Pour liquid from tin salmon into saucepan, add a little chopped parsley, one onion, one carrot, few peppercorns, cloves, and small piece mace, add one cup water, one-half cup vinegar. Boil gently until liquid is flavoured by ingredients added, take gelatine out of water and add to hot liquid, stirring till dissolved (never add gelatine to boiling liquids, it makes it cloudy). Strain over the salmon to which have been added two tablespoons bread crumbs and a hard-boiled chopped egg mixed well through. Set in a mould. Turn out and serve either with rings of hard-boiled eggs, parsley, or beetroot. —Miss Rehn, W.C.T.U., Adelaide.

SALMON CAKES

One small tin salmon, one cupful mashed potatoes, one dessert-spoon chopped parsley, half teaspoon lemon juice, quarter tea-spoon salt, one-eighth teaspoon pepper.

Remove bones from salmon and mash well. Add the other ingredients and mix well. Take small portions of the mixture, roll in flour and form into cakes. Coat with egg and bread crumbs and fry for three minutes in a saucepan of smoking hot fat. Drain well on kitchen paper. Serve on a hot dish and garnish with lemon and parsley. —A. Sharman.

SARDINE PUFFS

Six large sardines, one egg, 1 oz. butter, 1 lb. of mashed potatoes, and pepper.

Mix the mashed potatoes with the butter, a little of the beaten egg and pepper. Roll each sardine in a thick covering of the potatoes, keeping the shape of the fish. Brush with the remainder of the beaten egg, roll in fine bread crumbs, fry in smoking hot fat till they are brown and puffed out, drain on kitchen paper, and dish garnished with parsley.

—Mrs. W. Schmidt, Railway Town, Broken Hill.

SOUSED FISH

Put into a large pie-dish or casserole some cutlets or fillets of fish, and cover with vinegar. Cut one large onion in thin slices and place on the fish with a little ground allspice, cloves and ginger. Bake in a slow oven till well cooked. Serve cold, and garnish with cucumber, tomatoes and chopped parsley.

—Miss A. Sharman, Black Forest.

In an Electric Cooker bake at 400°.
Bake in Gas Cooker at 350° F.

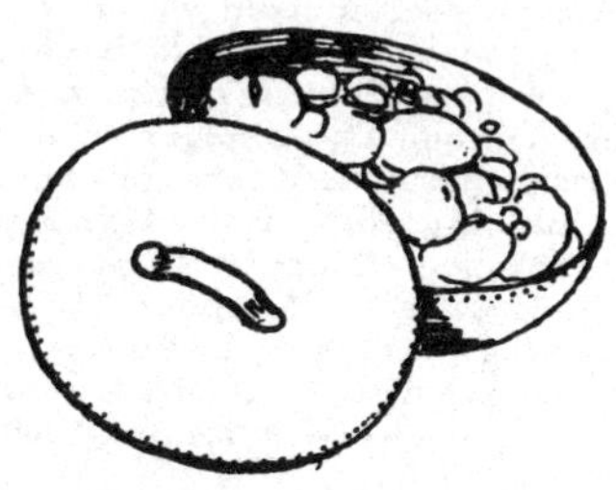

MADE-UP DISHES — ENTREES, STEWS, Etc.

MADE-UP DISHES, STEWS, etc.

BEEF OLIVES

One pound beefsteak cut thin in small squares, fill with seasoning and sew up.

Seasoning: Bread crumbs, a little dripping, salt, pepper, thyme, and parsley or finely chopped onions. Brown in saucepan with little dripping, add sufficient water to cover and simmer for two hours. — E. Whitelaw, North Norwood.

BEEF RISSOLES

One lb. steak, ½ cup bread crumbs, 1 egg, a few leaves of thyme, pepper and salt.

Mince the steak, add bread crumbs, thyme, pepper and salt; mix together with the unbeaten egg. Divide into patties, and roll in flour. Fry with two onions sliced. Make gravy, then simmer all together in a saucepan for about an hour. — M. Brice.

CHICKEN PIE

Remove all the flesh from the bones of a cooked chicken, and mince finely. Add an equal amount of bread crumbs, a little grated onion, pepper and salt; mix all together with the yolk of an egg. Whip the white of an egg to a stiff froth, and add that. Then put the mixture in a small pie-dish and spread mashed potatoes over the top. Bake in a moderate oven until potatoes are brown and crisp. Serve hot with tomato sauce.

— Mrs. A. Williams, Congregational Manse, Semaphore.

CORNISH PASTIES

One pound pastry, ½ lb. lean steak, ½ lb. potatoes, onions, salt and pepper to taste.

Cut up finely, and sprinkle with a little gravy or water. Roll out pastry. Cut in round pieces about 6 in. Put meat and vegetables in centre. Press edges into a frill. Bake half an hour. A little carrot or turnip may be added. — M. Higginbottom.

In Electric Cooker bake at 450°.

Bake in Gas Cooker at 425° F.

CORNISH PIE

One lb. leg chops, 4 turnips, 4 potatoes, 1 large onion, salt and pepper.

Cut meat into small pieces; line pie-dish, cover with sliced onion, then turnips, and on top potatoes. Cover, and boil slowly for 1½ hours. Make crisp piecrust cover, and cook three-quarters of an hour. Enough for six people, with green vegetables.

— C. J. McRitchie.

In an Electric Cooker bake at 450°.

CORNISH PASTY

Three cups of flour, ½ lb. lard or dripping, three potatoes, one onion, small swede or turnip, 1 lb. good beef or mutton. Put flour in bowl, mix dripping or lard well with flour and a pinch of salt; make it with milk or water to a stiff paste, then roll it out. Put the potatoes, onion, and turnip on the paste; cut the meat up finely or mince; add a little pepper and salt to season it, then close both ends together and crimp with fingers by holding paste in one hand and crimping it with the other.

Bake for one hour. — Mrs. G. Roach, Kadina.

In an Electric Cooker bake at 450°.

Bake in a Gas Cooker at 400° F.

CURRIED KIDNEYS

Four or five sheep's kidneys, 1 oz. butter, 1 dessertspoon rice-flour, 1 teaspoon curry powder, 1 onion, 1 small apple, ½ pint stock, a little chutney, salt, pepper, and a squeeze of lemon juice.

Skin and split kidneys and remove fat. Heat butter and brown kidneys; lift out into a saucepan. Slice onion thinly and chop apple and brown in butter. Add flour, curry powder, chutney, salt, pepper, and lemon juice. Stir well, and pour in gradually the stock. Boil three minutes; pour over kidneys and simmer for three-quarters to one hour. Serve on a hot dish with a border of boiled rice.

CURRIED RABBIT

Fry two sliced onions until brown in one tablespoonful of hot dripping; peel, core, and grate one apple and add to onion; mix one tablespoonful of curry powder with two cups of water; add one-quarter teaspoon of salt; add to and boil with onion and apple; chop one tablespoonful of stoned raisins and add, when the curry is boiling, with one rabbit cut into neat joints

Simmer gently for two hours; and 10 minutes before serving add one tablespoonful of flour and the strained juice of half a lemon. — S. R. Smith, Congregational Manse, Kadina.

CURRY AND RICE

One pound cooked meat, one apple, one onion, one dessert-spoon sultanas, half teaspoon salt, one-eighth teaspoon pepper, one teaspoon lemon juice, one dessertspoon flour, one dessert-spoon curry powder, one teaspoon sour jam, three-quarters of a pint stock or water, one tablespoon dripping.

Remove skin, gristle and fat from meat, and cut into small pieces. Cut the apple and onion in dice and fry in the hot fat. Add the flour and curry powder, and stir well till brown. Add the liquid gradually, and boil three inutes. Add the flavourings, and simmer for 15 minutes. Cool slightly. Add the meat, and cook slowly till heated (do not boil), about 10 to 15 minutes. Serve on a hot dish. Place a border of boiled rice round, garnish with slices of lemon and finely-chopped parsley. — C.S.

EXETER STEW

Two pounds blade or chuck steak, one onion (large), 1 oz. dripping, 1 oz. flour, a pint and a half water, four cloves, one small piece, mace, quarter teaspoon pepper, one teaspoon salt.

Cut the onion in thin slices and cook in the hot fat till brown. Add the flour and brown well. Stir in the water gradually, and boil for three minutes. Slightly cool and put into a saucepan with mace and cloves (tied in muslin), salt, pepper and meat cut into suitable pieces. Simmer slowly for two hours.

GRILLED CHOPS ON STEAK

Short loin chops, one or two inches thick; rump or undercut steak. Remove the skin from the chops, make into a round shape, and fasten with a skewer. Heat gridiron, and grease. Expose meat to a great heat on each side for one minute to seal up the outside and keep in juices. Cook 10 to 12 mins., turning grill every 3 mins. Remove skewer, place on hot dish, put little butter, salt and pepper or green butter on the meat, and serve at once.

In an Electric Cooker heat grilling pan for 5 minutes. Expose meat to a great heat on each side for one minute to seal up the outside and so keep in the juices. Grill with the current high for 10 to 12 minutes.

Heat the fret bars on a Gas Cooker, place meat under to grill; keep frets hot the whole time and turn the meat every 2 or 3 mins.

HARICOT MUTTON

One pound neck chops, 1 oz. dripping, 1 oz. flour, one onion, one pint stock or water, one carrot, one small turnip, one piece celery, one teaspoon salt, quarter teaspoon pepper.

Mix the flour, salt and pepper together. Wipe and trim the chops and coat with the seasoned flour. Heat the fat and brown chops, and lift into stewpan. Slice onions finely and fry till brown. Add remainder of flour and brown well. Add the liquid gradually and boil for three minutes. Cool slightly and pour over the chops. Add the diced vegetables. Simmer one and a half to two hours. Serve on a hot dish and garnish with chopped parsley.

INDIAN DEVIL

One tablespoon of chutney, one tablespoon ketchup, one tablespoon cold gravy, one tablespoon butter, 1½ teaspoons salt, pepper or mustard to taste.

Mix all well together and in it place thin slices of cooked meat. Stir gently until well heated and serve. Ketchup need not be used if preferred without. — D. Evans, Keyneton.

IRISH STEW

Required.—1 lb. neck chops, one teaspoon salt, quarter teaspoon pepper, half pint water or weak stock, one onion, one small turnip, 2 lb. potatoes.

Wipe the chops, and remove spinal cord and surplus fat. Put the meat into stewpan or casserole with the salt, pepper and liquid, and bring slowly to the boil. Remove the scum, and add the turnips, cut in half-inch dice, the onion in thin rings, and the potatoes in half-inch slices. Simmer for an hour and a half. Serve on a hot dish, the meat in the centre and the potatoes round the edge. Garnish with finely-chopped parsley.

MARINADED STEAK

Put 1½ lbs. of undercut into a casserole and rub into it two tablespoons of flour, one tablespoon sugar, a little pepper and salt. Add one tablespoon vinegar, one tablespoon tomato sauce, one-half tablespoon Worcestershire sauce. Leave steak soaking in this for several hours, turning it occasionally. Before putting in the oven add two cups of boiling water, then bake slowly for 2½ hours.

— Edith E. Rutt.

In an electric cooker put in oven at 450°, reset thermostat to 400°.

Bake in Gas Cooker at 350°F. for 2 hours.

MEAT—BEEF EN CASSEROLE

One and a half lb. stewing steak, 1 onion, 1 cup carrot, 1 cup turnip, ½ cup celery, ¾ pint water or stock, small bunch of herbs, salt and pepper.

Wipe meat and cut into small pieces. Heat 1 oz. dripping in a frying pan and brown meat. Cut vegetables in dice, onions in thin rings. Put a layer of vegetables in the bottom of a casserole and the meat on top; add seasoning, remainder of vegetables and stock. Cook slowly for two to two and a half hours. Mutton may be done the same way, using a piece cut from the leg.

MEAT PIE

Take 1 lb. steak diced or minced, one onion, three cloves, salt to taste, and a pinch of sugar. Roll the meat in flour, cut the onion up finely, and put them both in a saucepan with sufficient cold water to cover them well. Add the cloves and the pinch of sugar, and the salt when it is almost at boiling point. Don't let it boil, only simmer until cooked enough. Prepare a pie-dish with short pastry, and bake a nice brown. Serve hot with mashed potato. Onion may be omitted.

— Miss E. Jones, Port Elliot.

In an Electric Cooker bake at 450°.

Bake in Gas Cooker at 425° F.

MINCED VEAL STEAKS

One lb. veal, 3 oz. ham or bacon, 2 oz. chopped suet, 2 tablespoons bread crumbs, grated rind of half a lemon, 1 dessertspoon chopped parsley, a pinch of nutmeg, salt and pepper.

Mince veal and ham finely and mix other ingredients with it; bind together with a little beaten egg. Form into flat cakes on a floured board; coat with egg and bread crumbs. Fry in hot fat and drain well. Serve hot with tomato or brown sauce, and garnish with lemon.

MIROTON OF BEEF

One pound cold meat, half onion, salt, pepper to taste, one dessertspoon flour, one tablespoon butter or dripping, half pint stock.

Brown onions in butter. Add flour. Stir well. Add gradually the stock, salt, pepper. Cover. Boil gently three-quarters of an hour. Cut meat into neat pieces. Warm through. Place the meat in the dish, bread crumbs on top. Bake.

— M. Higginbottom.

MUTTON AND MACARONI

One lb. neck chops, 1 onion, 1 teaspoon salt, ⅛ teaspoon pepper, ½ pint water, ¼ lb. macaroni.

Trim meat and place in a saucepan with liquid and seasoning. Bring slowly to the boil; remove scum, and add onion cut in thin rings. Simmer 1½ to 2 hours.

Cook macaroni in fast-boiling salted water for 10 minutes; strain and add to meat half an hour before serving. This may be cooked in a casserole.

OX TONGUE IN JELLY

After skinning tongue cut it in halves, lengthways; put into a round cake tin or mould. Boil some of the liquid with the trimmings from the tongue; strain, and pour over. Turn out when cold and set.

RABBIT PIE

Cut the rabbit into joints and put into a pie-dish. Cover with milk and cook slowly in oven for about two hours. Take out and add salt and pepper and thicken with flour. Lay a few slices of bacon on the top. Cover with an inch or so of veal stuffing and bake for another hour. — Daisy E. L. Evans, Keyneton.

In an Electric Cooker bake at 400° for two hours and then for another hour at 350°.

Bake in Gas Cooker at 375° F.

RISSOLES

Cold minced meat, mashed potatoes, seasoning. Make into cakes and fry in boiling fat. Add a little butter.

— M. Higginbottom.

ROMAN PUDDING

Boil one rabbit until tender. Take the meat off the bones, and cut it up small. Mix it with 2 oz. boiled macaroni, 2 oz. grated cheese, one small onion chopped fine, one-half pint milk, pepper, and salt. Put in a pie-dish and bake with a little butter on the top. —Mrs. W. Simmons, Ardrossan.

In an Electric Cooker bake at 400°.

Bake in Gas Cooker at 375° F.

RUSSIAN STEAKS

Half pound tender steak, ½ lb. fillet of veal, 1 shallot, yolk of 1 egg, 1 teaspoon chopped parsley, salt and pepper to taste, a pinch of mace.

Put meat twice through mincer; add seasonings, and mix with yolk of egg. Spread on a plate and allow it to set for half an hour. Divide into eight or ten pieces, form into flat cakes on a floured board. Egg and bread crumb and fry. Serve with gravy or tomato sauce.

SAVOURY BALLS

Six ounces flour, one teaspoon baking powder, 2 oz. suet, one pinch salt, one teaspoon chopped parsley, one pinch dried herbs.

Chop suet finely, add other ingredients, and mix to a soft dough with water. Form into balls and cook in the stew for 20 to 30 minutes.

SAVOURY CHOPS

One pound chops, 1 teacup each of chopped carrot and turnip, 2 tablespoons of chopped onion, ½ pint stock, seasoning, 1 tablespoon rice. Put vegetables, rice, seasoning, and stock in a saucepan; bring slowly to the boil. Wipe chops and trim off fat. Simmer till done—1 to 1½ hours. Serve vegetables on a hot dish, the chops on top, and garnish with sippets of toast.

SAVOURY PIE

One pound chuck or skirt steak, 1 onion, 1 tablespoon Worcestershire sauce, a sheep's kidney, 1 tablespoon flour, 1 dessertspoon finely chopped parsley, salt, pepper, half pint water.

Cut the steak into inch squares and roll in seasoned flour. Slice the onion and add to the meat. Skin the kidney and chop finely.

Put all the ingredients into a saucepan and simmer for 1½ hours. Pour into a pie-dish and allow to become cool before covering with the following:—

CARROT ROUNDABOUTS

Make a short pastry, roll it out thinly, brush with milk and sprinkle thickly with grated carrot and chopped parsley. Roll up as for Swiss Roll, cut in slices and place in overlapping layers on the meat. Bake in a hot oven till cooked, about 20 minutes.

—Mrs. J. Wilson, Black Forest.

SAVOURY STEAK

Ingredients.—1 lb. bladebone steak, one teaspoon salt, one-eighth teaspoon pepper, one teaspoon sugar, one tablespoon flour, half nutmeg, grated, one tablespoon vinegar, one tablespoon Worcestershire sauce, one tablespoon tomato sauce, half pint of water.

Method.—Mix flour, pepper, salt and nutmeg together. Rub into steak, and sprinkle remainder on top after placing in a casserole. Mix water, vinegar and sauces together with sugar and pour over meat, etc. Cover and cook in a slow oven for two hours. — R.M. — J.C.C.

In an Electric Cooker put in oven at 450°, reset thermostat to 400°.

Bake in Gas Cooker at 350° F. till tender.

SAVOURY ROLY-POLY PUDDING

Prepare a suet crust with ¾ lb. flour and ¼ lb. suet. Roll out thinly and cover it first with a layer of chopped raw potatoes, then some finger lengths of fresh uncooked beef, a little parsley and onion, and a good seasoning of pepper and salt. Wet the edges, tie up in floured cloth, and boil for three hours. Cooked meat may be used, in which case the pudding will not need so much boiling. — J.S.

SAUSAGE ROLLS

Take some sausage meat, a little stock or gravy. Stir together in a pot over a gentle heat. Make a nice puff paste, roll out in squares. Put some of the meat on each. Roll up, glaze with egg, and bake 20 minutes. — M. Higginbottom.

In an Electric Cooker bake at 500° for 20 minutes.

Bake in a Gas Cooker at 450° F.

SEA PIE

A pound and a half steak, one teaspoon salt, one-eighth teaspoon pepper, one turnip, one carrot, one onion, one pint water.

For Crust—Half lb. flour, one pinch salt, half teaspoon baking powder, quarter pint water, 3 oz. suet.

Cut meat in small pieces and put in a saucepan with salt, pepper and water. Bring slowly to the boil. Add vegetables cut in dice, and simmer for an hour and a half. Roll out suet crust to fit saucepan, put over meat, and cook slowly for another half hour. Serve on a hot dish, the meat in centre, and the pastry round.

STEAK AND KIDNEY PIE

One pound blade, chuck or skirt steak, one sheep's kidney, half tablespoon flour, half teaspoon salt, one-eighth teaspoon pepper, 1½ gills water, ½ lb. flake or rough puff pastry.

Prepare the meat as for pudding; put into a saucepan with the water and simmer for an hour and a half. Place a pie cup in the centre of the pie-dish, and pour in the cooked meat. Allow to cool. Roll out pastry a little larger than the pie-dish. Cut off a strip of pastry and put round the wet edge of the pie-dish. Moisten this and cover with remaining pastry. Trim the edges and cut. Ornament the top with a rose and leaves; make three incisions in the pastry, and glaze with egg yolk. Bake in a hot oven till the pastry is done—20 to 30 minutes. If meat is not done place in a cooler part of the oven. Send to the table with a jug of hot water or the extra gravy.

If liked, the meat need not be cooked first. Cover with pastry, bake in a hot oven for 20 to 30 minutes, then in a cooler part or on top of the stove for an hour to an hour and a half. If on the top of the stove, return pie to oven for five minutes to crisp the pastry.

In an Electric Cooker bake at 450°.

Bake in a Gas Cooker at 425° F., then reduce temperature to 375° F.

STEAK AND KIDNEY PUDDING

Two pounds blade, chuck or skirt steak, two sheep's kidneys, one tablespoon flour, one teaspoon salt, quarter teaspoon pepper, 12 oz. suet crust.

Wipe the meat, remove fat, and cut into strips 2 in. by 1 in. Roll in seasoned flour. Skin and wash and dry the kidney, and cut into small pieces. Roll a piece of kidney into piece of steak. Line a greased pudding basin with two-thirds of the pastry. Put in the meat and half a pint of water, and cover with pastry. Place a piece of greased paper over the pudding, then tie on firmly a pudding cloth. Boil for two or three hours. Serve on a plate with a serviette folded round the basin.

STEWED STEAK

Two pounds blade or chuck steak, one teaspoon salt, quarter teaspoon pepper, a pint and a half water, two carrots, half turnip, 1 piece celery, 2 or 3 tomatoes, 2 tablespoons pearl barley.

Wipe meat, remove fat, and cut into pieces about 3 in. square. Put into saucepan with water, salt and pepper. Bring slowly to boil, add vegetables, onions cut in thin rings, carrots, turnips, celery in dice, and tomatoes in slices, and washed barley. Simmer 2 hours. —Mrs. T. C. Sharman.

SHEPHERD'S OR POTATO PIE

Any cooked meat, small onion (minced), one dessertspoon flour, quarter pint stock or gravy, mashed potatoes, one dessertspoon tomato sauce, pepper, and salt, one dessertspoon butter.

Remove skin, gristle and some fat from meat; mince or chop finely. Put in a saucepan with gravy, flour and flavourings, and cook slowly for five minutes. Put into a greased pie-dish and cover with mashed potatoes. Spread butter on top. Place in a hot oven till browned.

If there is no stock or gravy, heat 1 oz. dripping in a pan, slice one small onion thinly and brown. Add ½ oz. flour, brown well. Stir in gradually half a pint of water. Boil three minutes. Season and strain.

In an Electric Cooker bake at 450°.

Bake in Gas Cooker at 375° F.

SPICED MUTTON

One pound leg chops, 4 oz. celery, 1 oz. dripping, one teaspoon chutney, quarter teaspoon ground ginger, one teaspoon salt, half pint stock or water, 4 oz. onions, quarter teaspoon curry powder, quarter teaspoon allspice, 1 oz. ground rice, quarter teaspoon cloves, one tablespoon sultanas.

Cut meat into neat pieces and sprinkle with spices. Brown meat and onions in hot fat. Add the ground rice and stir well. Add gradually the liquid and celery. Simmer slowly till tender—about an hour and a half. Half an hour before serving, add sultanas; five minutes before serving add chutney.

STEWED CHOPS

One pound neck chops, one onion, one carrot, one turnip, one teaspoon salt, one-eighth teaspoon pepper, half pint water, ½ oz. flour.

Wipe the meat, remove the fat, and put into a saucepan with the water, salt and pepper. Bring slowly to the boil and remove the scum. Add the vegetables, the onion cut in thin rings, the carrot and turnip diced. Simmer an hour and a half to two hours. Lift chops on to a hot dish, thicken gravy with the flour mixed to a smooth paste. Pour over meat and garnish with chopped parsley. — Miss D. Chenoweth, Willaston.

STEWED OX KIDNEY

One ox kidney, 2 tablespoons flour, ½ teaspoon mixed spice, 1 teaspoon salt, ⅛ teaspoon pepper, ¾ pint stock or water, 1 tablespoon chopped onion, 1 dessertspoon ketchup, 2 oz. dripping.

Wash, scald and dry kidney. Cut in thin slices, removing fat. Mix flour, rice, salt, and pepper, and coat kidney well. Heat fat in saucepan, brown kidneys and onion well. Add stock and ketchup, and stir till it boils. Simmer slowly for 1½ to 2 hours. Serve on a hot dish with a border of rice or mashed potatoes. A little bacon, a few mushrooms, or tomatoes are an improvement.

STEWED OX TAIL

One ox tail, 1 pint brown stock or water, 1 carrot, ½ turnip, 1 onion, small bunch herbs, 2 oz. flour, 2 oz. dripping, salt, pepper, juice of half a lemon.

Wash the tail, cut it at joints in 2 in. lengths, and trim off superfluous fat. Put in a saucepan with a little salt; cover with cold water and bring to the boil. Boil 10 minutes; strain and rinse. Dry well and coat with flour. Heat dripping in a stewpan and brown meat; add vegetables, cut in dice, the stock and seasoning. Cook slowly till tender (3 to 4 hours), skimming when necessary. Lift meat on to a hot dish; skim gravy, add lemon juice, and strain over tail. Garnish with fancy shapes of carrot and turnip, which have been cooked separately.

STEWED RABBIT

One rabbit, one onion, one pint and a half water, 1 oz. flour, 1 oz. dripping, one teaspoon salt, quarter teaspoon pepper, three slices of bacon, one carrot, one turnip, one stick celery, one blade mace.

Soak the rabbit in cold salted water for half an hour. Dry and cut into joints and coat with the seasoned flour. Brown in the hot fat. Place in a saucepan. Slice onion thinly and brown. Add remainder of flour and stir till a dark brown. Stir in gradually the liquid and boil three minutes. Cool and pour on to rabbit. Add vegetables cut in dice; the mace and bacon in small pieces. Simmer an hour and a half. Serve on a hot dish, and garnish with chopped parsley.

STEWED TRIPE AND ONIONS

One pound tripe, 1 onion, ½ pint milk, 1 teaspoon salt, 1 tablespoon flour, 1 teaspoon butter, 1 dessertspoon finely chopped parsley.

Wash tripe, scrape under side if necessary, and cut into pieces 1 in. square. Blanch by putting into a saucepan, covering with cold water, and bringing to the boil. Add ½ pint water, ½ pint milk, salt, butter, and onion sliced thinly. Cook slowly for three-quarters to one hour. Thicken with flour, mixed to a smooth paste. Simmer 5 minutes; add parsley, and serve with toast.

STUFFED STEAK

One and a half lb. topside steak cut with a pocket, veal forcemeat (see page 52). Fill pocket with forcemeat; fasten securely with skewers or sew up. Bake 1 to 1¼ hours.

In an Electric Cooker bake at 400°.

VEAL OLIVE PIE

One and a half lb. fillet of veal or veal cutlets, ¼ lb. bacon or ham, 4 oz. bread crumbs, 1 teaspoon salt, ¼ teaspoon pepper, grated rind of 1 lemon, ½ teaspoon grated nutmeg, 1 dessertspoon of finely chopped parsley, 1 oz. butter or dripping, 3 tablespoons of milk.

Cut the veal in strips 4 ins. by 2 ins., and the bacon in small pieces. Mix the other ingredients together. Place a piece of bacon on a piece of veal; spread on some seasoning, and roll up. Put in a saucepan with ½ pint of stock or water, and simmer for 1½ hours. Put into a pie-dish and allow to cool before covering with flaky or rough puff pastry. Bake in a quick oven for 20 minutes, and then in a slower oven till meat is thoroughly heated.

In an Electric Cooker bake at 450°.

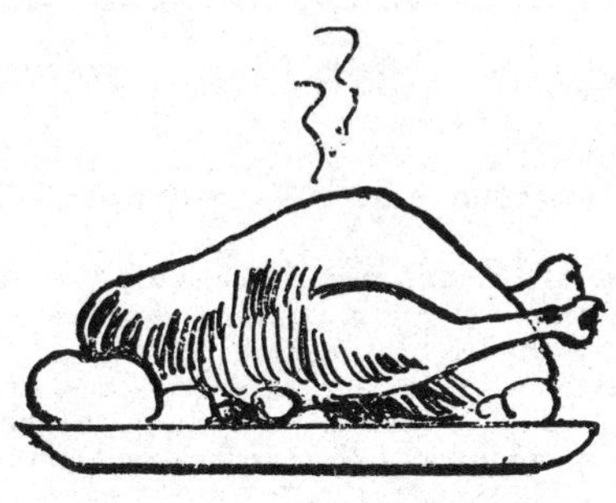

POULTRY

MEAT

SAVOURY SAUCES

POULTRY

DIRECTIONS FOR DRAWING AND TRUSSING POULTRY

1. Pluck and singe the bird.

2. Scald feet and legs. Remove nails and horny skin, and truss.

For Roasting.—Break legs between foot and knee, then twist foot until the sinews are exposed. Draw out sinews with a skewer. Leave leg on while cooking to prevent flesh from shrinking and exposing bone. After cooking cut off leg at knee. Press legs well against body of fowl and secure with string or skewer. Secure flap of skin left on neck with wings.

Ducks and Geese.—Leave feet on when trussing, and twist legs round the body in such a way that feet lie flat on the back. Remove tips of wings of ducks and geese before trussing.

For Geese and Ducks forcemeat is placed in the body of birds.

For Fowls and Turkeys, put forcemeat in neck.

Boiled ham or grilled bacon should be served with poultry and game, as they lack fat.

Trussing for Boiling.—Sever legs at knee joint, then loosen skin of leg so that the legs can be pressed right back into the body.

Boning Poultry.—Birds should be undrawn when boned. Begin at back of bird and lift the flesh with a sharp knife from each side until the legs and wings are reached. Legs and wings should be severed from the body, but the bony carcass should be intact. Bone legs and wings separately.

ACCOMPANIMENTS

Roast Fowl and Roast Turkey.—Celery, tomato or oyster sauce, brown gravy. Bread sauce is always served with fowl.

Roast Goose or Duck.—Apple or tomato sauce, brown gravy.

Boiled Turkey or Boiled Fowl.—Celery, bechamel or any good white sauce.

Geese or Ducks.—Sage and onion stuffing.

TO ROAST A TURKEY

Stuff with veal stuffing and a little sausage meat. Sew up neck. Cover breast with buttered paper and place on meat, stand in baking dish with a plentiful supply of fat in the dish under stand. Give turkey 15 minutes in a hot oven, and then cook slowly to preserve the juices. Baste frequently after the fat has become very hot. Fifteen minutes before serving remove paper to allow breast to brown. Time required for a large turkey, one and a half to two hours. Serve with bread sauce, and garnish with lemon.

In an Electric Cooker place turkey in oven at 425°.

Bake in Gas Cooker at 425° F. for the first 10-15 minutes, then reduce heat to 400° F.

SEASONING FOR FOWLS AND TURKEYS

Ingredients.—Three tablespoons bread crumbs, half tablespoon chopped parsley, one teaspoon herbs, grate of nutmeg, grate of lemon rind, salt and pepper to taste, one egg.

Method.—Mix all together and bind with a well-beaten egg. Place in neck of bird.

BREAD SAUCE FOR FOWLS

Ingredients.—One slice of onion, 12 peppercorns, one pint milk, 4 oz. bread crumbs, 1 oz. butter, salt and pepper.

Method.—Soak peppercorns and onion in milk for 20 minutes. Bring slowly to the boil and strain. Sprinkle on bread crumbs; allow to stand for five minutes and slowly bring to the boil. Stir in butter and flavour.

SAGE AND ONION STUFFING FOR GEESE AND DUCKS

Ingredients.—Four onions, nine sage leaves, 4 oz. bread crumbs, 1 oz. butter, salt and pepper.

Method.—Blanch and boil onions until tender, then drain and mince. Add sage leaves, and cook for five minutes. Mix minced onion and sage leaves with bread crumbs, butter, and salt to taste. Stuff in body of bird.

VEAL FORCEMEAT

Four tablespoons bread crumbs, one tablespoon chopped suet or dripping, one teaspoon chopped parsley, half teaspoon dried herbs, salt and pepper, egg or milk to bind, grated lemon rind, one tablespoon chopped onion. Mix well together and bind with the beaten egg.

GUIDE FOR MEATS

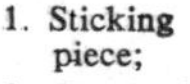

1. Sticking piece;
2. Chuck ribs;
3. Middle ribs;
4. Fore ribs;
5. Sirloin;
6. Rump (silverside, middle and chump end);
7. Aitchbone;
8. Buttock (including topside);
9. Flank;
10. Brisket;
11. Leg of mutton piece;
12. Clod;
13. Mouse buttock and shin;
14. Leg;
15. Tail.

GUIDE FOR BUYING BEEF.

Cuts arranged in order of their prices per lb.

Prime Cuts for Grilling, Roasting or Frying.

Fillet Steak	Wing Rib
Rump Steak	Ribs (for boning and rolling)
Sirloin	Topside (for best cuts)

Best Cuts for Boiling and Stewing.

Silverside Thick Flank	Best pieces for salting and boiling.
Chuck Steak Blade Bone Steak	Very good for stewed or braised steak, ragouts and mince.
Leg of Mutton Cut	Excellent for braising whole.

Cheap Cuts for Stews, Casserole Dishes and Stock.

Leg and Shin of Beef, thick end (boneless)	This is somewhat sinewy, but can be used for stews and ragouts if cooked very slowly until tender. Excellent for meat roll and for beef tea, because it has no fat.
Ox Tail	For stewing, and thin end for soups.
Back Ribs	Use the best meat for stewing, braising, or *en casserole*. The bones and "tail" pieces will make nutritious soups.
Clod and Sticking Piece	Use the meatiest portions for stews and casserole dishes, and the other portions for stock and beef tea. The latter should be cooked the day before, so that the fat may cool and can be lifted.
Brisket	This usually despised and very inexpensive cut makes an excellent joint, stuffed and rolled, and very slowly cooked in a tightly covered roaster. Brown quickly when quite cooked.
Aitchbone	Carries a large proportion of bone, but may be slowly roasted, boiled or used *en casserole*.
Thin Flank	Very cheap cut, but good for braising.
Cheeks	Can also be used for cold meat mould.

Compliments of Mrs. Alex Flint.

— English Homes & Gardens.

TIME-TABLE FOR COOKING MEATS

BEEF AND MUTTON.—15 minutes to each pound and 15 minutes over.

MEAT WITHOUT BONE.—20 minutes to each pound and 20 minutes over.

PORK AND VEAL.—25 minutes to each pound and 20 minutes over.

CORNED ROUND.—25 minutes to each pound and 25 minutes over.

CORNED BRISKET.—30 minutes to each pound and 30 minutes over.

PICKLED PORK.—25 minutes to each pound and 25 minutes over.

HAM.—25 minutes to each pound and 25 minutes over.

TONGUE.—Two to three hours, according to size.

JOINTS AND THEIR ACCOMPANIMENTS

ROAST BEEF.—Yorkshire pudding; horseradish sauce; thin brown gravy; baked vegetables.

CORNED BEEF.—Carrots; turnips; suet dumplings.

BOILED MUTTON.—Carrots; turnips; caper, onion and parsley sauce.

ROAST MUTTON.—Baked vegetables; thin brown gravy; red currant jelly.

ROAST LAMB.—Baked vegetables; green peas; mint sauce; thin brown gravy.

ROAST VEAL.—Boiled ham, bacon, or pickled pork; thick brown gravy; forcemeat.

ROAST PORK.—Sage and onion seasoning; baked vegetables; apple sauce; thin brown gravy.

Oven Temperature Guide

The Celcius (°C) and Fahrenheit (°F) temperatures in this chart relate to most electric ovens. Decrease by 10°C or 25°F for gas ovens or refer to the manufacturer's temperature guide. For temperatures below 160°C (325°F) do not decrease the given temperature.

Oven Description	°C	°F	Gas Mark
Cool	100	200	¼
Very slow	120	250	½
Slow	150	300	2
Warm	160	325	3
Moderate	180	350	4
Moderately hot	200	400	6
Hot	220	425	7
Very hot	230	450	8
Extremely hot	250	500	10

MEATS

CUTS OF MEAT AND HOW TO COOK THEM

ROASTING OR BAKING

BEEF.—Sirloin; wing rib; ribs (rolled); topside.
MUTTON.—Leg; shoulder; loin; saddle.
PORK.—Leg; loin.
VEAL.—Shoulder; loin; leg; fillet

BOILING

CORNED BEEF.—Silverside; round; aitchbone; brisket; ox tongue.
MUTTON.—Leg; neck; sheep's tongues; corned breast.
PORK.—Pickled hand; breast; pig's cheek; ham.

GRILLING

Rump or fillet steak; skirt steak. Short loin chops; cutlets. Small fish. Small birds. Bacon.

STEWING

BEEF.—Skirt; buttock; topside; bladebone and chuck steak; ox tail; ox kidney; tripe.
MUTTON.—Breast; neck; chops; brains; kidneys.

FRYING

Sausages; cutlets; liver; kidney; pork chops; veal cutlets; brains; bacon.

SOUP BONES

Shin of beef; knuckles and shanks of mutton; scrag end of neck; knuckles of veal; sheep's heads.

BAKED MEAT

Place the meat on a trivet in a baking dish with three or four tablespoons of fat. Put in a hot oven for 10 minutes to set the surface albumen, thus keeping in the meat juices. Reduce the heat. Baste every 20 minutes. Salt may be sprinkled on the meat after the first 10 minutes.

In an Electric Cooker bake at 400°.
Bake in Gas Cooker at 425° F.

TO MAKE GRAVY

Carefully strain off the fat from the baking dish, leaving behind the sediment. Add one dessertspoon flour, salt and pepper to taste, and brown over the fire. Add three-quarters to a pint of stock or water (if cold add all at once; if hot or boiling, gradually). Stir till boiling and boil for three minutes. Strain, if necessary, into a gravy boat.

BRAISED NECK AND BREAST OF MUTTON

Three pounds boned neck and breast of mutton, veal forcemeat, root vegetables, two tomatoes, stock or water.

Remove any superfluous fat and beat the meat. Spread on the forcemeat, roll up and tie with string or tape. Cut the vegetables in dice, and put in a saucepan with half a teaspoon salt and enough stock to cover. Bring to the boil. Place meat on the bed of vegetables, which should be 2 in. high, and simmer for two hours; baste occasionally with the stock, and turn once. Remove from saucepan and brown in oven. Strain the vegetables, remove fat from the liquid, and boil quickly to form a glaze. Remove string from meat and place in a hot dish. Garnish with vegetables and pour over the liquid.

SALTED MEATS

Wash the joint to remove some of the salt. Put into tepid water and bring slowly to the boil; this helps to draw out the salt and soften the tough fibres. Simmer for rest of time. Remove scum as it rises. Salted meats should be allowed to cool in the water in which they are cooked; this makes them tender and juicy. A little vinegar added to the water will help make the meat tender.

TO PICKLE MEAT

Mix one cupful salt, one tablespoonful dark sugar, one teaspoonful saltpetre. Mix and rub this well into the meat; next day turn over and rub more salt on. Let stand for three or four days.

To make brine: One pound salt, 2 oz. brown sugar, 1 oz. saltpetre to each gallon of boiled water. When quite cold put in the meat. This will keep quite a long time.

TO COOK A HAM

Soak the ham in cold water for several hours. If very dry and salted, from 12 to 24 hours; the water should be changed two or three times. Scrape the ham and remove all rust and discoloured parts. Put into a large vessel with sufficient lukewarm water to cover. Bring to boil and simmer till done—allow two hours for a ham weighing 8 to 10 lb. and two and a quarter hours for 12 lb. Leave in water till cold. Remove rind, smooth fat, and sprinkle thickly with brown bread crumbs and decorate with cloves. Put a paper frill round knuckle of ham.

BOILED MEAT

Put the meat into fast-boiling water without salt (salt helps to draw out the juices). Boil for five or ten minutes to set the surface albumen and so keep in the meat juices. Remove scum. Simmer till done to make tender. Root vegetables should be cooked with the meat.

REAL YORKSHIRE PUDDING

One egg, two tablespoonfuls flour, one saltspoon salt, one breakfast cup milk and water mixed.

Method.—Beat up the egg, then add milk and water. Sprinkle flour into the liquid, stirring all the time. Give the batter a good beating. It is then ready to bake. Put some dripping in the tin, so that when melted it will be a quarter of an inch deep. Let it stand on stove until it is piping hot, then pour in the batter. Slip it quickly into the oven, and bake for half an hour. A quick oven first ten minutes; after that it will only require soaking.

— Mrs. G. H. Lang, Gawler South.

In an Electric Cooker bake at 450°.

BOILED OX TONGUE

Wash the tongue well and put into a saucepan of lukewarm water. Bring slowly to the boil; skim and simmer till done—2 to 2½ hours for a small tongue; 3 hours for a larger one. When done, plunge into cold water (this enables skin to be easily removed), and skin.

MOCK DUCK

Bone a shoulder of mutton, leaving in the knuckle. Fill with sage and onion stuffing (see page 52), and fasten securely, arranging the joint to look like a duck, the knuckle forming the head.

Allow 20 minutes for each lb. and extra 20 minutes over. Serve with gravy and baked vegetables. — Mrs. T. C. Sharman.

SAVOURY SAUCES

Foundation—Melted Butter Sauce

One ounce butter, 1 oz. flour, half to one pint milk or stock, white pepper, salt, lemon juice.

Melt butter. Add flour, and blend well together with wooden spoon, and cook for a minute or two. Draw pan off fire and add liquid, then stir until boiling. Add seasoning, and simmer at least five minutes. Add lemon juice when sauce is off the fire. When sauce is to be served with vegetables, use half milk and half the liquid in which the vegetables were cooked.

BECHAMEL

Use seasoned milk and add a little cream. (For seasoned milk, put as much milk as is required into a saucepan, and add small quantity carrot, turnip, onion, celery, parsley, one or two cloves, blade of mace. Let this stand by the side of the fire to infuse, then strain and cool before using.)

ANCHOVY OR SHRIMP

To half a pint of white sauce made with fish stock and milk add one teaspoon of anchovy or shrimp essence.

CAPER

To half pint white sauce made with fish stock or meat liquor add one tablespoon of chopped capers and one tablespoon of vinegar.

EGG

To half pint of white sauce add one or two hard-boiled eggs finely chopped.

PARSLEY

Add finely-chopped parsley.

ONION

Add chopped Spanish onions which have been cooked until tender.

APPLE SAUCE

Two apples, one teaspoon butter, one tablespoon sugar, one tablespoon water and juice of one-quarter lemon.

After peeling and slicing the apples place them in a saucepan with the other ingredients and stew till tender. Beat with wooden spoon until smooth. To be served with roast pork, roast goose, or roast duck. — F.M.S.

BROWN SAUCE

One oz. dripping, 1 oz. flour, one blade mace, one small onion, one piece carrot, one piece turnip and celery, 12 peppercorns, four cloves, half teaspoon salt, bouquet garni, one pint brown stock or water.

Cut onion thinly and brown in the hot fat. Add the flour and brown well. Stir in gradually the stock or water, and boil five minutes. Add vegetables, roughly cut up, and flavourings. Simmer slowly for half to three-quarters of an hour. Strain through a fine strainer.

HORSERADISH SAUCE

Two tablespoons of grated horseradish, one teaspoon made mustard, one teaspoon sifted sugar, one teaspoon salt, one tablespoon vinegar, and three tablespoons of cream.

MINT SAUCE

One tablespoon chopped green mint, one tablespoon white sugar, one tablespoon boiling water, two tablespoons vinegar.

Wash and dry mint, chop finely after removing stalks and put in tureen. Boil sugar and water for one minute. Add to mint and vinegar as well. Allow to stand for 15 minutes. Stir well before using. To be served with roast lamb. — F.M.S.

TOMATO SAUCE

One and a half cups tomatoes (canned ones may be used), ¼ pint water, 1 clove, 1 bay leaf, 1 onion, salt and pepper, 1 oz. butter.

Cook together slowly for half an hour; strain and thicken with 1 oz. flour mixed to a thin, smooth paste.

VEGETABLES

(ROOTS, GREENS, DRESSED VEGETABLES)

VEGETABLES

(Roots, Greens, Dressed Vegetables)

JERUSALEM ARTICHOKES BOILED

Wash, brush and peel the artichokes. Put into clean cold water with a few drops of lemon juice or vinegar to preserve the colour. Cook in boiling salted water (one teaspoon salt added to one pint water). Cook slowly till done. Test with a skewer. Drain in a colander and serve in a hot vegetable dish. Pour over white sauce. If liked, the artichokes may be cooked in milk or milk and water. The liquid should be used for the sauce.

BOILED BEETROOT

Wash the roots carefully; do not cut the skin; leave on the tops. Cook in boiling salted water, and cook gently till done—one to two hours. Remove skin. Beetroot may be served hot with white sauce, or cold as salad.

BOILED CARROTS

Wash the carrots and scrape thinly. Drop into cold water. Cook in boiling salted water, and cook slowly till tender—20 to 30 minutes. Drain in a colander, and serve in a hot vegetable dish with parsley sauce.

BOILED ONIONS

Remove the outer skin. Blanch the onions by putting into a saucepan of cold water and bringing to the boil. Strain and cook slowly in boiling salted water (one teaspoon to one pint) till done—three-quarters of an hour to an hour and a half, according to size. Drain in a colander, and serve with white sauce.

BOILED PARSNIPS

Wash and scrape the parsnips and drop into cold water. Cut off ends and cut thick parts in halves lengthways. Cook slowly in boiling salted water till done—20 to 30 minutes. Drain in a colander and serve with parsley sauce.

If preferred, the parsnips may be mashed with a little butter and pepper.

TO SCRAPE NEW POTATOES

Soak in cold water to which has been added a small piece of common soda for a few minutes. The skin scrapes off easily without staining hands.

NEW POTATOES

Choose potatoes of one size. Scrub the potatoes well and scrape, removing all specks. Cook in boiling salted water with a sprig of mint, and cook slowly till done—15 to 25 minutes. Drain against the lid of a saucepan. Place a clean cloth over the potatoes and stand the saucepan in a warm place. This absorbs all the moisture. Shake over the fire with one teaspoon butter, one dessertspoon chopped parsley and a little pepper.

OLD POTATOES

Choose potatoes of one size. Scrub and peel thinly. Put in a saucepan with sufficient salt and enough cold water to barely cover them. Bring slowly to the boil and cook slowly till done—20 to 30 minutes. The potatoes should be firm and unbroken. Drain against the lid of the saucepan. Cover the potatoes with a cloth, and stand on the side of the stove for a few minutes. Lift out carefully on to a hot vegetable dish.

Note.—If potatoes are cooked in too much water and allowed to boil too rapidly they will not remain whole.

MASHED POTATOES

After draining the potatoes, break up with a fork. Add two tablespoons of hot milk and one teaspoon of butter and a little pepper to each pound of potatoes. Beat well with a wooden spoon till smooth and creamy. Pile in a hot vegetable dish.

SWEDE TURNIPS

Peel the turnips thickly and drop into cold water. Cut if necessary, and cook slowly in boiling salted water till soft—about three-quarters of an hour. Drain in a colander, return to saucepan, mash them with one dessertspoonful of butter and a little pepper.

WHITE TURNIPS

Peel the turnips very thickly to remove the woody portion. Wash in cold water. Cook slowly in boiled salted water till tender—20 to 40 minutes. Drain in a colander. Serve in a hot vegetable dish with butter and pepper. White sauce may be poured over them. Garnish in either case with finely-chopped parsley.

BAKED ONIONS

Skin the onions and blanch if necessary. Cook in boiling salted water for half an hour, drain well. Bake in hot fat until done—test with a skewer. Baste every quarter of an hour.

BAKED PARSNIPS

Prepare the parsnips as for boiling. Boil in salted water for 10 minutes; strain. Place in a baking dish with the meat and cook till done—20 to 30 minutes.

BAKED POTATOES

Scrub, peel, wash and dry the potatoes. Cut in halves lengthways, and sprinkle with salt. Put in a baking dish with the meat and baste with the hot fat. Cook for 30 to 40 minutes, keeping well basted, and turn once. Drain free from fat, and serve in a hot vegetable dish.

If liked, the potatoes may be boiled for five or ten minutes before baking.

POTATOES BAKED IN THEIR SKINS

Take potatoes of medium and equal sizes. Scrub well, remove eyes, and prick. Bake in a hot oven till soft—three-quarters to one hour. Turn the potatoes occasionally so that they cook evenly.

GREEN VEGETABLES

Green vegetables must always be put into fast-boiling salted water, brought quickly to the boil and boiled with the lid on. If this is not done, the greens lose their bright colour, and are apt to be tough.

BOILED APPLE CUCUMBERS

Peel the cucumbers and cook slowly in boiling salted water with the lid partly off till tender. Drain free from water and serve with white sauce.

ASPARAGUS

Scrape each stick of asparagus well, being careful not to break the tops. Tie into bundles, keeping tops all together, and wash well. Stand upright in boiling salted water which comes about two-thirds up the bundles. Add half a teaspoon of lemon juice or vinegar, and cook gently for 20 or 30 minutes. Make a piece of toast and place it in a hot vegetable dish. When asparagus is soft, lift on to toast. Pour melted butter over the tops, and serve.

BROAD BEANS

Shell and wash the beans. Cook in fast-boiling salted water till tender. Strain in a colander. Melt one dessertspoon butter in a saucepan. Add the beans, a little salt and pepper, and shake over the fire for a few minutes. Serve in a hot vegetable dish.

If beans are old, remove the skins before cooking; put in a basin of boiling water, cover and leave a few minutes; drain and remove skins.

When broad beans are very young they may be prepared and cooked in the same way as French Beans.

CABBAGE

Remove the coarse outside leaves and stalk. Cut the cabbage in halves or quarters and soak in cold salted water for one hour. Cook in fast-boiling salted water, with lid on, until tender—20 to 40 minutes. Drain in a colander and press well with a plate. Serve in a hot vegetable dish. Add one teaspoon butter and sprinkle with pepper.

CAULIFLOWER

Remove outside tough leaves and cut stalk in four. Soak in cold salted water for half an hour. Put into large saucepan of fast-boiling salted water, stalks downwards. Boil slowly with the lid off till tender. Lift out carefully and serve on a piece of toast placed in a hot vegetable dish. Pour melted butter sauce over top.

BOILED CELERY

Separate the sticks, wash well, scrape and cut into suitable pieces. Cook quickly, with the lid partly off, in boiling salted water till tender—a half to three-quarters of an hour. Drain in a colander and serve with white sauce. Use some of the liquid to make the sauce.

FRENCH BEANS

Wash the beans, cut off ends and string; slice in thin strips. Cook in fast-boiling salted water. Cook quickly, with lid on, for 15 to 20 minutes. Drain in colander. Serve in a hot vegetable dish. Add one teaspoon butter and sprinkle with pepper.

When French beans have become limp through having been picked a day or two, pour hot (nearly boiling) water over them before cutting them for use; they will then slice easily.

—Mrs. R. G. Abbott, Port Elliot, S.A.

BOILED LETTUCE

Three large lettuces, three large bunches of parsley, one teaspoon of salt. Wash the lettuce and parsley well, and put it into a saucepan half full of boiling water. Add the teaspoon of salt. Steam well, and after cooking for 20 minutes add a small piece of butter, and pepper to taste. Make the following sauce, pour it over the greens, and serve:—One cup milk, one teaspoon mustard, one teaspoon sugar. Bring these to the boil and thicken with flour. Radish and turnip tops, cooked like ordinary greens, are very tasty.

MARROW OR TROMBONE

Cut marrow or trombone into suitable pieces and peel thinly so as to show the green. Drop into cold water. Cook in boiling salted water with the lid partly off till done—15 to 20 minutes. Lift out with a slice and serve on toast placed in a hot vegetable dish. Pour over melted butter sauce and garnish with finely chopped parsley.

GREEN PEAS

Shell the peas. Put into almost boiling water with half dessertspoon salt, one teaspoon sugar, and a sprig of mint added to each quart. Simmer till done—15 to 30 minutes. Drain in a colander. Remove mint. Return to saucepan and shake over the fire with one teaspoon butter.

SPINACH

Remove the white stalk and discoloured leaves. Put into a saucepan with the water that clings to the leaves. Add one teaspoon salt and cook with the lid on till tender—about 20 minutes, stirring occasionally. Drain in a colander, press out water with a plate, and chop. Return to saucepan. Add one teaspoon butter, lemon juice, and pepper to taste. Serve on pieces of toast.

SILVER BEET

Prepare the same way as spinach, and if young, cook the same way. If old, cook in half pint boiling salted water. Drain free from water, and serve the same as spinach.

SAVOURY CARROTS

One bunch carrots, a little butter, salt and pepper to taste, one teaspoonful of finely chopped parsley, one tablespoonful of finely chopped onions.

Wash and scrape the carrots and cut them into rings about quarter inch thick. Put butter into saucepan and when it is melted add the other ingredients. Toss over fire till the carrots are well saturated with the butter, then add one-half pint of stock and simmer gently till tender. — Mrs. Geo. Heath, Keyneton.

STEWED MUSHROOMS

One pound mushrooms, 1 oz. butter, a gill and a half of stock or water, lemon juice, one teaspoon flour, salt and pepper.

Peel and trim, wash and dry the mushrooms; if large, cut. Put into a saucepan with the butter, salt, pepper, liquid, and a squeeze of lemon juice. Stew slowly for 10 minutes. Thicken with the flour mixed to a smooth paste, and stew for another quarter of an hour. Serve on buttered toast. If liked, the mushrooms may be cooked in half milk and half water.

ANNA POTATOES

Cut some peeled potatoes into thin slices, and after leaving them in cold water for a quarter of an hour dry on a soft cloth. Butter a dish and put in an even layer of sliced potatoes. Spread a small quantity of butter or dripping over them, and sprinkle with a little salt, pepper and grated nutmeg. Then add rest of potatoes in same way, layer on layer. When dish is full, place a piece of paper on top and cook in moderate oven for one hour. Half an hour before potatoes are done pour some milk under paper, but do not touch potatoes. Serve them turned out on hot dish. — B.A.S.

In an Electric Cooker bake at 400°.

Bake in Gas Cooker at 350° F.

POTATO CAKES

These may be eaten without meat, but usually with poultry.

Mash two or three pounds hot boiled potatoes. Add slice butter and two or three beaten eggs. Rub mash with wooden spoon until quite smooth, then spread out in layer three-quarter inch thick. Stamp out with paste cutter. Brush cakes over with beaten egg, cover with bread crumbs, and dust with grated cheese Fry cakes in hot fat until they are brown. Drain on kitchen paper and serve very hot. — Miss B. Skewes, Victor Harbour

POTATO CHIPS

Peel potatoes, wash and dry. Cut into thin slices or strips and dry thoroughly. Place in a frying basket and deep fry in smoking hot fat for two or three minutes. Lift out basket, and allow fat to get smoking hot. Put chips in fat again and fry till a golden brown. Drain on kitchen paper, sprinkle with salt and serve hot.

POTATO PUFF

Two breakfast cups of cold mashed potatoes, two tablespoons of oiled butter, two eggs, one teacup of milk, salt to taste.

Stir butter into potato and beat to a white cream. Add eggs, whipped very light, the milk and the salt. Beat well. Pour into a deep dish and bake in a hot oven till brown.

—Miss B. Skewes, Victor Harbor.

SMOTHERED POTATOES

Six medium potatoes, a cup and a half of milk, two tablespoons butter, three tablespoons flour, half teaspoon salt, one onion, pepper.

Slice potatoes quarter inch thick. Place a layer of potatoes on the bottom of a baking dish, sprinkle with flour, dot with butter. Scrape a little onion and pepper slightly. Fill the dish up with layers of this kind, ending with uncovered potatoes. Fill the dish with milk, and bake in a moderate oven for an hour and a half. The potatoes should be browned on top.

In an Electric Cooker bake at 400°.
Bake in Gas Cooker at 350° F.

BAKED CABBAGE

One firm cabbage well boiled, pressed and cut, two eggs, pepper and salt, two tablespoons chopped cold bacon, two tablespoons milk, one tablespoon butter.

Mix well together. Place in buttered fireproof dish. Put small pieces butter on top. Bake till brown and hot.

Note.—A good way to use up cold left-over cabbage.—W.G.T.

In an Electric Cooker bake at 400°.
Bake in Gas Cooker at 325° F.

TOMATO PIE

Butter a dish and fill up with alternate layers of sliced tomatoes, sliced onions, and bread crumbs, with a little butter or dripping on top of last layer of crumbs, and bake to a nice brown. Use with roast beef, mutton, etc. —Mrs. A. H. Kerr, Mitcham.

In an Electric Cooker bake at 400°.
Bake in Gas Cooker at 350° F.

TOMATOES AU GRATIN

Dip three or four tomatoes into boiling water for a minute or so. Dry and remove the skins. Cut in slices, season with pepper and salt. Mix three tablespoons bread crumbs and two tablespoons grated cheese together. Place tomatoes and bread crumbs and cheese alternately in a greased pie-dish, having crumbs for the last layer. Put 1 oz. butter in small pieces on top of dish, and bake for 20 minutes. — Mrs. J. Colliver.

In an Electric Cooker bake at 400°.

Bake in Gas Cooker at 350° F.

STUFFED POTATOES

Four or five potatoes, three or four tablespoonfuls cooked meat, one teaspoon chopped parsley, two tablespoons sauce or cream or one egg, seasoning.

Choose potatoes of equal size and of good shape. Prepare and cook the same as potatoes baked in skins (page 63). Cut a piece from the top of each potato and scoop out the centre without damaging the skin. Add this to the finely chopped meat and parsley. Season well and bind with the sauce, cream or beaten egg. Refill the skins, piling high in the centre, sprinkle bread crumbs over the top, and put a little butter on each one. Heat in the oven, and serve garnished with sprigs of parsley.

STUFFED TOMATOES

Half ounce bread crumbs, 1 oz. butter, two level tablespoons chopped parsley, two teaspoons grated cheese, one level tablespoon chopped onion, salt, pepper, browned crumbs, one level tablespoon thick gravy or sauce.

Mix all except cheese and browned crumbs. Scoop out some of soft part of tomatoes and fill with mixture, putting a little cheese and browned crumbs on top. Bake. — E. F. Benskin.

Six large tomatoes, two tablespoons bread crumbs, three tablespoons cold meat (chopped finely), one dessertspoon chopped parsley, grated nutmeg, salt and pepper, butter.

Cut the tops off the tomatoes and scoop out the inside. Mix together the meat, bread crumbs, flavouring and two tablespoons of tomato pulp. Fill tomatoes with mixture, place a little butter on, and replace tops. Bake in a moderate oven. Serve on slices of fried bread or toast.

In an Electric Cooker bake at 400°.

Bake in Gas Cooker at 350° F.

SCALLOPED PARSNIPS

Two or three cooked parsnips, half pint white sauce, one tablespoon chopped onion, two tablespoons bread crumbs, seasoning.

Cut the parsnips into thin slices. Into a greased dish place layers of sauce, parsnips and chopped onion, making the top layer sauce. Sprinkle with the bread crumbs and put small pieces of butter on the top. Bake in a hot oven until brown. If liked, the onion may be omitted and grated cheese used.

In an Electric Cooker bake at 400°.
Bake in Gas Cooker at 400° F.

STUFFED ONIONS

Scoop out the middle of the onions, and chop finely some lean beef and a little fat bacon, bread crumbs, chopped parsley or sage, salt and pepper to taste, and a little melted dripping. Put this mixture into the onions and stand side by side in a saucepan and pour in enough water to barely cover. Cover pan closely and steam for three hours. The onions must not break. When done take them out carefully and thicken the gravy with a little flour and pour round the onions. — Miss B. Skewes.

STUFFED VEGETABLE MARROW

Cook the marrow in boiling salted water for 15 minutes. Drain, peel thinly, and cut in half lengthwise and remove the seeds. Fill the marrow with the following stuffing: Mix together one cooked onion finely chopped, 1 oz. butter, one dessertspoon chopped sage, ¼ lb. bread crumbs, salt and pepper to taste, and moisten with the yolk of an egg. Place the pieces of marrow into original shape and lay in a buttered dish; brush with butter. Bake in a hot oven for three-quarters to one hour, according to size and age of marrow.

In an Electric Cooker bake at 400°.
Bake in Gas Cooker at 350° F.

STUFFED POTATOES AU GRATIN

SUITABLE FOR LUNCHEON OR TEA

Six potatoes, 1 oz. butter, 3 to 4 tablespoons grated cheese, salt, cayenne, half teacup milk.

Choose good, sound potatoes of medium size, wash them well, then dry and prick with a fork or skewer. Bake in a slow oven till done, 1 to 1½ hours or longer, according to size. To tell if done, press with the thumb and finger. Cut a slice off top of each potato, then scoop out centres without breaking the skins. Mash the potato. Heat the milk and butter, add to the potato with the cheese and seasonings. Beat till smooth and creamy. Refill cases with the mixture, piling high. Sprinkle over a little grated cheese. Replace in a hot oven and leave till thoroughly heated and nicely browned. — A. L. Sharman.

BAKED PUDDINGS

BOILED PUDDINGS

STEAMED PUDDINGS

SWEET SAUCES

MILK PUDDINGS AND CUSTARDS

BAKED PUDDINGS

BAKED RAISIN PUDDING

One pound flour, ½ lb. suet, pinch salt, grated nutmeg, ¾ lb. raisins, 1 oz. sugar, milk.

Chop suet finely, stone raisins and cut in halves. Mix these with the suet and add the salt, sugar and nutmeg. Moisten whole with sufficient milk to make it into a thick batter. Put the pudding into a buttered pie-dish and bake 1½ hours. Turn it out and sprinkle sugar over it. Improved by one or two eggs.

In an Electric Cooker bake at 450°.

Bake in Gas Cooker at 400° F.

BREAD FRITTERS

One cupful stale bread (crusts can be used). Cover with milk and soak for an hour. Put into basin and mash well with fork, then add one egg, one tablespoon flour, half teaspoon salt, grate of nutmeg. Fry spoonfuls of the mixture in boiling fat, and serve hot with sugar and slices of lemon. (This quantity makes about nine small fritters.)

CAKE PUDDING

Half cup sugar, one tablespoon butter, two tablespoons milk, three tablespoons self-raising flour, one egg and a few drops of vanilla essence.

Beat sugar and butter together, break in egg, and beat again. Add milk and essence, and lastly flour. Fill pie-dish three parts full of cooked apples, with plenty of syrup. Drop the mixture in spoonfuls on top. Bake in hot oven. Test as for cake. Any kind of fruit may be used.— Mrs. Cockington — Miss Ruth Stacy.

In an Electric Cooker bake at 375° for 30 minutes.
Bake in Gas Cooker at 375° F.

CHAMPAGNE CRUST

Boil enough fruit to half fill medium sized pie-dish.

A batter: Mix half cup sugar, two ounces butter. Add one egg and half cup of milk. Sift in one cup of self-raising flour. Pour over fruit, which must be boiling. Cook for 20 minutes in oven.

— Mrs. W. J. Vandepeer, "Waringa," Ardrossan.
— Miss E. Cooper, Farrell's Flat.

In an Electric Cooker bake at 375°.
Bake in Gas Cooker at 375° F.

BAKED ROLY-POLY

Two cups self-raising flour, one cup dripping; rub in flour and mix with water, roll out and spread with jam, and place in a pie-dish (buttered).

Dissolve one-half cup sugar and two tablespoons of butter in two cups of boiling water and pour over roly-poly and bake till brown. Half this quantity is enough for a small family.

— Mrs. C. Elfenbein, Port Elliot.

Chopped apples, fruit or jam may be used, and more sugar.

— Mrs. B. L. Henderson, Ardrossan.

In an Electric Cooker bake at 450° for 1 hour.
Bake in Gas Cooker at 400° F.

CROUTES OF APRICOTS

One tin of apricots, bread, butter, sugar.

Method: Cut some oval-shaped pieces of bread and butter about one-quarter inch thick. Arrange them in a greased fireproof dish, put half an apricot on each, hollow side up. Sprinkle with sugar and put in a small piece of butter on each; bake in a moderate oven until nicely browned. When cooked sift sugar over and serve. Stale cake may be substituted for bread, and when cooked a spoonful of whipped cream in the centre of each apricot improves the flavour greatly.

— S. R. Smith, Congregational Manse, Kadina.

COTTAGE PUDDING

Beat one cup of sugar and 2 oz. of butter to a cream. Add two eggs well beaten and one and a half cups of milk, then two cups self-raising flour. Flavour with essence of lemon.

Grease a pie-dish and bake for one hour in fairly hot oven.

In an Electric Cooker bake at 375°.
Bake in Gas Cooker at 400° F.

CARDINAL PUDDING

Three eggs, 4 oz. sugar, 4 oz. S.R. flour (or add 1½ teaspoons baking powder to ordinary flour), lemon or vanilla flavouring (one-quarter teaspoon).

Beat eggs and sugar together as for a sponge cake, stir flour in until thoroughly mixed, then add flavouring if liked. Have ready some dariole tins or small cups well buttered, fill about two-thirds full with mixture and bake in moderately hot oven about 20 minutes. Turn out, cover tops with stiff red jam or jelly and serve immediately with good white sauce.

— Mrs. C. R. Morris.

In an Electric Cooker bake at 375°.
Bake in Gas Cooker at 375° F.

ELIZABETH APPLE PUDDING

Partly fill a buttered baking dish with peeled and sliced apples, or with stewed apples. Over the top pour a thick batter made with 1½ cups S.R. flour, three teaspoons butter, one egg, ¾ cup milk, cup sugar, and a little salt and cinnamon.

Bake the pudding slowly for ¾ hour. Before serving, baking dish should be inverted and the pudding removed, so that the apples will be on top. This pudding should be served hot with cream or sweet sauce.

In an Electric Cooker bake at 375°.

— Mrs. T. W. Neill, McLaren Vale.

GOOD COVERING FOR FRUIT

The weight of one egg in sugar, butter, flour, and ground rice (cornflour will do).

Beat sugar and butter together, add the egg and the other ingredients with one teaspoon baking powder. Cover your cooked fruit, and bake for 20 minutes or half an hour. Eat either hot or cold. Sprinkle with sugar.

— Mrs. E. M. Evans, Keyneton.
— Mrs. J. E. Creswell.

In an Electric Cooker bake at 375°.

Bake in Gas Cooker at 375° F.

KATE'S BATTER PUDDING

One and a half ounces butter, three dessertspoons flour, one cup and a half milk, two eggs, one dessertspoon sugar, flavouring to taste.

Mix flour, butter, sugar in boiling milk. Stir a minute or two. Let stand till cold, then add beaten eggs, flavouring. Bake in moderate oven. Sultanas or fresh fruit may be added if liked.

— M. Higginbottom.

ORANGE SOUFFLE

Stir together in a saucepan the yolks of four eggs with half a breakfast-cup of sugar, add grated rind of one and juice of two oranges, the grated rind of half and juice of one lemon.

Stir over fire until boiling, add the stiffly beaten whites of four eggs, and pour the whole into a dish previously lined with strips of sponge cake. Steam or bake in a moderate oven, and serve at once.

In an Electric Cooker bake at 375°.

Bake in Gas Cooker at 350° F.

INDIAN FRITTERS

Mix three tablespoons flour into stiff paste with boiling water, let cool; then mix in one egg. Beat well and drop spoonfuls into smoking hot fat. Drain on paper and sandwich together with jam.

— A. L. Lillecrapp, Hill Ridge.

UNCOMMON PUDDING

One and a half cups of flour, one-half teaspoon of soda, one teaspoon of cream of tartar, pinch of salt, three-quarter teaspoon of butter. Sift the cream of tartar, soda and flour; rub in butter and mix to a dough with milk; roll out to a thickness of about one half-inch, then spread the following mixture; mince two apples, one tablespoon of sultanas, one and a half tablespoons of currants and a little peel; add two tablespoons of sugar and a little grated nutmeg; mix well and spread on the paste, roll up and place in a pie-dish. Make a syrup of three-quarters cup of sugar and a little more than one-quarter of a cup of butter; pour this round the roll.

Bake in a moderate oven for one hour until a golden brown.

— S. R. Smith, Congregational Manse, Kadina.

In an Electric Cooker bake at 450°.
Bake in Gas Cooker at 375° F.

WAFER PUDDING

Two eggs, 1½ oz. butter, 2 oz. flour, half pint of milk.

Method.—Rub butter into flour. Beat eggs and mix with milk into the flour. Pour in buttered plates and bake till pale brown. Serve hot with jam between.

Bake in an Electric Cooker at 400°.
Bake in Gas Cooker at 375° F.

WROTESLY PUDDING

Cream one tablespoon of butter with one tablespoon sugar. Stir in yolks of three eggs, beat whites separately. Add two tablespoons of flour to the previous mixture, then mix in the whites, and lastly stir in one pint milk. Stir well before putting in oven. Bake in a moderately hot oven for three-quarters of an hour.

In an Electric Cooker bake at 375°.
Bake in Gas Cooker at 375° F.

CUP PUDDING

Half pint milk, 1 oz. butter, one tablespoon sugar, 4 oz. bread crumbs, 1 oz. peel, a little essence.

Boil milk, pour over crumbs. Let cool. Add sugar, butter creamed. Let stand half hour. Add peel cut finely, essence, eggs beaten. Three parts fill cups. Bake 30 minutes in moderate oven.

— M. Higginbottom.

In an Electric Cooker bake at 375°.
Bake in Gas Cooker at 325° F.

BOILED PUDDINGS

These puddings are wholesome and nourishing and suitable for the winter.

Suet is the fat used, but butter or clarified fat may be used. Bread crumbs added to the mixture help to make the pudding light. Boiled puddings are cooked in a cloth or in a greased basin and covered with a cloth; if the latter is used, the mixture must fill the basin. The water must cover the pudding and be kept boiling. Always dip the pudding cloth in boiling water and sprinkle with flour. To prevent the pudding sticking to the cloth, allow it to stand a few minutes before removing the cloth. Pudding cloths should not be washed with soap.

AMERICAN PUDDING

Two large cups of flour, one of chopped suet, one of golden syrup, one teaspoon of cream of tartar, one of carbonate of soda, one of ground ginger, and a pinch of salt. A few currants or sultanas are an improvement.

Mix all together. Tie in a cloth, leaving room for swelling. Put quickly into a saucepan of boiling water, not lifting the lid for half an hour. Boil steadily for three hours. Serve with maizena sauce or cream. — Mrs. Kentish, Port Road.

APPLE PUDDING

Twelve ounces suet pastry, 2 lb. apples, 6 oz. sugar, flavouring (ground ginger, cloves, cinnamon, or lemon rind).

Line a greased pudding basin with two-thirds of the pastry. Add half the apples, the sugar, and the flavouring, then the remainder of apples. Half fill the basin with water. Cover with remainder of pastry. Cover with greased paper, then a pudding cloth. Boil for an hour and a half or two hours. Serve with custard sauce or cream.

AUNT NELLY'S PUDDING

Half pound flour, ½ lb. treacle, ½ lb. suet, the rind and juice of one lemon, a few strips of candied lemon peel, three tablespoons of cream, two eggs.

Chop the suet finely, mix with it the flour, treacle, lemon peel (minced). Add the cream, lemon juice and two well-beaten eggs. Beat the pudding well, and boil in buttered basin for two and a half to four hours.

BACHELOR'S PUDDING

The weight of an egg in flour, sugar, bread crumbs, dripping (or butter), raisins (or currants), chopped fresh apple, teaspoon carbonate of soda.

Mix flour, sugar, bread crumbs, raisins, dripping and apple together. Then mix with the egg and a little milk into which the soda has been well stirred. Boil in buttered basin for about three hours.

BELL PLUM PUDDING

Two tablespoons dripping, pinch of salt, two tablespoons sugar, one egg, one teaspoon carbonate of soda in a half cup of boiling water, one large cup of flour (plain), handful bread crumbs, currants, raisins, or dates.

Put in buttered basin. Mix all together. Boil for two and a half hours. — Miss Niehuus, King's Park.

CAFFON PUDDING

The weight of three eggs in S.R. flour, butter, sugar, and raspberry jam. Mix butter, flour and sugar together. Then mix a teaspoon of soda into the jam and add other ingredients. Beat three eggs well and then mix in. Tie in a pudding cloth and boil 2½ hours. Serve hot or cold with fresh or scalded cream.

This pudding can be baked instead of boiled, if preferred.

— Miss E. Norman, Kadina.

CARROT PUDDING

Half pound bread crumbs, 4 oz. suet, ¼ lb. raisins, ¾ lb. carrot, ¼ lb. currants, 3 oz. sugar, three eggs, quarter nutmeg, milk.

Method.—Boil carrot until tender enough to mash to a pulp. Add remaining ingredients, and sufficient milk to make the consistency of thick butter. Time.—Two and a half hours to boil or one hour to bake. Sprinkle sifted sugar over before serving, and have white sauce or boiled custard with it.

— Mrs. E. R. Ingham, Highgate.

DATE PUDDING

Ingredients.—One cup flour, one cup dates, half cup suet, half cup sugar, half cup milk, one teaspoon ground cinnamon, one teaspoon nutmeg, one teaspoon carbonate soda (dissolved in the milk), one apple (sliced), one banana (sliced).

— Miss E. Prince, Medindie.

One pound dates chopped fine, 6 oz. finely chopped suet, ½ lb. bread crumbs, one cup sugar, two eggs, one teaspoon cinnamon, a little milk.

Mix well, put mixture in greased basin or pudding mould, and boil three hours. — Mrs. Chas. Coote, Port Elliot.

CALIFORNIA PUDDING (Boiled)

One cup flour (plain), 1 cup currants, ½ cup sultanas, ½ cup sugar, 1 to 2 tablespoons chopped lemon peel, 1 teaspoon soda bicarb. Mix all together, and then mix in 2 tablespoons butter dissolved in a cup of hot water. Mix thoroughly, put in a greased basin, cover securely, and boil three hours.

—Mrs. T. W. Neill, McLaren Vale.

CHRISTMAS PUDDING

Half pound raisins, currants, S.R. flour, suet, bread crumbs, three eggs, three tablespoons brown sugar, same of treacle, one teaspoon spice and one of cinnamon, 1 oz. lemon peel, pinch of salt and flavouring, half teaspoon carbonate soda mixed in a little milk.

Mix all dry ingredients. Add beaten eggs with warm treacle and the milk. Boil for five hours in cloth dipped in boiling water and well floured. —R. H. Cropley, Rosefield.

CHRISTMAS PLUM PUDDING

One pound currants, 1 lb. raisins, ¼ lb. lemon peel, ¼ lb. almonds (blanched and cut up), half packet mixed spice, one teaspoon ground ginger, 1 lb. sugar, 1 lb. suet (or good dripping), 1 lb. plain flour (or half plain and half S.R.), ¼ lb. bread crumbs, half teaspoon carbonate soda in one tablespoon of hot water, eight eggs, one tablespoon brandy.

Boil for eight hours, or can be made up into four or five puddings and boil for six hours. Can be kept for weeks if hung in a dry place. —Mrs. E. R. Ingham, Highgate.

PLUM PUDDING

One cup of flour, one cup bread crumbs, one cup suet, one cup raisins, one cup currants, one cup dark sugar, one tablespoon of treacle, two teaspoons of carb. soda, five eggs, one-half packet spice, and ½ lb. lemon peel.

Boil eight hours if made into one pudding. This mixture will make three small puddings if for small family.

—Mrs. Fred Thorn, Angaston.

JOE'S PUDDING

One cup of common flour, one tablespoon of dripping mixed together, half cup of sugar, teaspoon carbonate soda, half cup of currants, pinch of salt, half teaspoon of spice.

Mix to thick paste with boiling water. Tie loosely in a cloth and boil for two hours. —Mrs. L. A. Williams, Mile End.

GINGER PUDDING

One-half pound flour, $\frac{1}{4}$ lb. suet, one-half teaspoon carbonate soda, pinch salt, one teaspoon ground ginger, two tablespoons sugar, one good tablespoon treacle, and one-quarter cup milk.

Method.—Sift flour, soda, ginger, and salt; shred and rub in suet, and add sugar; blend treacle and milk together and add to dry ingredients. Put into a floured cloth and boil at least $1\frac{1}{2}$ hours. Serve with warmed treacle or white sauce.

— Mrs. Alfred Anderson, Blythwood.

JAMAICA PUDDING (No Eggs)

Half pound flour, $\frac{3}{4}$ lb. moist sugar, suet or dripping, one dessertspoon ground ginger, a pinch of salt. No moisture needed. Pack in a greased basin. Boil or steam three hours. Serve with jam or jam sauce.

— M. Higginbottom.

MARMALADE PUDDING

Two eggs, their weight in self-raising flour, and half the weight in sugar, one tablespoon butter, two tablespoons marmalade.

Beat butter and sugar to a cream. Add the eggs and marmalade. Beat in the flour, pour into a buttered mould, and boil for two hours.

— Mrs. Pearce, Port Pirie.

POOR MAN'S PUDDING

One cup suet, one cup flour, one cup bread crumbs, one cup currants and raisins, one cup sugar, one cup milk, one teaspoon carbonate of soda, a little lemon peel.

Boil for two and a half to three hours.

— E. L. Pledge, Laura.

PLUM PUDDING (Without Eggs)

Two cups of plain flour, one cup of sugar, one cup raisins, one cup currants, two cups boiling water, one teaspoon carbonate soda, piece of butter the size of an egg.

Pour one cup of boiling water on to the butter and one cup of boiling water on to the soda. Mix well, and steam for three hours, or two hours to boil. This makes a very thin mixture and a large pudding, cheap and very nice.

— Mrs. E. R. Ingham, Highgate.
— Mrs. Agnes Bowering, Prospect.

RASPBERRY PUDDING

Fig, Plum, Marmalade can be used in the same way.

A cup and a half flour, half cup sugar, half cup milk, half cup dripping, two tablespoons of jam, one teaspoon carbonate of soda. When made with dripping melt it and stir in the sugar, then mix the jam into the milk, into which the soda has been added. Then add the flour, stirring well all the time. If too thick, add a little more milk, and boil in buttered basin for about four hours.

ROLY-POLY PUDDING

Six ounces suet pastry filling. Roll the pastry out about ¼-in. thick. Spread on filling within one inch of edge; moisten edges and roll up; fasten ends securely. Put in a scalded pudding cloth. Tie the ends firmly, sew the middle. Boil for three-quarters of an hour. Serve with sweet sauce.

Suitable fillings.—Jam; chopped apples, 2 oz. currants, one tablespoon sugar, half teaspoon mixed spice; chopped dates, treacle or golden syrup. When using treacle or golden syrup sprinkle bread crumbs on top of it.

SHIP PUDDING

Two cups flour, half cup sugar, one cup any fruit, one teaspoon soda, one tablespoon dripping, lemon peel or one tablespoon marmalade.

Stir soda and dripping in a cup of boiling water. Mix all dry ingredients together and put in boiling water last. Boil two hours.

— J.M.A.

ST. GEORGE'S PUDDING

Mix together ½ lb. each of bread crumbs, minced apples, cleaned sultanas and chopped suet, ¼ lb. flour, the grated rind and juice of two lemons, one teaspoon of baking powder, pinch of salt, two beaten eggs, and a gill of milk. Boil three hours in a greased dish. Serve with any sweet sauce. — B.A.S.

THIRTY MINUTES' PUDDING

One cup S.R. flour, one dessertspoon butter, quarter cup milk, one dessertspoon sugar, one egg, pinch of salt.

Cream butter and sugar; add beaten egg, then milk, and lastly flour. Put in buttered mould and boil 30 minutes.

— Miss Niehuus, King's Park.

STEAMED PUDDINGS

Steaming is the lightest method of cooking puddings. They may be cooked in two ways:—

1. In a steamer placed over a saucepan of boiling water.

2. In a saucepan in which the water only comes half-way up the basin.

Steamed puddings should be put in a greased bowl and covered with greased paper. The bowl should be only three parts full.

The fat used should be butter or clarified fat. Suet puddings may be steamed; they take much longer to cook than when boiled. The water should boil quickly enough to give sufficient steam. When steaming in a saucepan be careful that no water enters the pudding.

AUNT MARGARET'S PUDDING

One-half pound flour, ½ oz. baking powder mixed into flour, 3 oz. castor (sifted) sugar, ¼ lb. lard or dripping rubbed into the flour, one egg, and five tablespoons of milk.

Put thick layer of any kind of jam at bottom of greased bowl, pour mixture on top of jam, cover bowl with greased paper, and steam from one and a half to two hours.

— Miss C. Norman, Wayville.

BONNY PUDDING

One large cup of flour, four tablespoons brown sugar, four tablespoons butter, one cup milk, one teaspoon carb. soda, little salt, one-half cup seeded raisins, a little mixed spice. Steam for three hours.

— Mrs. M. A. Luck, Croydon Park.

BROKEN HILL PUDDING

Two cups flour, one cup sugar, one cup currants, dates or figs, one large tablespoon butter, one dessertspoon carb. soda dissolved in one cup boiling water, a little essence of lemon and lemon peel. Mix all together and boil or steam for two and a half hours.

— Mrs. W. Simmons, Ardrossan.

CANARY PUDDING

One tablespoon butter, half cup sugar, one cup S.R. flour, one egg, half cup milk.

Directions.—Mix butter and sugar to a cream. Then add egg, milk, and flour. Steam for two hours

— Mrs. Campbell, Brisbane.

SAGO PLUM PUDDING

Soak four tablespoons of sago overnight in a little milk, one large cup bread crumbs, one cup sugar, one cup sultanas, raisins (stoned), or dates, two tablespoons butter (melted), one egg (beaten) and essence lemon, one small teaspoon carb. soda.

Mix well; pour into a buttered basin and steam two and a half hours.

— Miss E. Norman, Kadina.
— Miss R. Burke, Maitland.

Mix together one cup flour, half cup sugar, two tablespoons dripping, one tablespoon marmalade, half cup raisins, pinch salt, half teaspoon carbonate soda, dissolved in half cup milk. Steam until done.

One tablespoon of butter or dripping, one cup bread crumbs, one cup mixed raisins and currants, half cup sugar, three tablespoons sago, one teaspoon carb. soda, a little mixed spice or cinnamon or nutmeg.

Method.—Soak sago in milk or water one hour; mix other ingredients; mixture must not be too wet. Steam for two to three hours.

Use two cups bread crumbs and one egg.

— M. E. Sibley, Angaston.

One cup sago soaked for two hours in milk or water.

— Mrs. O. Stribling.
— Miss T. Wheare, Cunningham.

Two heaped tablespoons sago soaked overnight in enough milk to cover it, one cup bread crumbs, one cup raisins, half cup sugar, two tablespoons butter, one teaspoon soda dissolved in boiling water.

Mix with enough milk to make pretty wet. This is very rich; if double quantity is required the same amount of butter and raisins will be sufficient for a plainer pudding. Boil for three hours. — Mrs. Alfred Anderson, Blythwood.

CHEESWICK PUDDING

Two cups flour, one cup sugar, two large tablespoons dripping or butter, one cup fruit, currants, raisins and peel.

Rub butter into flour, then add sugar and fruit, one teaspoon soda, one cup milk. Dissolve soda in milk. Steam two hours; serve with sweet sauce. — M. Sharples, Kadina.

CHOCOLATE PUDDING

One cup flour, half cup sugar, one tablespoon butter, two tablespoons cocoa sifted through with the flour, and one teaspoon baking powder, one-quarter teaspoon vanilla, one egg, half cup milk. Mix together and steam for two hours. — M. McRae.

CLAYWORTH PUDDING

One-quarter pound suet, $\frac{1}{4}$ lb. raisins, $\frac{1}{4}$ lb. flour, $\frac{1}{4}$ lb. sugar, $\frac{1}{4}$ lb. currants, $\frac{1}{4}$ lb. ground rice, one teaspoon soda, two teaspoons cream tartar, one teaspoon cinnamon, one cup of milk.

Mix to a batter and steam three or four hours.

COLLEGE PUDDING

One cup flour, one tablespoon of butter, half cup sugar, one egg, one wineglass milk, one teaspoon baking powder, and a small cup of jam. Grease a basin and put the jam in first, then the other ingredients, after they have been well mixed. Steam for $1\frac{1}{2}$ hours. Serve either hot or cold.

— Miss E. Jones, Port Elliot.

CUT CAKE PUDDING

Mix two teaspons of baking powder and half teaspoon of salt with two cups of flour. Cream one tablespoon of butter with half cup of sugar, add one egg well beaten, and one cup milk.

Stir in the flour mixture and beat well. Turn into small buttered moulds or cups and steam one hour.

— Mrs. J. E. Creswell, College Park.

DATE PUDDING

Half packet flour, ¾ lb. dates, ¾ lb. butter, ¼ lb. preserved ginger, ½ lb. sugar, five eggs, pinch salt, quarter cup milk.

Rub the butter into flour. Add sugar. Beat eggs well, mix with flour, add dates, ginger, and milk. Put into well-greased mould, steam five hours. — (Mrs.) C. Stanley, Mitcham.

EGGLESS AND BUTTERLESS DATE PUDDING

One cup flour, one cup dates, one small cup sugar, one teaspoon cinnamon, one dessertspoon dripping dissolved in two tablespoons boiling water, one teaspoon soda dissolved in a little milk, small quantity lemon peel.

Mix thoroughly and steam for two hours.

— S. R. Smith, Congregational Manse, Kadina.

DELICATE PUDDING

One egg, one cup sugar, one cup milk, two teaspoons baking powder, one cup raisins, piece butter the size of an egg, flour to make a stiff batter (about two cups).

Mix, put in buttered mould, and steam one hour. Allow plenty of room for rising. —Mrs. N. Miller, Port Pirie.

FREE KIRK PUDDING

Two tablespoons currants, two tablespoons raisins, two tablespoons sugar, three tablespoons suet, three tablespoons flour, half teaspoon of soda, half teaspoon spice, pinch of salt, lemon peel. Mix with one egg and a little milk. Steam three hours.

— J. M. Adams, Port Elliot.

Three tablespoons of flour, three tablespoons of sugar, three tablespoons of raisins, three tablespoons of currants, five tablespoons suet, six tablespoons of bread crumbs, a little spice and peel, one teaspoon of carbonate of soda. Mix with milk fairly stiff.

GINGER PUDDING

One cup plain flour, two oz. dripping, one tablespoon of sugar, one teaspoon ground ginger, one tablespoon treacle, one egg, half teaspoon carbonate soda dissolved in boiling water, and a little milk. Steam two hours.

HIGH CHURCH PUDDING

Take ½ lb. flour, three ounces butter, one cup raspberry jam one cup milk with one teaspoon carbonate soda dissolved in it.

Mix the flour and butter well, add the jam, then the milk. Steam for three hours and serve with sauce.

— M. Millar, Renmark.

Three ounces suet, one cup flour, half cup sugar, half cup jam (any sort), half teaspoon carbonate soda. Boil for 2½ hours.

— Mrs. Cross, Kadina.

LEMON PUDDING

Two ounces butter or dripping, two ounces sugar, one egg, one lemon, four ounces flour, quarter teaspoon carbonate soda, one pinch salt.

Cream butter and sugar, and add well-beaten egg. Add the grated lemon rind and juice, flour (sifted with soda and salt). Put into a greased basin and cover with greased paper. Steam for an hour and a quarter. Serve with sweet or lemon sauce.

MARGUERITE PUDDING

Two ounces butter, 2 oz. sugar, ¼ lb. self-raising flour, one egg, and a very little milk.

Line a basin with apricot jam, pour in the mixture and steam one hour. Serve with jam sauce. — Miss Ruth Stacy.

Plain flour with one teaspoon baking powder may be substituted for S.R. flour; raspberry jam for apricot.

— Anonymous.

One tablespoon butter, one egg, one cup sugar, half cup new milk, one heaped cup self-raising flour, one cup jam.

Place the jam at the bottom of the greased pudding mould, pour mixture in and boil for two hours.

— Mrs. A. Treasure, Georgetown.

KESWICK PUDDING

One and a half cups flour, three tablespoons sugar, three-quarters of a cup currants, one teaspoon soda, two tablespoons dripping, one cup milk, one nutmeg, pinch of salt.

Method.—Rub dripping into flour, then add dry ingredients, lastly the milk. Steam two hours.

MOUNT LOFTY PUDDING

One cup self-raising flour, two tablespoons butter, two tablespoons sugar, one egg, three tablespoons milk, jam.

Cream butter and sugar, beat egg and add. Add flour and milk alternately. Have ready a greased basin, and put one tablespoon jam in the bottom, then half of mixture. Spread over another tablespoon jam, then rest of mixture. Cover with a greased paper, and steam two hours. Serve with milk sauce or custard.

— Miss H. Spencer, Wayville.

Two eggs, their weight in butter, sugar and flour, tablespoon of marmalade, teaspoon baking powder.

Method.—Beat the butter to a cream, and add to it the sugar, then the flour, in which the baking powder is added, then the marmalade. Beat eggs well, yolks and whites separately. Add the whites last. Pour into a well-greased basin. Steam for one and a half hours. Serve with sweet sauce.

MARMALADE PUDDING

Ingredients.—4 oz. clarified fat or butter, 4 oz. sugar, two eggs, four tablespoons milk, 8 oz. flour (plain), half teaspoon carbonate soda, two tablespoons marmalade, good pinch salt.

Method.—Prepare basin, and put water on to boil under steamer. Cream fat and sugar. Add well-beaten eggs. Mix marmalade and milk well, and add to mixture. Add flour, salt and soda sifted. Stir, but do not beat the mixture. Steam for two and a half hours

RASPBERRY PUDDING

Two eggs, their weight in flour and butter, and weight of one in sugar. Beat butter and sugar to a cream; add eggs well beaten. Stir in the flour and 2 tablespoons raspberry jam. Before putting in the mould stir in ½ teaspoon of carb. soda. Steam for 1½ hours.

RASPBERRY PUDDING

Two ounces butter, one cup of sugar, one egg, one cup milk, 1½ tablespoons raspberry jam, one cup S.R. flour, one teaspoon soda.

Beat sugar and butter to a cream. Add egg, milk, and the other ingredients. Steam two and a half hours.

— M.B., St. Peters.

SNOWDON PUDDING

Quarter pound raisins, 3 oz. suet, 3 oz. marmalade, grated lemon rind, one pinch salt, $\frac{1}{4}$ lb. bread crumbs, $\frac{3}{4}$ oz. ground rice. two eggs, $\frac{1}{2}$ gill milk, 3 oz. sugar.

Sprinkle raisins inside a greased basin. Mix together suet, crumbs, ground rice, sugar, salt and lemon rind. Add marmalade, eggs and milk. Put in the prepared basin, cover with greased paper and steam one hour.

FRENCH RICE PUDDING

Three ounces rice, one pint milk, $\frac{1}{4}$ lb. raisins, 2 oz. candied peel, 2 oz. suet or butter, 3 oz. sugar, two eggs, one pinch of salt.

Wash the rice and cook in the milk with the pinch of salt till soft. Add the stoned raisins, chopped peel and suet, sugar and beaten eggs. Put in a greased pudding basin, cover with greased paper and steam two hours.

—Miss A. Sharman, Black Forest.

STEAMED DATE PUDDING

One cup S.R. flour, 1 pinch salt, 1 egg, 1 tablespoon butter, tablespoon sugar, $\frac{1}{2}$ cup milk.

Method.—Melt butter, add sugar, then beat, next add egg and milk; put into flour and then add dates. Steam 1 hour.

— Mrs. N. Boynes.

PLUM PUDDING

One cup squeezed bread, one heaped tablespoon plain flour, half cup sugar, one tablespoon dripping, one cup mixed fruit or dates, and any spare jam, salt, nutmeg, a little spice, one teaspoon carb. soda and the dripping in one cup boiling water. Beat well together and put in greased basin. Let stand three or four hours before cooking. Steam three hours.

— Mrs. Pulford, Adelaide.

MAY PUDDING

Half pint of milk, two eggs, 3 oz. bread crumbs, one teaspoon of castor sugar, two dessertspoons golden syrup.

Put the golden syrup in the bottom and sprinkle the bread crumbs over it. Beat up the eggs, adding milk and sugar gradually. Pour the mixture into the cooker on top of bread crumbs. Steam quickly for 30 minutes.

MARY ANN PUDDING

Two eggs, weight in butter, sugar, flour, two tablespoons jam (raspberry or some dark jam without stones), teaspoon of carb. soda.

Beat butter and sugar to a cream, break eggs, add other ingredients, and steam two and a half hours.

STEAMED PUDDING

Quarter pound sugar, flour, bread crumbs, two teaspoons ginger, 1½ teaspoons cinnamon, one teaspoon carbonate soda in little milk, dessertspoon butter or dripping, three tablespoons warmed syrup. Steam two and a half hours. — M. Higginbottom.

RAISIN PUDDING

Into a cup and a half of plain flour rub one tablespoon of butter or good dripping. Add three-quarters of a cup sugar, a pinch of salt, little spice, teaspoon Parisian essence and some grated nutmeg. Stone half a pound raisins (or dates) and add to other ingredients. Dissolve one teaspoon carbonate soda in good half cup of milk, and well mix the whole. Put into greased basin, cover with greased paper and steam two and a half hours.

— Mrs. Arbon, Brighton.

GOLDEN PUDDING (STEAMED)

Two ozs. flour, 6 ozs. bread crumbs, 1 pinch salt, 4 ozs. suet, 1 teaspoon baking powder, 2 ozs. sugar, 3 tablespoons of marmalade, 1 egg, ¾ of a gill of milk.

Method.—Chop suet finely and mix with it the other dry ingredients, add the well beaten egg, then milk, and mix to a stiff batter. Put in a well greased basin, cover with greasepaper, and steam 1½ hours. Heat 3 tablespoons of marmalade with 3 tablespoons of water and serve with the pudding.

— Mrs. N. Boynes.

CHOCOLATE NUT PUDDING

Ingredients.—1½ oz. cocoa, 2 oz. flour, 2 oz. suet, 1 flat teaspoon baking powder, 2 oz. bread crumbs, 2 oz. sultanas, 3 oz. shelled walnuts, 3 oz. sugar, 1 egg, milk.

Method.—Wash, pick over, and dry the sultanas. Chop the walnuts finely. Make the bread crumbs, and mix with the cocoa, flour, and baking powder.

Chop the suet finely and mix in thoroughly. Add the sugar, prepared walnuts and sultanas and mix all together.

Beat up the egg, and add with sufficient milk to mix to about the consistency of a cake. Put into a greased basin or mould, cover with a well-greased paper, and steam for about two hours. Turn on to a hot dish and serve.

SWEET SAUCES

BOILED CUSTARD

Three eggs, one pint milk, 1 oz. sugar, flavouring.

Heat milk and sugar, but do not boil. Pour on to beaten eggs, stirring well. Return to saucepan and cook over a low heat till custard coats back of spoon. Add flavouring and serve in a sauce boat.

JAM SAUCE

Half pint water, one tablespoon sugar, one tablespoon red jam, half teaspoon lemon juice, two or three drops carmine of cochineal.

Put all the ingredients in a saucepan and boil quickly till reduced to half. Add the colouring and strain.

LEMON SAUCE

Half pint water, one dessertspoon arrowroot, one or two tablespoons sugar, rind and juice of a lemon.

Blend arrowroot with a little of the water. Put rest of water and thinly peeled lemon rind on to boil; boil slowly for three minutes. Strain on to blended arrowroot, stirring well. Return to saucepan, and boil for three minutes. Add sugar and strained lemon juice.

If liked, the arrowroot may be omitted. Put all ingredients in the saucepan and boil till reduced to half. Strain into sauce boat.

SWEET SAUCE

One dessertspoon cornflour, one dessertspoon sugar, half pint milk, flavouring, one teaspoon butter, if liked.

Blend the cornflour and sugar with some of the milk, and put rest on to boil. Stir in the blended cornflour and boil three minutes. Add flavouring and butter. Serve in a sauce boat.

CHOCOLATE SAUCE

One teaspoon cornflour, one teaspoon cocoa, half teaspoon vanilla essence, half pint milk, two tablespoons sugar. Mix cornflour and cocoa with a little of the cold milk and boil the rest. Add blended mixture to boiling milk and boil ten minutes. Add sugar and essence.

MILK PUDDINGS AND CUSTARDS

MILK PUDDINGS AND CUSTARDS

BAKED CUSTARD

Two eggs, 1 oz. sugar, one pint milk, flavouring.

Beat the eggs and sugar together. Put in a greased pie-dish with the milk and flavouring, and bake in a slow oven till custard is set.

In an Electric Cooker bake at 325°.

Bake in Gas Cooker at 250° F.

ECONOMICAL BOILED CUSTARD

One egg, half pint milk, ½ oz. sugar, one teaspoon cornflour, flavouring.

Mix the cornflour with a little milk. Put rest of milk on to boil. Add the blended cornflour and boil three minutes. Add sugar and cool. Pour on to beaten egg, stirring well. Return to saucepan and cook over a low heat till custard coats back of spoon. Add flavouring and pour in a custard boat.

BARLEY KERNEL PUDDING

Two tablespoons barley kernels, one to two tablespoons sugar, one pint milk.

Put all ingredients in a greased pie-dish, and bake in a slow oven for one and a half to two hours. If pudding becomes too stiff, add more milk.

In an Electric Cooker bake at 375°.

Bake in Gas Cooker at 300° F.

BREAD AND BUTTER PUDDING

Two thin slices bread and butter, one tablespoon sugar, one pint milk, two eggs, one tablespoon currants or sultanas, grated nutmeg or cinnamon.

Cut the buttered bread into squares and put in a greased pie dish. Sprinkle with sugar and currants. Beat the eggs well, add the milk and pour over. Grate nutmeg over top, and bake in a slow oven till set—30 to 45 minutes.

In an Electric Cooker bake at 325°.

Bake in Gas Cooker at 300° F.

CABINET PUDDING

One slice bread and butter ½-in. thick, 1 oz. sugar, half pint milk, one or two eggs, 2 oz. raisins, flavouring.

Stone raisins, cut in halves and decorate a greased basin. Carefully put in the bread and butter cut in fingers, the sugar and rest of raisins. Pour over the beaten eggs, milk and flavouring. Cover with greased paper and let stand one hour. Steam slowly till set—about one hour. Let pudding stand one minute before turning out on to a hot dish. Serve with custard or jam sauce.

CUSTARDS WITHOUT EGGS

Sweeten one pint of milk to taste. Place one tablespoon of custard powder in a basin and add sufficient of the sweetened milk to make a smooth paste. Boil remainder of the milk, and while still boiling pour the milk quickly into the contents of the basin. Stir well, allow to cool slightly before pouring into custard glasses.

— Mrs. Reusch, Grassmere.

WALDEN CHOCOLATE PUDDING

Ingredients.—½ lb. flour, 5 ozs. butter, 3 ozs. cocoa, ½ teaspoon salt, 3 ozs. finely ground nuts, ¾ gill milk, 3 ozs. sugar, 2 teaspoons baking powder, 3 eggs, ½ teaspoon almond essence.

Method.—Cream butter and sugar, add an egg and one-third of dry ingredients, mixing well. Add second egg, then the third, lastly milk and remainder of dry ingredients. Stir in nuts and essence. Pour into a greased pie-dish. Serve with chocolate sauce.

In an Electric Cooker bake at 375°.
Bake in Gas Cooker at 350° F.

CARAMEL PUDDING

For the Caramel.—Three tablespoons of loaf sugar, three tablespoons of cold water, one teaspoon of lemon juice.

For the Custard.—One pint of fresh milk, three eggs, one tablespoon castor sugar, essence of lemon or vanilla to flavour.

Method.—Put sugar, water and lemon juice on to heat. Stir now and then, but do not let it boil till all grains of sugar are dissolved. Then allow to boil till a dark amber colour, and the consistency of golden syrup. Now put the milk on to heat. Beat up eggs and sugar, add the milk and stir. Have a plain mould heating, and when very hot pour the caramel in and twist round and round till the sides are well coated. Then pour in the eggs and milk and cover with buttered paper. Steam quickly for 40 minutes. The water should only be allowed to simmer while cooking. — Mrs. Atkins, New Mile End.

BOILED RICE

Quarter pound rice, half pint water, one pinch salt, one quart milk, 2 oz. sugar.

Wash the rice in three waters and put in a saucepan with salt and water, and cook till water is absorbed. Add milk and cook slowly until rice is soft. Add sugar. A cup of stoned raisins added to the above is a great improvement.

In an Electric Cooker use current turned to low.

QUEEN PUDDING

One breakfast cup of bread crumbs, one to two tablespoons sugar, 1 oz. butter, one pint milk, two eggs, flavouring, two tablespoons jam.

Put the bread crumbs, butter and half the sugar in a basin, and pour over the hot milk. Let stand 15 minutes. Add the beaten yolks of eggs. Pour into a greased pie-dish and put in a slow oven till set. Spread the top with jam. Beat up whites of eggs stiffly. Add rest of sugar, pile on top of pudding. Place in oven till a golden brown. — F.M.S.

— Mrs. T. W. Neill, McLaren Vale.

In an Electric Cooker bake at 325°.
Bake in Gas Cooker at 300° F.

PRINCESS PUDDING

Three thin slices of bread, marmalade, desiccated coconut, two eggs, one pint milk, 1 oz. sugar.

Spread the bread with marmalade, put into a buttered pie-dish and sprinkle with coconut and sugar. Add the beaten eggs and milk and bake in a moderate oven till set. — K.S.

In an Electric Cooker bake at 325°.
Bake in Gas Cooker at 300° F.

RICE CUSTARD

Two ounces rice, half pint water, one pinch salt, one pint milk, two eggs, one ounce sugar, flavouring.

Wash the rice in three waters, and soak in half pint water for one hour. Cook till water is absorbed. Add salt and half the milk, and cook till rice is soft. Put in a buttered pie-dish. Add sugar, beaten egg, rest of milk and flavouring. Cook in a slow oven till custard is set. If the pie-dish is stood in a dish of water while cooking, the custard will not curdle. Sago or tapioca may be used instead of rice. — K. Sharman.

In an Electric Cooker bake at 325°.

Bake in Gas Cooker at 300° F.

RICE PUDDING

Two ounces rice, one pinch salt, 1 oz. sugar, one pint milk, nutmeg, quarter pint water.

Wash the rice in three waters, and leave soaking in quarter pint of water for at least one hour. Put in a greased pie-dish with the other ingredients, and cook in a slow oven till the rice is done. Sago or tapioca may be used instead of rice.

In an Electric Cooker bake at 400°.

Bake in Gas Cooker at 300° F.

VERMICELLI CUSTARD

Two ounces vermicelli, 1 oz. sugar, two eggs, one pint milk, 1 oz. sugar, lemon essence.

Cook the vermicelli in plenty of boiling salted water for 20 minutes; strain and put in a greased pie-dish. Add sugar, beaten eggs, milk and essence, and cook in a slow oven till set.

In an Electric Cooker bake at 325°.

Bake in Gas Cooker at 300° F.

SAGO CREAM

Put two heaped tablespoons sago into a breakfast cup of milk and boil for a few minutes. Add the beaten yolks of two eggs, two tablespoons sugar and another cup of milk beaten together. Stir over the fire until it thickens. Take off and add the beaten whites of the eggs and a little flavouring. Pour into a glass dish or very wet mould, and serve cold. — F. Laughton.

BLANC MANGE

Two ounces cornflour, 1 oz. sugar, one pint milk, flavouring.

Mix cornflour with some of the milk to a smooth paste. Put rest of milk and sugar on to boil. Add blended cornflour away from heat, return to stove and boil three minutes. Add flavouring and pour into a wet mould. When cold turn out. Serve with jam or stewed fruit. — K. E. Sharman.

COLD SWEETS, PUDDINGS, Etc.

REFRIGERATION RECIPES

COLD SWEETS, PUDDINGS, etc.

AMBER PUDDING

One pint water, two eggs, 2 oz. cornflour, 1 oz. butter, ½ lb. sugar.

Put cornflour in bowl, add yolks of eggs and just enough water to mix to a thin cream. Put water and a strip of thinly cut lemon rind (or lemons grated), the juice and butter into saucepan and bring to a boil; add cornflour and yolks and stir well; add sugar, boil one minute. Pour into a pie-dish, whip whites to a stiff froth, with one tablespoon castor sugar. Spread on top, and bake light brown. Serve cold. — M. R. Keynes.

ANGEL'S FOOD (Eggless)

One tablespoon powdered gelatine, 1½ cups sugar dissolved in 1 cup cold water. Let stand for some time before continuing.

In another bowl mix 1 tablespoon plain flour in cup cold water. Add juice of 1 lemon and 2 large oranges. Boil all together two or three minutes, stirring all the time, and allow to become quite cold; then whip for half an hour. Pile it on a dish, and drop strawberries or crystallised cherries on top.

— Mrs. Slane, North Unley.

APPLE AND RICE MERINGUE

Stewed apples; boil rice, mix with the yolk of an egg and milk and a little sugar. Put all in a pie-dish. Beat white of egg well with a little castor sugar. Pile on top and brown in oven.

APPLE SAGO

Peel and core some apples and put small piece of butter in each, put in a pie-dish and between each apple put a slice of lemon and teaspoonful of sago. Almost fill the dish with water and bake steadily. — Mrs. P. R. Evans, Keyneton.

In an Electric Cooker bake at 375° for 1 hour.

Bake in Gas Cooker at 325° F.

APPLE SNOW

Stew four large apples with the rind of a lemon, take out rind when apples are soft. Beat whites of four eggs with a little sugar. Beat lightly with apples. Place mould in oven a few minutes to set. — M. Sharples, Kadina.

APPLE SPONGE

One pound apples, one pint water, two dessertspoons gelatine, four dessertspoons sugar, one lemon, two eggs (whites only).

Cook apples until tender with water and grated lemon rind. Pass through a sieve. Add the juice of lemon, with the gelatine dissolved in a little of the hot liquid. When cold, whisk in white of eggs, beaten to a stiff froth. Then place in mould to set or pile roughly in glass dish. Serve with custard or whipped cream.

— Miss B. Colliver.

APPLE WASHINGTON PIE

Work quarter cup butter until creamy. Beat in half cup sugar, add one egg well beaten. Sift a cup and a half self-raising flour, and add alternately with half cup milk to the first mixture. Beat vigorously, turn into two sandwich tins, spread evenly, and bake for 12 minutes. Put apple cream between and on top.

Apple Cream.—Peel, core and cut apples into quarters—there should be a quart. Put in a fireproof dish. Sprinkle with three-quarters of a cup of sugar, one-third cup water, and a few grains of salt. Cover and bake in a slow oven for three hours. When cold, rub through a sieve. Beat half a pint of cream till nearly thick, then beat in the apple pulp. When it is stiff add one teaspoon lemon juice.

— Miss D. Cochrane, Auburn, Victoria.

In an Electric Cooker bake at 400°.
Bake in Gas Cooker at 325° F.

A COLD CHRISTMAS PUDDING

Three dessertspoons gelatine, 1½ squares of chocolate or three tablespoons cocoa, 1½ pints milk, one cup raisins, one cup sugar, one-half cup chopped lemon peel and nuts, one-half cup currants, one-half cup dates or figs, one-half teaspoon vanilla, pinch salt.

Place milk, chocolate, or cocoa, and gelatine in saucepan over heat and stir until dissolved, but do not boil. Now add sugar and salt and after further stirring remove to a cool place. When the mixture begins to thicken add essence, fruit and nuts. Turn into a mould which has been rinsed in cold water and place aside to set. When required decorate with holly and serve with whipped cream or custard. Be sure and wash the dried fruit thoroughly and allow to soak before mixing. This is an ideal pudding for occasions quite apart from Christmas.

BUTTERCUP PUDDING

Two tablespoons maizena, two eggs, two lemons, one large cup of sugar, one dessertspoon of butter.

Mix maizena with a little cold water, then add the grated rind and juice of the lemons, sugar, butter and yolks of eggs (not beaten). Stir well, then add one pint of boiling water. Set on stove until quite thick. Put in a mould and let get cold. Beat the whites of the eggs to a stiff froth. Then turn the pudding into a glass dish with the whites around it.

—Mrs. W. Wise, Prospect.

In an Electric Cooker use current turned to low.

BANANA ICE PUDDING

Peel and mash eight ripe bananas; mix with them the strained iuice of two oranges and one lemon, half a pint of cream and half a pint of custard (the cream may be omitted and one pint of custard used). Add 2 oz. castor sugar, and freeze lightly as the mixture has to be moulded.

Put some of this mixture in an ice mould holding a pint and a half, and on this arrange a few whole strawberries taken from jam and a tablespoon of chopped nuts. Place alternate layers on until the mould is full. Put the lid on, and stand in the refrigerator to finish freezing. To turn out, dip the mould in hot water while you count five; it will turn out easily. Stoned cherries may be used instead of strawberries.

— Mrs. Atkins, New Mile End.

COLD CABINET PUDDING

With the yolks of four eggs, 5 oz. sugar, one pint milk, and half lemon, make some lemon cream. Beat the yolks in a saucepan, add the sugar and milk, and stir over heat. As it thickens, add the grated lemon rind. Pour into a basin, and while hot add two tablespoons of fine gelatine previously dissolved in a little water. Mix together and keep liquid. Have ready half a pound small candied fruits (cherries, apricots, citron and orange peel), cut in small pieces and soak in a few tablespoons of brandy. Butter a mould and place it in a basin surrounded with pounded ice. Decorate the bottom with candied fruits of various shades. Add a layer of grated sponge cake, more fruit and cover with some of the lemon cream liquid. Let this set. Continue until all the mould is full. Leave for half an hour in packed ice. Turn out, mask with the lemon cream liquid and serve with cream.

— Mrs. R. A. Waller, Port Adelaide.

CHERRY MERINGUE

Beat together one cup of bread crumbs, half a cup of sugar, the yolk of one egg, and a pint of milk; bake in a pie-dish; when set cover with stewed cherries (stoned and well sweetened). Beat up the white of an egg with one tablespoon of castor sugar until very stiff; spread over the fruit.

Put in a cool oven for five minutes to set; serve cold.

— Miss M. Treasure, Black Forest.

In an Electric Cooker bake at 325°.

Bake in Gas Cooker at 300° F.

CONVENT CREAM

Half ounce gelatine, half pint cold water, half cup castor sugar, 1 cup boiling water, juice of two lemons, stiffly beaten whites of four eggs; custard of one pint of milk and yolks of four eggs.

Dissolve gelatine in hot water. Add sugar and lemon juice and cold water. Stir well until sugar dissolves. Add whites of eggs. Pour in glass dish and leave to stand till set. Then pour the custard over.

CREAM PIE

Beat two eggs well. Add one cup sugar, one tablespoon melted butter, one cup milk, two teaspoons baking powder, with a cup and a half of flour, and stir into the mixture. Flavour with one teaspoon lemon essence.

Bake in sandwich tins. When cool fill with prepared custard or cream.

Cream for Pie.—Boil one cup milk. Wet one tablespoon maizena in a little cold milk. Stir into the boiling milk and cook over hot water for 10 minutes, stirring often. Beat one egg lightly. Add two tablespoons sugar and pinch salt, and stir into the thickened milk. Cook one minute. Stir one teaspoon butter and one teaspoon vanilla and set away to cool. Put between cakes. Whip a cup of cream. Pour right over cake, and serve.

— A. L. Lillecrapp, Hill Ridge.

In an Electric Cooker bake at 375°.

Bake in Gas Cooker at 350° F.

CHOCOLATE PUDDING

Into one pint of milk add 1 oz. sugar, 1 oz. chocolate, 2 oz. ground rice. Put all together in a saucepan and stir constantly over a low heat until it boils for five minutes. Put into a wet mould and when firm serve with custard.

— Miss Morphett, Torrens Park.

DUNCAN PUDDING

Three-quarter cup sugar, 1½ tablespoons cornflour mixed with the juice of a large lemon, two cups boiling water, bring to the boil and stir into it the snow made by the whites of two eggs. Then make custard with yolks of eggs and pour round when cold.

FAIRY SHAPE

One and a half breakfast cups of water, 1½ tablespoons of cornflour, three tablespoons of sugar, half a lemon, and two eggs.

Put water, sugar, juice and grated lemon rind into a saucepan and boil five minutes. Strain and add to cornflour which has been mixed to a smooth paste with water. Return to saucepan and boil three minutes, then stir in the stiffly beaten whites of eggs and put into a wetted mould to set. Serve with custard made from the yolks of eggs.

— Mrs. W. Schmidt, Railway Town, Broken Hill.

FRUIT CHARTREUSE

Ingredients.—One pint packet of orange or lemon jelly, a few bananas, one or two peaches if preferred, one tablespoon of castor sugar, one tablespoon of gelatine, two gills of fresh cream, and juice of a small lemon.

Method.—Dissolve the jelly according to directions given on packet, but using about a gill less water than usual. Put it aside till almost cold. Then line a wetted mould with some of it, and arrange in it two or three thinly sliced bananas and the peaches stoned and sliced, putting in some more of the jelly. Rub three bananas through a coarse sieve. Mix them with the sugar. Dissolve the gelatine in some warm water, sufficient to cover it, and add the strained juice of the lemon. Whip the cream stiffly. Mix the dissolved gelatine and cream to the banana. Pour this mixture into the mould and leave aside in a cool place until set. If preferred, the chartreuse may be garnished with little heaps of whipped cream and bunches of red currants or strawberries.

— Mrs. A. Atkins, New Mile End.

LEMON PUDDING

One cup bread crumbs, two cups milk, one-half cup sugar, yolks of two eggs, 2 oz. butter, grated rind of lemon, lemon juice to taste.

Method.—Put crumbs, sugar, butter and rind in basin, make milk warm (not hot), pour over crumbs, etc. Beat yolks of eggs and stir in, add gradually enough lemon juice to taste. Pour in pie-dish, bake half an hour in moderate oven. Have ready white of eggs beaten to froth, with two tablespoons sugar beaten in. Pour over pudding when done, put in oven to set just on three minutes. — Miss Lewis, Joslin.

Take two tablespoons cornflour, mix with a little water, add one cup sugar, one dessertspoon butter, juice and rind of two lemons (grated), yolks of two eggs.

Beat all well together, add 2½ cups boiling water, put into a saucepan until boiling. Beat whites of eggs with a little sugar and put over the top, or the whites of the eggs can be beaten into the pudding with the yolks. — B.S.

In an Electric Cooker bake at 325°.

Bake in Gas Cooker at 300° F.

LEMON SAGO JELLY

One cup sago, five cups water, two tablespoons golden syrup, two lemons, one cup sugar.

Boil the sago in water till clear, add the other ingredients, boil together a few minutes, add a few drops lemon essence. Pour into a mould and set in refrigerator.

— Miss E. Norman, Kadina.

LEMON SPONGE

Soak half an ounce of gelatine in three-quarters of a pint of cold water, then dissolve over fire. Add rinds of two lemons thinly pared, the juice and three ounces of sugar. Stir well with wooden spoon, and boil all together for three minutes. Strain and let remain in a bowl until nearly set. Beat well, then add the beaten whites of two eggs. Beat until it becomes the consistency of sponge. Pile lightly into a glass dish, leaving it in appearance as rocky as possible. — F. Laughton.

ITALIAN CREAM

Dissolve half an ounce of gelatine in ¼ pint hot water. Make a custard with half a pint of milk, yolks of 3 eggs, ½ oz. sugar. Stir in a few drops of brandy, a few drops of vanilla. When cool add dissolved gelatine and half a pint of cream which has been whipped till it has thickened. Put in a well oiled mould and freeze. Colour part pink. Cut in squares to serve.

DAINTY CHOCOLATE MOULD

Ingredients.—One tin preserved pears, slices of sponge cake, 1 pint milk, 2 dessertspoons cocoa, 3 tablespoons sugar, 1 level tablespoon gelatine, vanilla, whipped cream and glacé cherries (for decoration).

Method.—Line bottom and sides of mould with fingers of sponge cake, leaving half an inch space between each. Heat milk and sugar till boiling, dissolve cocoa with a little of the hot milk, return to pan and boil for one minute. Take off and leave to cool. Dissolve gelatine in a little hot water and stir into chocolate mixture. Flavour delicately with vanilla. When nearly cold whisk mixture for 5 minutes; pour into prepared mould and leave to set. Turn out on a dish, decorate top and base with mounds of whipped cream, stick half a glacé cherry on top of each, and serve with pears

LEMON CREAM PIE

Heat one quart milk and stir into it one-third cup of flour, wet with a little cold milk. Let this get hot, stirring all the time. Beat the yolks of five eggs with five tablespoons sugar, and add milk and flour to this.

Let all cook together for one minute after they come to the simmer. Take from fire and add juice and grated peel of large lemon. Bake in open shells of puff paste, and as soon as the custard is set, cover it with a meringue made of whites of five eggs beaten stiff and three tablespoons powdered sugar. Brown lightly and serve cold.

MILK JELLY

One cup milk, 1 dessertspoon of gelatine, 1 tablespoon sugar, rind of half a lemon.

Put gelatine in saucepan with milk, add sugar; stir gently until gelatine is melted—do not boil it. Pour into wet mould, put into cool place to set. Serve with flavoured cream.

—Mrs. A. Rowland, Warrnambool.

Two dessertspoons gelatine, 1¾ cups milk, ¼ cup warm water, 3 dessertspoons sugar, essence vanilla to taste.

Place milk, sugar and flavouring in a bowl and stir till sugar is dissolved. Dissolve gelatine in warm water, cool a little and add to the milk, and stir well together. Pour into wet mould to set.

—Mrs. H. P. Harris.

PINEAPPLE SNOW

One pineapple (tinned will do), 2 tablespoons castor sugar, ½ lemon, ½ oz. gelatine, 2 eggs.

Soften gelatine in 1 oz. water (1 tablespoon), add ½ pint of pineapple syrup, dissolve gelatine over fire, and put to cool. Arrange a few slices pineapple in bottom of dish in which pudding will be served. Shred the rest of the fruit, beat whites of 2 eggs stiff and add sugar. Add the cold syrup, lemon juice and gelatine, beating all the time, and stir lightly into shredded pineapple, and pile up in a mound on sliced fruit in the dish. Serve with boiled custard made from the yolks of eggs.

—Mrs. H. P. Harris.

NARCISSUS BLANC MANGE

Ingredients: One quart milk, 1 oz. gelatine, yolks of 4 eggs, ¼ lb. white sugar, vanilla or rose water for flavouring, ¼ pint cream.

Method: Dissolve gelatine in ¼ cup hot water. Heat milk to boiling point, pour on to beaten egg yolks, add sugar. Return to the saucepan and heat until the mixture boils. Remove from the fire, cool, add dissolved gelatine and flavour to taste. Pour into a mould which has an open centre; set aside till firm; turn out on a glass dish and fill the hollow with whipped cream.

PRUNE WHIP PIE

Fill baking dish with following paste mixture. Mix ¼ lb. cornflour with ¼ lb. flour, a small teaspoon baking powder, and a tablespoon of icing sugar. Now rub in 4 ozs. butter or lard. Beat up the yolk of an egg with ¼ pint milk, and stir in. Knead into a light dough. Roll out and put in dish, and bake in a hot oven till a golden colour. Fill with the following:—Wash and soak ½ lb. prunes, simmer in water till tender, and liquid practically cooked away. Stone prunes, cut small. Add two tablespoons sugar and same of walnuts (walnuts may be omitted). Mix together, and, lastly, add whites of two eggs beaten stiff. Fill pastry case, and continue baking in moderate oven for 20 minutes. When cold, garnish with whipped cream.

— Miss D. Cochrane, Auburn, Victoria.

In an Electric Cooker bake at 425°.

Bake in Gas Cooker at 400° F.

RASPBERRY SPONGE

Half ounce gelatine, half cup raspberry jam, one lemon, good half pint water, little sugar.

Mix jam with two tablespoons water and rub through fine sieve. Soak gelatine in rest of water, add the juice of lemon (also peel if liked), and sugar. Stir over fire till dissolved. Pour into bowl and mix with jam. When cold and beginning to set, add well beaten white of egg. Pour into wet mould and turn out when set. Serve with custard. (Home-made raspberry jam need not be strained.)

BANANA TRIFLE

Cut a sponge cake in thin slices and spread each slice with jam. Peel some bananas and cut into strips. Put a layer of cake in glass dish, pour over it a spoonful or two of custard. Next a layer of bananas. Grate on them a little lemon rind. Then put layer of cake, and so on till used up. You will require a pint of custard. Whip some cream, sweeten to taste, heap roughly over trifle.

— Mrs. P. R. Evans, Keyneton.

FLOATING ISLAND

Put a pint of milk into a double saucepan, heat to boiling point, then add well beaten yolks of three eggs mixed with three tablespoons sugar. Stir well and when done turn into dish from which it is to be served.

Beat whites to froth and drop by spoonfuls into hot water. Let them stand, then turn over, do not let them harden. Put as islands on top of the custard and serve with jelly.

HEAVEN PUDDING

Two tablespoons cornflour. Mix with a little water, one dessertspoon butter, one cup sugar, juice of two lemons, grated rind of lemon, yolks of two eggs.

Beat together, add two and a half cups boiling water. Put into saucepan. Let simmer for five minutes and pour into wet mould. Beat up whites with some icing or castor sugar, and spread over the top.

— Mrs. Lloyd Prince.

— Miss B. Colliver.

ORANGE PUDDING

Peel and slice five oranges. Put over this a large cup of sugar. Heat a pint of milk and add yolks of two eggs and tablespoon cornflour mixed in cold water. As soon as it has thickened, pour hot over the fruit. Beat whites to a stiff froth. Add teaspoon sugar, and spread on the top. Place in slow oven to set meringue.

— J.M.A.

RICE SNOWBALLS

Boil one cup of rice in four cups of water with half a teaspoon of salt, until quite soft, then add three-quarters of a cup of sugar. Put it in small cups, having them quite full. When perfectly cold, turn them into a dish. Take the yolks of three eggs, one pint of milk, one teaspoon cornflour, eight level teaspoons of sugar. Flavour with lemon and cook as soft custard. Turn over the rice half an hour before serving it.

— Miss E. Hill, St. Peters.

PINEAPPLE CREAM

One pint lemon jelly, half pint cream (whipped), pineapple chunks chopped up.

Mix jelly (prepared) and chunks. When nearly set, work in cream. — E. F. Benskin.

RHUBARB JELLY

To 2 lb. rhubarb allow half a pint of water, ½ lb. sugar, one lemon, carmine, and some gelatine. Wash rhubarb and cut into small pieces. Put into saucepan with peel and strained juice of lemon, water and sugar. Stew slowly till a pulp, strain and press out juice. To each pint of juice allow about 1 oz. gelatine. Put both into saucepan and stir over fire till gelatine is dissolved. Strain into basin, add two or three drops carmine, cool slightly, then pour into a wet mould and set aside till firm. Serve with whipped cream or custard.

— Miss D. Cochrane, Auburn, Victoria.

RHUBARB SPONGE

Is made with same recipe as Rhubarb Jelly, and whipped whites of three eggs beaten into it.

— Miss D. Cochrane, Auburn, Victoria.

SOLID CUSTARD

Ingredients.—Half oz. powdered gelatine, 1 pint milk, 2 eggs, ¼ cup sugar, essence of vanilla to taste.

Method.—Dissolve gelatine in ¼ cup hot water. Beat yolks and egg whites separately. Boil milk, remove from fire, stir in the yolks of eggs. Place back on fire and stir until boiling again. Remove, cool. Add dissolved gelatine and stir in beaten whites. Pour into a wet mould and let stand overnight.

SUMMER TRIFLE

Ingredients.—Quarter pound stale sponge cake, one small packet jelly crystals, one tablespoonful custard powder, half pint milk.

Lay cake in a pudding-dish; dissolve the jelly and pour over the cake. Make a custard of the custard powder and the milk. Pour custard over the cake and grate nutmeg over the top. Chill and serve with stewed or preserved fruit.

— Mrs. G. Barnes, Adelaide.

TO PREPARE DRIED PEACHES FOR DESSERT

Place ½ lb. fruit in large dish. Sprinkle saltspoon of carbonate of soda on them and cover with boiling water. Soak for one hour only. Pour water off, cover with cold water and soak for 24 hours. Remove skins, which will now readily come off, make syrup, pour over fruit when boiling, and serve when cold with cream or custard.

Syrup.—Quarter of a pound sugar to one pint of water. Boil for ten minutes. The juice of half a lemon added is an improvement. Soaking for a few hours in the syrup improves the fruit.

COCOA MOULD BLANC MANGE

Ingredients.—Three dessertspoons cornflour, 1½ dessertspoons cocoa, 1 pint milk (or milk and water). Pinch of salt. Sugar and vanilla flavouring to taste.

Method: Mix the cornflour and cocoa together, then mix to a smooth paste with a small quantity of the milk.

Heat the remainder of the milk, with the salt and sugar added, then stir in the cornflour, etc.

Return to the pan and bring to the boil, and boil gently for ten minutes, keeping it well stirred all the time. Add vanilla flavouring to taste.

Pour into a wet mould and leave until set, then turn out and serve.

NOTE.—If liked less stiff, use only 2½ instead of 3 dessertspoonfuls of cornflour.

SPANISH CREAM

Half ounce gelatine, three eggs, two cups milk, two tablespoons sugar.

Put the milk and gelatine in a saucepan, and heat till it dissolves. Beat the yolks of eggs and sugar together. Add to the milk and gelatine, and stir till it just boils. Cool and add the stiffly-beaten whites of eggs. Flavour with vanilla. Pour into a wet mould, and set aside to cool.

SPANISH PUDDING

Put some sponge cakes into a mould. Make a pot of raspberry jam boiling hot, and pour over the cake. Then let it stand till next day. Turn out of the mould and serve with whipped cream or custard.

— Miss D. Cochrane, Auburn, Victoria.

SUMMER PUDDING

Cut thin slices bread, not too fresh, and line pudding basin with them. See that every part is well covered with bread. It may be moistened with a little milk or cream before it is pressed round the mould so that it adheres closely to it.

Take any kind of fresh fruit, boil with sufficient sugar until cooked and then pour whole into mould. Cover with a plate and leave till next day, then turn out carefully. Serve with cream or custard. — B.A.S.

— Miss B. Colliver.

STEWED FRUIT

To each pound of soft fruit allow ¼ lb. sugar and a scant half pint water. Make a syrup of the above, boil one minute, add fruit, and cook slowly till done. If fruit is tart, do not add more sugar, add one pinch of carbonate soda. Hard fruits, such as quinces and stewing pears, after preparing, should be put in a saucepan and covered with cold water. Bring slowly to the boil. Add the sugar and cook slowly till fruit becomes red and is soft.

DRIED FRUIT DESSERT

Sprinkle one teaspoon of carbonate of soda over 1 lb. of dried fruit. Cover with boiling water. Stir three minutes, then rinse fruit several times in cold water. Place in saucepan. Add one pint of cold water, bring slowly to boil. Add ¼ lb. sugar, and boil for five minutes. — Mrs. J. A. Parkes, Malvern.

PRESERVED PEACHES

Saltspoon of washing soda to half pound of fruit. Cover with boiling water and let stand for a quarter of an hour. Skin, rinse in three waters and cook, using plenty of water. Add sugar last as it keeps a better colour. — B. L. Bowley.

STRAWBERRY SPONGE

One ounce butter, three-quarter cup sugar, three eggs, one cup flour, one teaspoon cream tartar, half teaspoon carb. soda. Beat the butter and sugar to a cream; add the well-beaten eggs and beat lightly for 15 minutes; add one cup flour sifted with one teaspoon of cream of tartar and half teaspoon of carbonate of soda (or self-raising flour). Bake 20 minutes in moderate oven. When cool have ready one-quarter pint cream whipped with a little icing sugar to sweeten, and spread half on each layer. Bruise a few strawberries and spread on top of cream and spread a little cream over the top; put a row of small strawberries along the edge, six or seven in the centre. Make some jelly (strawberry) from packet jelly crystals. When it begins to set pour over the top of the sandwich, first pinning a piece of butter paper round the edge a little higher than the cake and removing when the jelly is set.

—Miss M. Treasure, Black Forest.

In an Electric Cooker bake at 375°.

Bake in Gas Cooker at 400° F.

STRAWBERRY TRIFLE

One stale sponge cake, two eggs, one packet jelly crystals, one and a half pints milk, three dessertspoons cornflour, half cup sugar, 1 lb. strawberries.

Method: Lay the sponge cake at bottom of dish, pour over it the melted jelly crystals. When cool, add a layer of strawberries. Put custard on top of this, and then repeat another layer, putting custard last.

For Custard: Boil the milk. Add yolks of eggs and cornflour, which must be previously mixed with cold milk, and bring all again to the boil. When cold, pour over cake and fruit. Beat the whites of the eggs to a stiff froth and place in rounds on top of trifle.

—Mrs. A. Hill, St. Peters.

ICE CREAM (WITHOUT CREAM)

Beat four tablespoons powdered milk into 1 pint of milk. Add 2 dessertspoons sugar, half teaspoon gelatine dissolved in a little water. Beat until the consistency of cream. Place in wet trays for 1½ hours. Remove from refrigerator and beat well. Add 1 teaspoon vanilla or juice and grated rind of an orange or lemon.

APRICOT DELIGHT

Two cups of stewed apricots rubbed through sieve, 2 eggs, half cup of cream.

Beat egg yolks and add to the apricots. Place in trays and freeze to a mush. Remove to a chilled bowl and beat. Add egg whites, beaten, with a tablespoon of sugar. Fold in cream and return to refrigerator to freeze.

This can be made without cream. — F. M. Leslie.

PASSION FRUIT FLUMMERY

Two dessertspoons gelatine, 1 pint hot water, quarter cup sugar, 1 tablespoon flour, orange or lemon juice, 6 passion fruit.

Dissolve the gelatine and sugar in hot water. Mix flour to a thin, smooth paste with the orange or lemon juice. Add to the above liquid and stir over a slow heat till boiling. Boil three minutes. Pour into a bowl. When cold, put into refrigerator and leave till the mixture begins to thicken. Beat to a stiff cream, add passion fruit, and stir thoroughly. Pour into a serving dish and serve with cream or custard.

MARSHMALLOW MERINGUE (PAVLOVA)

Whites of 3 eggs, 1 teaspoon vinegar, 1 cup sugar.

Beat egg whites. When stiff, add sugar gradually, then vinegar and vanilla essence (if liked). Put on to greaseproof paper on slide, make into a circle and flatten top. Decorate with cream and fruit.

In an Electric Oven cook for 1¼ hours at 300°, turn thermostat off.

This recipe can also be used for small meringues. Time ¾ hour to 1 hour. — M.B.

REFRIGERATION RECIPES

CHOCOLATE ICE CREAM

Two dessertspoons cocoa, ½ cup water, ¼ cup milk, 1 cup cream, whipped, ⅛ teaspoon salt, ⅛ cup sugar, 2 teaspoons vanilla.

Combine cocoa and water in top of double boiler. Heat until mixed. Add milk, salt, sugar. Cool. Add vanilla, fold slowly into cream, whipped just stiff enough to hold its shape. Pour into freezing trays of refrigerator, freeze to desired consistency.

CHOCOLATE SAUCE

One dessertspoon cocoa, ½ cup cold water, ½ cup sugar, ⅛ teaspoon salt, 1 tablespoon butter, 1 teaspoon vanilla.

Mix cocoa with water and when quite smooth, stir in sugar and salt. Cook 3 or 4 minutes. Remove from flame and stir in butter and vanilla. Serve hot on ice cream.

CARAMEL SAUCE

One cup brown sugar, ½ cup cold water, 1 teaspoon vanilla, 1 tablespoon butter, ⅛ teaspoon salt.

Combine sugar and water in saucepan. Boil 6 or 7 minutes, or until mixture begins to thicken and become syrupy. Remove from flame just before it reaches the soft-ball stage. Add butter, salt, vanilla and beat about 1 minute, or until it becomes lighter in colour and begins to thicken. Serve hot on vanilla ice cream.

APRICOT SNOW

One jar preserved apricots or stewed apricots, 2 egg whites, pinch salt, 1 gill custard, 3 tablespoons cornflour, 2 tablespoons sugar, 3 tablespoons cold water.

Mix the cornflour and sugar to a paste with the cold water. Drain the syrup from the apricots and stir into the cornflour. Bring to the boil, stirring constantly; cook thoroughly for about 5 minutes. Sieve most of the apricots and stir the puree into the cornflour mixture. Cool. Beat the egg whites until stiff and fold into the apricot mixture. Fold in the custard lightly. Pour into glasses, and set in refrigerator. When set and chilled garnish with remainder of apricots and mock cream.

PINEAPPLE FOAM

Dissolve 4 teaspoons of gelatine in 1 cup of hot pineapple syrup. Then beat 4 egg yolks with 4 tablespoons of sugar until creamy, then add to the cooled gelatine, stand in ice, and when beginning to set add 1 cup of chopped pineapple and the four stiffly beaten egg whites. Mix well but lightly. Pour into moulds and chill in refrigerator. Serve with cream.

MOULDED HAM SALAD

One level tablespoon powdered gelatine, 4 level tablespoons cold water, 1½ gills boiled salad dressing, 2 breakfast cups chopped ham, ½ cup chopped celery, shredded lettuce, slices of tomato, beetroot or hard boiled egg.

Soak gelatine in cold water, then mix with the salad dressing and leave till beginning to set. Add the chopped ham and celery, pour into a wet mould and leave to set in refrigerator. Turn on to a dish and garnish with shredded lettuce, tomato slices and beetroot or hard-boiled egg.

ICE CREAM RECIPES

Mix 4 heaped tablespoons powdered milk with 3 tablespoons cold water to a paste. Add ½ cup sugar and 2 cups of cow's milk and vanilla essence. Lastly add 2 teaspoons gelatine dissolved in ¼ cup hot water. Beat well, place in trays in refrigerator. When the ice cream is beginning to set, remove from trays and beat, return to trays and freeze.

One pint milk, 2 whole eggs, 1 tin condensed milk, 2 ozs. castor sugar, 2 egg yolks, vanilla.

Heat the milk and sugar. Beat egg yolks and add, stirring over a low gas for a few minutes. Remove from flame, add essence and condensed milk, and beat well and pour into refrigerator trays to chill. When setting around the edges take out and whisk again. Then return to cabinet and freeze.

Quarter pint cream, 2 egg whites, 2 tablespoons icing sugar, ½ teaspoon vanilla.

Whip whites stiffly. Whip cream slightly, stir in sugar and vanilla. Fold in egg white lightly but thoroughly. Pour in ice block tray with small compartments removed. Set temperature control at maximum 1 hour before freezing and leave at maximum during freezing. Time: 3 to 4 hours.

SUGGESTED FLAVOURINGS

One teacup chopped mixed nuts.
Half ounce walnuts and 2 teaspoons coffee essence.
One ounce melted chocolate.
Half ounce crystallised ginger and ½ oz. walnuts.
One teacup crushed fruit as strawberries, bananas, pineapple (not plums or gooseberries).

GOLDEN SYRUP ICE CREAM

Half cup milk, ½ pint cream, 2 egg yolks, 2 tablespoons golden syrup.

Make a custard with the milk, egg yolks and golden syrup. Cool. Slightly beat the cream. Add to the custard and freeze in the refrigerator without stirring.

APPLE ICE CREAM

Four good-sized cooking apples, ½ teaspoon orange rind, juice of ½ orange, sugar to taste, 3 tablespoons sherry, 4 tablespoons apricot jam, 1 tablespoon red currant jelly, ½ pint cream, juice of ½ lemon.

Peel apples and cook gently in a covered saucepan with half the lemon juice. When cooked, sweeten to taste, and puree them; then add the rest of the lemon juice, rind and juice of the orange, apricot jam and sherry. Mix well and chill. Whip the cream (keeping out a little for decoration), and add to the puree. Mix and freeze, but on no account freeze too hard — it must be softish. Serve in fruit glasses. Decorate with a spot of the cream and a dab of red currant jelly.

PASTRY RECIPES AND PASTRY DISHES

PASTRY RECIPES

PASTRY DISHES

PASTRY

FLAKY PASTRY

Half-pound plain flour, one pinch salt, one gill water, 2 oz. butter, 2 oz. lard.

Sift the flour and salt, mix the fats together, and divide into four parts. Rub one part into the flour, and mix to a stiff dough. Knead well and roll out in an oblong strip three times as long as it is broad. Spread second part of fat two-thirds down the pastry, sprinkle lightly with flour and fold in three. Fasten ends with the rolling-pin and turn pastry round so that the sides now become the top and bottom. Roll out into an oblong shape and repeat twice. All rolling must be done the same way—i.e., from the person. Roll pastry to required size.

Three-quarters pound of S.R. flour, 6 oz. butter, one tablespoonful sugar, one saltspoon salt, and cold water.

Mix flour, salt, sugar, and sift twice. Rub 2 oz. butter into flour, then mix to a dough, not too soft. Roll out ½ in. thick. Cut the rest of the butter into thin shreds. Spread this over the paste. Roll and fold twice. Then roll out again, and using the remainder of the butter, roll and fold as before. Edges should be cut with a sharp knife. Cook in a hot oven, and pastry should cool off in a warm room. —E. C. Honeyman, Ki Ki.

In an Electric Cooker bake at 500°.
Bake in Gas Cooker at 450° F.

SHORT PASTRY

Eight ounces plain flour, one pinch salt, 4 oz. shortening (lard, butter, clarified dripping or margarine), quarter pint water.

Sift flour and salt; rub in shortening with tips of fingers. Mix to a stiff dough, turn on to a light-floured board, and roll to required shape.

Half a teaspoon of baking powder may be used, then 3 oz. of shortening is sufficient. If the pastry is to be used for sweet dishes, add one teaspoon of castor sugar.

SUET PASTRY

Six ounces plain flour, one teaspoon baking powder, one pinch salt, 2 oz. suet, gill water.

Sift the flour, salt, and baking powder. Skin, flake and chop the suet finely (a little sifted flour will assist). Rub suet into the flour, add water gradually, making a dry dough. Turn on to a floured pastry board and knead well.

PUFF PASTRY (Economical)

One pound flour, ¾ lb. good beef dripping or lard, ½ lb. butter, half teaspoon salt, about half a cup of water.

Rub dripping into the flour and mix into paste with water. Roll out paste on to a board, and spread with bits of butter. Fold up. Roll out, and spread. Fold and roll out again, and spread with butter. Leave for 10 minutes or more, then roll out again and spread with the rest of the butter. It is better to let this stand for some little time—say half an hour—before rolling out and using. — Miss D. Cochrane.

PUFF PASTRY

Half pound plain flour, ½ lb. hard butter, one pinch salt, yolk of one egg, a squeeze of lemon juice, less than quarter pint water.

Sift the flour and salt, add the lemon juice, and mix to a paste with the egg and water. The paste must not be too dry or too wet. Place the butter on a floured towel and form into a flat cake (this removes water from the butter and makes it easier for working). Place the butter on the paste, fold over the other half and press the edges together. Place folded edges of the paste to the sides, press the paste lightly three or four times, and roll into a strip three times as long as wide. Fold in three, but do not press the edges. Place in a cool place, and leave for a quarter of an hour. This is called giving the pastry a "turn"; the pastry requires seven turns. Give two more turns and leave for a quarter of an hour. Repeat until the pastry has had seven turns. The object of cooling between the rolls is to keep the butter and flour in distinct and separate layers. The rolling must be even, and always done away from person. This pastry will keep several days in cold weather if wrapped in greased paper.

ROUGH PUFF PASTRY

Half pound plain flour, one pinch salt, ¼ lb. hard butter, one squeeze lemon juice, one gill cold water.

Sift flour and salt; chip the butter into pieces the size of an acorn, and chop into the flour. Add the lemon juice and mix to a stiff paste. Knead well and roll into a long strip three times as long as it is wide. Fold in three, fasten ends, and turn round so that the sides become the top and bottom. The pastry should be rolled, folded, and turned three times, it is then ready to use.

EGG TART OR CHEESE CAKE

Two eggs, half cup sugar, one tablespoon of water, quarter teaspoon acid, 10 drops essence of lemon.

Beat well, pour into a plate lined with pastry. Bake for 20 minutes or till quite set. — E. L. Pledge, Laura.

In Electric Cooker bake at 450°.

Bake in Gas Cooker at 400° F.

BANANA ROLLS

Remove the peel from some fairly ripe bananas and sprinkle the fruit liberally with sugar. Prepare a short paste, roll it out thinly, cut into strips rather longer and more than double width the banana. Enclose banana neatly; after moistening and fastening edges of paste bake rolls lightly in moderate oven.

In an Electric Cooker bake at 450°.

Bake in Gas Cooker at 400° F.

CHIFFON PIE

Rub two ripe bananas through sieve. Add to them two tablespoons sugar, pinch of salt, and two unbeaten egg whites. Beat all together till stiff and frothy, flavour with almond essence and good squeeze of lemon juice. Bake in dish lined with pastry for 20 or 30 minutes or till firm to the touch, and lightly browned. Let it cool, and place brightly-coloured jelly on top and whipped cream sprinkled with chopped nuts.

— Miss D. Cochrane, Auburn, Victoria.

In an Electric Cooker bake at 450°.

Bake in Gas Cooker at 400° F.

DATE TART

Ingredients.—1 lb. dates, half gill water, juice half a lemon, ½ lb. good short crust.

Method.—Stone dates and put in a saucepan with water and lemon juice. Stir over fire until the consistency of thick jam. Turn on plate to cool. Make short crust and line a sandwich tin. Fill with date mixture and cover with pastry. Glaze with sugar and water and cook in moderately hot oven for 15 minutes

In an Electric Cooker bake at 425°.

Bake in Gas Cooker at 425° F.

APPLE AMBER PUDDING

Roll out some pastry thinly and line sides of pie-dish with it. Peel, core, and cut up 1½ lbs. of apples and put them in a saucepan with 2 oz. castor sugar and grated lemon rind; simmer very gently till apples are soft. They may need a little water to prevent burning. Beat smooth with a fork and add two yolks of eggs well beaten and one-quarter pint milk. Turn this mixture into the pie-dish and bake till pastry is done.

Beat the whites of eggs and 2 oz. castor sugar till quite stiff and put on top with some blanched almonds. Put in moderate oven till golden colour. — Mrs. Arbon, Brighton.

LEMON PIE

Ingredients.—Three eggs, 2 oz. butter, half pint water, juice and rind of three lemons, ¼ lb. sugar, two level tablespoons of arrowroot, ¼ lb. short crust.

Method.—Line sides and edges of pie-dish with pastry. Cut and ornament edges. Put yolks of eggs, water in which arrowroot has been blended, sugar, lemon rinds and juice, also butter, into a saucepan, and stir over fire until the mixture thickens. Then cook gently for three minutes. Pour into pie-dish. Decorate top with stiffly-beaten whites of eggs.

In an Electric Cooker first bake pastry shell at 450°. Return to oven to cook meringue at 350°.

Bake in Gas Cooker at 400° F.

LEMON TART

Line pie-dish with short pastry.

Filling.—Juice of two lemons and grated rind, two egg yolks, one cup sugar, one cup bread crumbs, one cup cold water.

Beat egg, sugar and lemon juice. Add rind, bread crumbs and cold water. Fill dish and bake till set. Make meringue of egg whites and sugar, and brown slightly in oven.

— Mrs. E. G. Harrison, Lower Mitcham.

In an Electric Cooker first bake pastry shell at 450°. Return to oven to cook meringue at 350°.

Bake in Gas Cooker at 400° F.

RAISIN TART

Half-pound seeded raisins, one dessertspoon sugar, juice of one lemon, one pinch cinnamon, one teacup water, one dessertspoon cornflour.

Stew raisins slowly with lemon juice, cinnamon, sugar and water. When soft add the cornflour, mixed to a smooth paste and boil for three minutes. Allow to cool. Line a tart plate with short pastry. Put on the mixture and cover with pastry. Bake in hot oven for 20 minutes. — F.M.S.

In an Electric Cooker bake at 450°.

Bake in Gas Cooker at 425° F.

CURRANT APPLE TART

Line a pie-plate with short pastry. Peel and core three or four large cooking apples, slice very thinly and put a thick layer of the sliced apple on the pastry, sprinkle over a handful of currants and seeded raisins or sultanas, and a few very thin slices of lemon peel. Then sprinkle over a handful of sugar; add another thick layer of sliced apples, sprinkle with sugar, cover with pastry, pierce the pastry half a dozen times with a fork, and bake in moderately hot oven for half an hour. A delicious tart.

In an Electric Cooker bake at 450°.

Bake in Gas Cooker at 425° F.

SULTANA SLICES

Make 1½ lb. short-crust, to which has been added one tablespoon sugar. Roll out about 12 in. square, mark half with back of knife, and spread evenly with following mixture:—Two tablespoons sultanas, half tablespoon spice, one tablespoon sugar, and one dessertspoon warm water and a few drops of essence of lemon. Blend well and cover half the paste with the mixture, fold over, and bake in a fairly hot oven till golden brown. When cold, cut into squares.

In an Electric Cooker bake at 450°.

Bake in Gas Cooker at 425° F.

PINEAPPLE CUSTARD TART

Grate 1 medium sized pineapple, add 1 cup water, 1 cup sugar, 1 egg, 1 tablespoonful butter, juice of 1 lemon. Bring to boiling point, then thicken with 2 tablespoons of flour blended in a little water. Line a pie-dish with good pastry, pour on the custard and cover with another layer of pastry and bake in a moderate oven.

—Mrs. H. G. Thompson, Killara, N.S.W.

In an Electric Cooker bake at 450°.

Bake the bottom layer of pastry first in a Gas Cooker at 400° F. for 15 minutes, then pour custard on top of pastry and finish baking.

MERINGUE TART

Line a tart-plate with short pastry and bake in a moderate oven for 15 minutes. Pour on a custard made as follows:—Melt in a saucepan 2 ozs. butter, remove from stove and stir in 2 ozs. flour; mix to a smooth paste, then add ½ pint milk and stir over a low flame till mixture boils; boil 3 minutes; add 1 oz. sugar, yolks of 2 eggs, and flavour with vanilla. Bake in the pastry for 5 minutes or until pastry is cooked. Spread 2 tablespoons apricot jam over custard; pile on top the stiffly beaten whites of 2 eggs, sweetened with 1 or 2 tablespoons castor sugar.

Set in a slow oven to set and brown meringue.

RAISIN AND RHUBARB TART

One pound cherry rhubarb, half packet seeded raisins, half cup sugar.

Cut rhubarb into small pieces, and stew for five minutes with raisins and sugar. When cool, place between short pastry in pie-plate. Bake in a hot oven. — Mrs. H. R. Adamson.

In an Electric Cooker bake at 450°.

Bake in Gas Cooker at 425° F.

JOHNNY CAKES

Make a short pastry, roll out thin; spread raisins or sultanas thickly on. Put layer of pastry on top; roll just enough to keep together. Mark into squares, and when baked they will separate easily where marked.

In an Electric Cooker bake at 450°.

Bake in Gas Cooker at 400° F.

SMALL CAKES

SMALL CAKES

AFTERNOON TEA

Four ounces chocolate, 3 oz. butter, 4 oz. castor sugar, three eggs, 3 oz. flour, a few drops of essence of almonds.

Grate the chocolate, and place it in a jar in the oven or in a saucepan of hot water, allowing it to melt slowly. Cream the butter and sugar, then add the yolks of eggs and chocolate, and beat for a few minutes. Whip the white of the eggs to a stiff froth, and sieve the flour with the baking powder. Add a little flour and a little white of egg alternately to the other mixture until all is lightly blended together. Half fill small prepared tins with the mixture, and bake in a moderate oven about 15 minutes.

In an Electric Cooker bake at 475°.

Bake in Gas Cooker at 375° F.

APRICOT CAKES

Weight of six eggs in butter, two in sugar, two in cornflour.

Beat butter and sugar to a cream. Add four eggs well beaten, enough S.R. flour to roll out a smooth paste. Stew dried apricots sweetened with sugar. Place apricot between paste, cut with tumbler. Bake in a moderate oven. When cold, ice and sprinkle desiccated coconut on top. —Mrs. G. H. Lang, Gawler South.

In an Electric Cooker bake at 425°.

Bake in Gas Cooker at 375° F.

ATHOL CAKES

Half-pound maizena, ½ lb. flour (S.R.), ½ lb. sugar, ½ lb. butter, three eggs, rind and juice of one lemon.

Cream butter and sugar together. Whisk eggs for five minutes and add. Sift maizena and flour and pinch of salt together, then finely grated lemon rind and lastly juice. Bake in paper cups for five minutes in a quick oven. Ice with lemon icing.

—Mrs. H. R. Adamson.

CHOCOLATE CAKES

Two eggs, their weight in butter, sugar, and flour, one teaspoon essence of vanilla, quarter teaspoon baking powder.

Beat butter and sugar to a cream. Add dry ingredients gradually, then the eggs and essence. Mix all thoroughly and put in patty pans and bake from 15 to 20 minutes.

Icing.—6 oz. icing sugar, 2 oz. cocoa, 12 drops essence of vanilla, and two tablespoons water. Mix smooth and stir over fire until warm, then dip the cakes into it.

—Mrs. M. L. Evans, Ivanhoe, Keyneton.

In an Electric Cooker bake at 475°.

Bake in Gas Cooker at 400° F.

COCONUT CAKES

Ten ounces flour, 5 oz. sugar, 5 oz. butter, 1 teaspoon cream of tartar, ½ teaspoon carb. soda, small cup coconut, 2 eggs.

Beat butter to cream. Add sugar, then eggs, then flour with cream of tartar in it, and soda dissolved in a little boiling water, coconut. Put on slide in little pieces. —Mrs. W. Simmons.

Three tablespoons dripping, 1 cup sugar, 1 cup coconut, 2 eggs, 3 cups S.R. flour, little milk.

Beat dripping and sugar to a cream, add eggs and milk, then coconut, and lastly flour. Drop little pieces on greased slide, and sprinkle with sugar. Bake in hot oven about 15 to 20 minutes. —Mrs. T. W. Neill, McLaren Vale.

In an Electric Cooker bake at 475°.
Bake in Gas Cooker at 375° F.

CREAM PUFFS

One cup hot water, half cup butter, boil together and while boiling stir in one cupful of dry flour. Take from the stove and stir to a smooth paste. After this cools stir in three eggs not beaten, stir five minutes. Drop in tablespoonfuls in a buttered tin and bake in quick oven 25 mins. Don't let them touch each other in pan. Do not open oven door more than absolutely necessary.

For the cream: One cup milk, half cup sugar, one egg, three tablespoons of flour or two tablespoons of cornflour. Mix cornflour with a little milk; put the rest of the milk on the stove, when hot put in the sugar and egg beaten together, and cornflour. Cook until thick, flavour with vanilla. When cream and puffs are cool, open one side of puffs and fill with cream.
—Mrs. Alfred Anderson, Blythwood.

Put half pint water and 2 oz. butter on to boil. When boiling add quickly 4 oz. S.R. flour, stir until a smooth paste is formed. Remove from the fire and when just warm add three eggs, one at a time, beat well as each one is added.

Bake in tins in a hot oven for half an hour, when cold fill with whipped cream and sprinkle with icing sugar. This makes about 18. —Mrs. Harry Arbon, Clarence Park. —T. Abbott. —Mrs. J. T. Farrow, Tea Tree Gully. —D. Jarrett, Angaston.

In an Electric Cooker bake at 500° 30 to 35 minutes to cook.
Bake in Gas Cooker at 375° F.

DATE BUNS

Three-quarter pound self-raising flour, ¼ lb. sugar, ¼ lb. butter, three eggs.

Mix into dough, take a spoonful and press a date into the centre, and make into a ball and bake. If liked, an icing is very nice. —Mrs. W. Simmons.

In an Electric Cooker bake at 425°.
Bake in Gas Cooker at 400° F.

CHOCOLATE CAKE DROPS

Three eggs (whites only), ½ lb. powdered chocolate, ½ lb. sifted sugar, vanilla flavouring.

Method.—Beat whites stiff, and mix in chocolate and sifted sugar. Drop from a teaspoon on a buttered tin. Bake in a moderate oven. — Dulcie Besanko, Clarence Park.

— M. Higginbottom.

In Electric Cooker bake 275° with current switched off.

Bake in Gas Cooker at 325° F.

CHEESE CAKES

For Pastry.—Six ounces flour, one pinch salt, 3 oz. butter or clarified fat, half teacup water, little jam.

Sift flour and salt. Rub in fat with finger tips. Mix to a stiff dough. Roll out thinly and cut in rounds. Line patties with pastry and put half teaspoon jam in each.

For Cake Mixture.—2 oz. butter, 2 oz. sugar, one egg, 4 oz. S.R. flour, a little milk, few drops essence.

Cream butter and sugar, and add the well-beaten egg. Stir in the sifted flour, essence and milk. Put a little of the mixture in each prepared patty. Decorate tops with strips of pastry. Bake in a hot oven for 20 minutes.

In an Electric Cooker bake at 475°.

Bake in Gas Cooker at 400° F.

CREAM LILIES

Four eggs, cup sugar, cup flour, one teaspoon cream tartar, half teaspoon carbonate of soda.

Beat eggs and sugar to a froth. Add flour with cream of tartar and soda. Beat well and cook on buttered paper. A small tablespoonful for each one. When cooked roll the shape of a lily, and when cold fill with whipped cream and a spoonful of jelly on top.

— A. Ellery, Sheridan Street, Woodville.

Three eggs, their weight in sugar; weight of 1 egg in cornflour; weight of 1 egg in S.R. flour.

Whip whites of eggs to stiff froth; stir in well-beaten yolks; then add sugar, flour, etc.

Drop teaspoonfuls on tray, only about 3 at a time, as they must be rolled to shape of lily immediately after coming from the oven. Bake in moderate oven. Fill with cream, and use small piece of jelly to represent tongue of lily. — Mrs. Slane, North Unley.

In an Electric Cooker bake at 375°.

Bake in Gas Cooker at 375° F.

DREAMS

Three eggs, their weight in sugar, butter, cornflour, two teaspoons baking powder.

Bake in patty pans for seven minutes in a hot oven. Also makes a nice loaf cake. — Mrs. G. H. Lang, Gawler South.

In an Electric Cooker bake at 475°.

Bake in Gas Cooker at 375° F.

DELECTABLE RICE MUFFINS

One cup boiled rice, one cup sweet milk, two eggs well beaten, five tablespoons melted butter, half teaspoon salt, one tablespoon sugar, one and a half cups flour.

Put rice in flour, add salt and sugar, stir in egg and milk, then the butter. Beat well. Bake in hot gem irons in a hot oven.

— Miss D. Cochrane, Auburn, Victoria.

In an Electric Cooker bake at 475°.
Bake in Gas Cooker at 425° F.

ECCLES OR BANBURY CAKES

Quarter pound currants, 1 oz. candied peel, 2 oz. castor sugar, oz. butter, ¼ teaspoon spice, 8 oz. flaky or rough puff pastry.

Clean the currants and chop the peel finely, place in a jar with other ingredients. Stand the jar in a saucepan of boiling water and boil for a quarter of an hour. Cool before using. Roll the pastry out thinly; cut in rounds three or four inches across, damp the edges and place some of mixture on half the pieces. Cover with the other pieces, and fasten round the edges. Make slits on the top, glaze and bake in a hot oven for 10 minutes.

— A.L.S.

In an Electric Cooker bake at 475°.
Bake in Gas Cooker at 400° F.

FRENCH CREAMS

Two eggs, two tablespoons sugar, and the weight of eggs in flour, half cup icing sugar, teaspoon butter, few drops vanilla.

Method.—Beat eggs and sugar together until stiff, lightly stir in flour, bake in patty pans in a brisk oven. When cool, cut out little pieces at the top and put in the cream made of icing sugar, butter and vanilla. Do not wet icing too much; it must be very stiff. Now place back the piece of cake which you cut out, leave the cream showing all round the piece. When all are finished, place all beside each other and sprinkle with dry icing sugar, then put a pink icing dot on top of each. These are very pretty for a supper table or afternoon tea.

In an Electric Cooker bake at 450°.
Bake in Gas Cooker at 375° F.

FRUIT CAKES

Half pound sugar, ½ lb. butter, four eggs, ¼ lb. sultanas, ¼ lb. dates, ¼ lb. currants, 2 oz. lemon peel, 1 lb. flour, two teaspoons cream tartar, one teaspoon carb. soda, one cup milk.

This makes two large cakes and can be also baked in little tins.

In an Electric Cooker bake at 475° for 15 minutes for small cakes. For large cakes 350°.
Bake in Gas Cooker at 300 F.

GEM CAKES

Two cups flour (S.R.), one cup sugar, half cup milk, one tablespoon butter, two eggs.

Beat sugar and eggs together. Add flour and melted butter last. Bake eight minutes in gem tins.

In an Electric Cooker bake at 500°.
Bake in Gas Cooker at 425° F.

GINGER ROUGHS

Four oz. sugar, 4 oz. butter, 1 egg, 1 cup (large) S.R. flour, 1 cup preserved ginger (cut small).

Cream butter and sugar, add beaten egg, then ginger. Add flour, then drop teaspoonfuls in cornflakes, and roll lightly. Place on greased slides and bake in moderate oven.

In an Electric Cooker bake at 425°.
Bake in Gas Cooker at 375° F.

HONEY BUNS

One cup S.R. flour, 1 cup arrowroot, 1 egg, 2 tablespoons butter, 1 tablespoon honey.

Mix all together, moisten with very little milk. Form into small balls, and bake in hot oven till brown.

In an Electric Cooker bake at 450°.
Bake in Gas Cooker at 425° F.

LITTLE CHOCOLATE CAKES

Take 4 oz. of flour, one egg, 2 oz. cocoa, half teaspoon of baking powder, 1½ oz. butter, vanilla essence, 1 oz. of sugar, a very little water.

Put the cocoa in a pan with the water, and stir over a gentle heat until it blends. Rub the flour, baking powder and salt through a sieve on to a piece of paper. Cream the butter and sugar, add the egg. Beat well. Add cocoa and vanilla, then stir the flour in. Drop in small quantities into gem scone tray and bake.

In an Electric Cooker bake at 475°.
Bake in Gas Cooker at 400° F.

MADELINE CAKES

One cup each of flour and cornflour, half cup sugar, three eggs, 4 oz. butter or half dripping and half butter, two teaspoons cream of tartar and one of carbonate soda.

Beat butter and sugar well together. Add eggs, one at a time. Beat well. Add flour, etc., and mix into a smooth dough. Put into well-greased patty pans. Bake a light brown in a moderate oven. When cold, brush tops with apricot jam, and sprinkle coconut on top. —Mrs. W. Greenwood, "Todmorden," Gawler.

In an Electric Cooker bake at 475°.
Bake in Gas Cooker at 400° F.

LENA CAKES

One and a half cups S.R. flour, ¼ lb. butter, one egg, three tablespoons sugar. Rub sugar and butter into flour and beaten egg. Add enough milk to make a stiff paste. Roll out and spread with jam. Roll up after style of jam roll and cut into slices not too thick. —Mrs. A. C. Ellis, Port Elliot.

In an Electric Cooker bake at 425°.
Bake in Gas Cooker at 400° F.

LAMINGTONS

Beat to a cream three-quarters of a cup of sugar and two tablespoons butter, then add two well-beaten eggs, lastly add one cup flour and one teaspoon baking powder. Bake in sandwich tin in moderate oven. When cold, cut into squares, dip in warm icing, and roll in desiccated coconut. The icing—one dessertspoonful cocoa, one cup sugar, quarter cup water. Boil three minutes. — Mrs. A. C. Ellis, Port Elliot.

In an Electric Cooker bake at 375° for ½ hour.
Bake in Gas Cooker at 325° F.

LAMINGTONS

One cup butter, 1½ cups sugar, 3 cups S.R. flour, 1 cup milk, 4 eggs.

Beat butter, sugar and eggs together. Add milk, then flour. Beat well, and bake in large square tin for about three-quarters of an hour. When cold, cut in squares, ice all over and dip in coconut. — T. Abbott, Rosslyn Park.

In an Electric Cooker bake at 375°.
Bake in Gas Cooker at 350° F.

ICING FOR LAMINGTONS

Sift 2 lb. icing sugar with 3 or 4 tablespoons of cocoa. Work in ¼ lb. butter and ½ cup hot water; more may be wanted. Flavour with essence of vanilla. Cut cake into suitable pieces, and coat with icing; cover with coconut.

TO ICE LAMINGTONS

Place basin containing icing over a saucepan of hot water. This keeps it soft. Hold cake on wire skewer or knitting needle, spread with icing, then cover with coconut.

LUNCH CAKES

Two ounces butter, 2 ozs. sugar, one egg, 2 oz. sultanas or currants, 4 oz. S. R. flour, one pinch salt, four tablespoons milk.

Cream the butter and sugar. Add the well-beaten egg and the prepared fruit. Stir in gradually the sifted flour and the milk. Put into patties and bake in a quick oven for 10 to 15 minutes. — Miss D. Chenoweth, Willaston.

In an Electric Cooker bake at 475°.
Bake in Gas Cooker at 400° F.

MYRA CAKES

A quarter pound butter, ¼ lb. sugar, two eggs, 6 oz. S.R. flour, one dessertspoon marmalade, one-quarter cup milk, raisins, currants, walnuts, and lemon peel.

Beat butter and sugar to a cream; add eggs, then fruit, marmalade, milk, and lastly flour. This makes about 3 dozen cakes. Use gem trays. Drop a piece of butter into each cup when they are hot, then the batter. Bake eight to ten minutes in a hot oven.

— Mrs. G. Rogers, Torrensville.

In an Electric Cooker bake at 475°.
Bake in Gas Cooker at 400° F.

MAID OF HONOR CHEESE CAKES

Line patty pans with pastry rolled thinly, and put in a teaspoon of raspberry jam. Then beat ¼ lb. butter to a cream with ¼ lb. sugar; then add two eggs well beaten. Stir in 4 oz. ground rice, previously mixed with 4 oz. S.R. flour. Put about a dessertspoon of this mixture on top of the raspberry jam, and bake until nicely coloured. Cornflour may be used instead of rice flour.

— Mrs. E. R. Ingham, Highgate.

Bake in Gas Cooker at 400° F.

TUNBRIDGE CAKES

Rub 6 oz. butter in to 1 lb. flour, then mix 6 oz. sugar and one dessertspoon caraway seeds. Beat two eggs and make the above into a paste; roll out and cut into rounds. Wash over with white of an egg and dust over with sugar.

Bake in a hot oven until a light brown colour.

— Miss Morphett, Torrens Park.

In an Electric Cooker bake at 425°.
Bake in Gas Cooker at 375° F.

VICTORIA BUNS

Two ounces butter, 2 oz. sugar, 2 oz. candied peel, 2 oz. currants, one pinch salt, ¼ lb. flour, 2 oz. ground rice, one teaspoon baking powder, 1 egg, little milk, essence lemon or grated lemon.

Cream butter and sugar and add well-beaten eggs. Add the prepared fruit and flavouring. Stir in gradually the flour and milk alternately. Bake in patties for 15 to 20 minutes.

In an Electric Cooker bake at 475°.
Bake in Gas Cooker at 400° F.
In an Electric Cooker bake at 475°.

PLAIN CAKES

Three cups flour, five eggs, ½ lb. butter, one cup sugar, one-quarter cup milk.

Beat sugar and butter to a cream, add eggs (separately well beaten), add flour (sifted), add flavouring, stir milk in last. Put in well-greased patty tins, bake five minutes in hot oven.

— Mrs. C. Stanley, Mitcham.

In an Electric Cooker bake at 475°.
Bake in Gas Cooker at 400° F.

QUEEN CAKES

Quarter pound butter and ¼ lb. sugar creamed together. Add three eggs one at a time, and 6 oz. S.R. flour. Add a few currants and some lemon peel, also a few drops of essence of lemon. Bake in patties in a hot oven.

— Mrs. W. Greenwood, Gawler.

In an Electric Cooker bake at 475° ¼ hour.
Bake in Gas Cooker at 400° F.

QUEEN CAKES

Three cups S.R. flour, one cup sultanas, 1 oz. lemon peel, three eggs, one cup sugar, ½ lb. butter, essence of vanilla, three-quarter cup of milk.

Beat butter and sugar to a cream, add eggs, then milk, then flour, and lastly fruit. Bake in patty pans. This mixture also makes an excellent cake baked in a large cake tin.

— Miss Morphett, Torrens Park.

Six eggs, ½ lb. sugar, ½ lb. butter, ½ lb. currants, one teaspoon cream of tartar, half teaspoon carbonate of soda, 14 oz. flour, essence of lemon.

Beat sugar and butter to cream. Beat eggs five minutes. Add to sugar and butter. Then add flour, etc. Bake in patty pans in quick oven, but not too hot to start.

In an Electric Cooker bake at 475° for 12-15 minutes.
Bake in Gas Cooker at 400° F.

RASPBERRY BUNS

Three-quarters of a pound of S.R. flour, ¼ lb. sugar, ¼ lb. butter, two eggs, one gill milk, grated rind of lemon.

Rub butter into flour. Add sugar. Add milk to eggs and mix all to stiff paste. Put on floured board and divide in 12 pieces. Roll each round. Fill one side with spoonful raspberry jam, fold over like a turnover. Pinch edges together. Bake for a quarter of an hour in moderate oven.

In an Electric Cooker bake at 450°.
Bake in Gas Cooker at 400° F.

TEA CAKES

Quarter pound butter, ¼ lb. sugar, two cups S.R. flour, two eggs, quarter pint milk, essence of lemon.

Beat butter, sugar and eggs to a cream. Add milk and essence, then sift in flour. Beat well. Add either fruit or nuts. Bake in hot oven.

Two ounces butter, 2 oz. sugar, ½ lb. S.R. flour, one gill milk, one egg.

Cream the butter and sugar. Add the egg (beaten). Add the milk. Mix flour in lightly. Bake in moderate oven in one sandwich tin for 20 minutes. Split and butter hot. — W.G.T.

In an Electric Cooker bake at 375°.
Bake in Gas Cooker at 350° F.

RICE CAKES

Four pounds flour, 2 lb. sugar, 1 lb. butter, eight eggs, four teaspoons cream of tartar, two teaspoons carbonate of soda, flavour with essence of lemon, a pint and a half of milk.

Mix butter, sugar to a cream. Add eggs, and beat again with milk. Then add flour and ingredients. Drop in tins and bake in hot oven.

In an Electric Cooker bake at 475° for 12 minutes.
Bake in Gas Cooker at 375° F.

ROCK BUNS

Six ounces S.R. flour, 2 oz. butter or dripping, 2 oz. sugar, one egg, 2 oz. currants, half teaspoon mixed spice or grated nutmeg, half teacup milk.

Rules.—Sift the flour and salt and add the butter or dripping. Add dry ingredients. Add moist ingredients. Place on a greased tray and bake for 10 minutes in a hot oven. — D. Besanko.

In an Electric Cooker bake at 425°.
Bake in Gas Cooker at 375° F.

ROCK CAKES

Half lb. butter, ¾ lb. plain flour, ¼ lb. castor sugar, 2 ozs. citron peel, ¼ lb. currants, teaspoon baking powder, 1 egg, 1 cup of milk, almonds.

Rub the butter into the flour, and add sugar, peel (chopped), currants, and baking powder. Beat egg with milk and mix with dry ingredients. Form the dough into little rough buns, place half almonds on top, and bake in hot oven for 15 to 20 minutes.

— Mrs. Pearce, Maitland.

In an Electric Cooker bake at 425°.
Bake in Gas Cooker at 375° F.

COCONUT PYRAMIDS

Quarter pound desiccated coconut, half teacup sugar, one egg.

Beat egg and sugar together. Add coconut. Form into pyramids with fingers, and bake in moderate oven till light brown.

— Mrs. S. P. Bond.

In an Electric Cooker bake at 350°.
Bake in Gas Cooker at 350° F.

COCONUT ROCKIES

Mix together 8 oz. flour, a good teaspoonful of baking powder, 3 oz. castor sugar. Rub in 3 oz. butter and 2 oz. desiccated coconut, and mix very stiff with a well-beaten egg and a little milk. Bake in rocky heaps on a greased tin about 15 minutes.

In an Electric Cooker bake at 425°.

Bake in Gas Cooker at 350° F.

JAM DROPS

Two cups flour, 1 teaspoon cream of tartar, ½ teaspoon of carb. soda, ¾ cup sugar, ½ cup butter, 2 eggs.

Beat butter and sugar to a cream; add eggs and beat well; add flour. Make into little balls with the hands. Press a hole in the centre; put in jam. Bake in a hot oven for 15 minutes.

In an Electric Cooker bake at 425°.

Bake in Gas Cooker at 375° F.

WAR BUNS

Rub ½ lb. dripping into 2 lb. flour, two heaped teaspoons cream of tartar, two flat teaspoons bicarbonate of soda (all sifted). Add ¾ lb. sugar, one cup currants.

Mix to paste with one cup milk, roll out and cut into shapes. Bake in hot oven about ¼ hour. — Mrs. W. H. Colliver.

In an Electric Cooker bake at 425°.

Bake in Gas Cooker at 400° F.

****

LARGE CAKES

LARGE CAKES

LARGE CAKES

AMERICAN APPLE SAUCE CAKE

Two and a half cups hot apple sauce unsweetened. Into this put half a cup each of lard and butter. When melted, add two cups white sugar. Into three cups flour put four level teaspoons soda, one teaspoon each of salt, cinnamon and allspice, 1 lb. chopped raisins, one cup nuts chopped, one teaspoon vanilla.

In an Electric Cooker bake at 375°.
Bake in Gas Cooker at 325° F.

AMERICAN POUND CAKE

One pound butter, 1 lb. sugar, 1 lb. raisins (seeded), 1 lb. currants, ½ lb. mixed peel, eight eggs, 1½ lb. S.R. flour, one packet spice, one nutmeg, half cup treacle, half cup strong coffee.

Beat butter and sugar together, add 1 egg at a time, then other ingredients, bake 3 or 4 hours. — Mrs Harry Arbon, Clarence Pk.

In an Electric Cooker bake at 325°.
Bake in Gas Cooker at 300° F.

APPLE CAKE

Two cups of S.R. flour, half cup sugar, half cup milk, one egg, 1½ tablespoons butter.

Mix well, roll out not too thick, then on one half spread stewed apples. Cover and bake in good hot oven.

— Mrs. Brokenshire, Broken Hill.

Take four large apples, pare, quarter and core them. Put into a saucepan with a little water, sweeten and flavour with ground cinnamon. Boil until you can beat to a pulp, and leave till cold. Make a light paste with two cups flour, ¼ lb. butter, half cup sugar, and a little cinnamon, one teaspoon baking powder, two eggs, and a little milk. Mix lightly and line a dish with the paste, then put in apple pulp, cover with layer of paste. Bake in hot oven, serve with whipped cream. — M. Theim, Beulah Park.

— Mrs. Ingham, Highgate.

In an Electric Cooker bake at 375°.
Bake in Gas Cooker at 350° F.

COCONUT SPONGE CAKE

Four eggs, their weight in sugar, butter and flour, one teaspoon cream tartar, half teaspoon soda, 4 oz. coconut, few drops vanilla.

Bake in moderate oven 40 mins. — M. Sharples, Kadina.

In an Electric Cooker bake at 375°.
Bake in Gas Cooker at 350° F.

BOILED CAKE or POOR SOLDIER'S

Ingredients.—One cup sugar, one cup water, half cup butter, ½ lb. seeded raisins, one teaspoon carbonate soda, one teaspoon ground cloves or other spice.

Method.—Put all ingredients into a saucepan and let just come to the boil. Allow to cool, and add just sufficient flour to make a thin batter (about a cup and a half flour). Bake in a moderate oven for one hour. — R.M.

— M. Theim, Beulah Park.

In an Electric Cooker bake at 375°.
Bake in Gas Cooker at 325° F.

BERLINA TORTOR

One pound flour, ½ lb. butter, ½ lb. sugar, three eggs, half teaspoon carbonate soda, one teaspoon cream of tartar, little essence of lemon.

Beat butter and sugar to a cream. Add eggs (beaten), stir flour through sifter with carbonate soda and cream of tartar. If too stiff, add a little milk. Roll and cut in rounds. Bake in a hot oven. Place five rounds together with jam or jelly between each layer. Ice top. — Mrs. Willshire.

In an Electric Cooker bake at 425°.
Bake in Gas Cooker at 350° F.

CANADIAN WAR CAKE

Eggless, Butterless, Milkless

Two cups brown sugar, one packet seeded raisins, two cups of hot water, two tablespoons lard, one teaspoon ground ginger, one teaspoon cloves, one teaspoon salt.

Boil all these ingredients together for five minutes after they begin to bubble. When cold add three cups of flour, one teaspoon soda dissolved in a teaspoon hot water. Bake in a meat tin for 40 to 50 minutes.

In an Electric Cooker bake at 375°.
Bake in Gas Cooker at 375° F.

COCOA CAKE

Half pound flour, ¼ lb. butter, ¼ lb. sugar, four tablespoons cocoa, six tablespoons milk, three eggs, one teaspoon cream of tartar, half teaspoon soda.

Method.—Cream butter and sugar. Add eggs and milk. Sift in flour, cream of tartar and soda, and cocoa. Bake ¼-¾ hour in moderate oven. When cool, ice with chocolate icing.

In an Electric Cooker bake at 375°.
Bake in Gas Cooker at 350° F.

CHRISTMAS CAKE

One lb. butter, 1 lb. dark sugar, 1¾ lb. plain flour, six eggs, two tablespoon of milk, one tablespoon of dark treacle, a nobbler of brandy, teaspoon baking powder, 1 lb. currants, ½ lb. sultanas, ¼ lb. peel, ½ lb. blanched almonds, teaspoon mixed spice, teaspoon ground cinnamon.

Beat butter and sugar to a cream, add eggs one at a time; then treacle and brandy, milk; then the spices, then the flour. Mix baking powder in the flour; last of all the fruit. Bake for three hours in a moderate oven.

You can keep this cake for quite a long time. Does not get dry. It is a lovely cake. — Mrs. J. Hawkes, Kent Town.

Five cups plain flour, three cups sugar, 1½ lb. butter, one dozen eggs, four cups sultanas, three cups currants, ½ lb. shredded lemon peel, ½ lb. finely-chopped almonds, one packet mixed spice, one cup treacle.

Beat butter and sugar to cream. Add eggs well beaten and treacle. Then mix in flour and fruit alternately. This will make three-tier Christmas cake. Bake three hours in moderate oven.

— Mrs. W. J. Smith, Fairfield, Maitland.

One lb. plain flour, ½ lb. S.R. flour, 1 lb. sultanas, 1 lb. currants, ½ lb. candied peel, ½ lb. almonds, ¼ lb. preserved ginger, eight eggs, 1 lb. butter, one teaspoon spice, half grated nutmeg, ½ lb. figs, 1 lb. brown sugar.

Beat butter and eggs to a cream. Add eggs one at a time, sugar, fruit, milk, spice, etc., lastly flour. Mix all thoroughly.

Put into hot oven. After 15 minutes reduce heat.

One and three-quarter pounds flour, 1 lb. sugar, 1 lb. sultanas, ½ lb. chopped almonds, 1 lb. butter, 1 lb. raisins, 1 lb. currants, ¾ lb. lemon peel, one level teaspoon each of carbonate soda, cinnamon and spice, 12 eggs.

Method.—Cream the butter and sugar, beat eggs thoroughly, sift the flour, soda and spices together and add alternately with the eggs. Mix all the fruit together. Add to the mixture. Put into well greased and papered tins and bake in a moderate oven. If all the mixture is baked in one tin it takes four hours.

— Miss E. Cooper, Farrell's Flat.

In an Electric Cooker bake at 325°.

Bake in Gas Cooker at 300° F.

COMMON CHRISTMAS CAKE

Three and a half pounds flour, $\frac{3}{4}$ lb. butter, $\frac{1}{2}$ lb. lard, 2 lb. sugar, $2\frac{1}{2}$ lb. currants, $\frac{1}{4}$ lb. candied peel, $1\frac{1}{2}$ oz. baking powder, and milk. Season with nutmeg to taste and mix with milk. Bake about two hours. — Mrs. C. Norman, Wayville.

In an Electric Cooker bake at 325°.

Bake in Gas Cooker at 300° F.

COFFEE CAKE

Two and a half cups of flour, two cups of sugar, one cup of butter melted, one cup milk, four eggs, two teaspoons cream of tartar, and one teaspoon soda.

Beat eggs and sugar together, add butter, then milk and flour, lastly cream of tartar and soda mixed in milk. Sprinkle top with cinnamon, sugar, chopped almonds and a little butter mixed together. — M. Treasure, Black Forest.

One and a half cups sugar, $\frac{1}{2}$ lb. butter, four eggs, three cups self-raising flour, one cup milk, pinch salt.

Bake in baking dish for half an hour. While hot spread top with butter, then sprinkle sugar and cinnamon on top.

— Mrs. Pearl Bowering, "Wheatley," Peterborough.
— Mrs. F. W. Roediger.

In an Electric Cooker bake at 375°.

Four pounds flour, 1 lb. sugar, 6 eggs, 1 cup yeast, pinch cinnamon, grated nutmeg, little essence of lemon, 3 cups milk.

Warm milk and butter together with sugar, then mix well, put to rise some hours in a warm place. After it has risen put dough on a slide and roll out, then let it stand for a while.

For Top of Cake: One-quarter pound of butter, a little essence lemon, one-half teaspoon of cinnamon, $\frac{1}{4}$ lb. sugar and a little flour. Rub together to form balls size of peas; spread on cake.

— Mrs. Fleming, Brighton.

In an Electric Cooker bake at 425°.

Bake in Gas Cooker at 325° F. Bake the mixture containing yeast at 375° F.

Two cups flour, half cup brown sugar, half cup golden syrup, barely half cup cold coffee, 3 oz. butter, 3 oz. dripping, two eggs, half teaspoon each nutmeg, cloves, and cinnamon, one large teaspoon baking powder.

Cream butter, dripping, sugar. Add eggs, then flour, etc. Bake in round tins as pound cake—a good substitute. — M. R. Keynes.

COCONUT CAKE

Half pound butter, ½ lb. sugar, three eggs, half cup milk, two cups flour, two teaspoons cream tartar, one teaspoon carbonate soda, half cup desiccated coconut, few drops essence of lemon.

Bake in a flat tin, in a hot oven for about three-quarters of an hour. When cold, ice over top and sprinkle thickly with coconut.

Coconut Icing for the above cake.—Two cups sugar, half cup of milk, three-quarters cup coconut. Boil sugar and milk five minutes. Add coconut, and boil for another minute. Beat till cool. Do not let icing get too cool before icing the cake.

— Mrs. Chas. Coote, Port Elliot.

In an Electric Cooker bake at 375°.

Bake in Gas Cooker at 350° F.

CREAM CAKE

Two cups self-raising flour, one cup sugar, one cup milk, one or two eggs, one tablespoon butter.

Beat the butter, sugar and eggs for 10 or 15 minutes. Add the milk, and beat gently for five minutes. Add the flour. Bake in shallow tin to a light brown, from 20 to 30 minutes.

— Mrs. A. E. Pudney, Largs Bay.

Mix two eggs, one cup sugar, one cup cream. Add two and a half cups flour, two teaspoons cream tartar, one teaspoon carbonate soda, half cup milk.

Topping.—Half cup sugar, good tablespoon butter (melted) and enough flour to crumble. Bake half an hour.

— Fanny G. Heath, "Heathvale," Keyneton.

In an Electric Cooker bake at 375°.

Bake in Gas Cooker at 350° F.

CURRANT LOAF

Sift 2 lb. flour into a basin, then rub in 6 oz. butter and ¼ lb. lard. Add ½ lb. each of currants and raisins, ¼ lb. sugar, 2 oz. lemon peel, 1 oz. ground almonds, 1½ tablespoons baking powder, and three well-beaten eggs. Add a little milk if too stiff

Put in a lined loaf tin and bake in a moderate oven for two and a half hours.

In an Electric Cooker bake at 375°.

Bake in Gas Cooker at 350° F.

DARK CAKE

Ingredients. — One breakfast cup butter, one breakfast cup brown sugar, two and a half breakfast cups flour, half cup currants washed and cleaned, half breakfast cup pudding raisins chopped a little, one breakfast cup sultanas, four or five pieces orange and lemon peel (shredded), five eggs, half cup almonds cut in half, quarter teaspoon salt, half teaspoon mixed spice, half teaspoon ground cinnamon, the juice of half a lemon.

Method.—Cream the butter and sugar with the hand. This is easier if castor sugar is used. Add the eggs one at a time, and beat each one in well. Sift the flour, salt and spice together and add a little of this also from time to time. When all the eggs are in add half the flour, then the fruit, then the rest of the flour. Add the lemon juice last and beat well. Line a large cake tin with four or five layers of buttered paper. Put in the mixture, smooth the top, making it a little lower in the centre than at the sides. Bake in a very moderate oven for about four hours. A thick layer of salt on the oven shelf will help to prevent the cake from burning underneath, but usually the layers of paper in the tin are enough. The almonds may be blanched or not, as preferred, and a few walnuts may be added if liked.

— Eileen Prince, Avenal Gardens, Medindie.

In an Electric Cooker bake at 325°.

Bake in Gas Cooker at 300° F.

DATE CAKE

Eight ounces sugar, 4 oz. butter, 12 oz. flour, one cup milk, ¼ lb. raisins and dates, four eggs, one teaspoon cream of tartar, half teaspoon carbonate soda.

Method.—Cream butter and sugar. Add egg and milk. Add flour sifted with cream of tartar and carbonate of soda. Add raisins and dates. Bake in moderate oven for 40 minutes.

Take ½ lb. flour, ¼ lb. sugar, 6 oz. butter, ½ lb. dates, three eggs, one teaspoon of baking powder.

Beat the butter and sugar to a cream. Add the eggs well beaten, then the dates, and lastly the flour, which has been well sifted with the baking powder. Bake for 35 to 40 minutes.

In an Electric Cooker bake at 375°.

Bake in Gas Cooker at 350° F.

DELICIOUS CHRISTMAS TUTTI-FRUITTI CAKE

One cup flour, one cup sugar, one tablespoon butter, three eggs, two teaspoons cream of tartar, one teaspoon carbonate of soda, three tablespoons cold water. (A sponge mixture.)

The Icing Filling.—Whites of four eggs, one cup water, two heaped cups of sugar, one level saltspoon cream of tartar, one cup each raisins, figs and almonds, vanilla to flavour. Seed raisins, blanch almonds, and chop all fine. Put sugar, water and cream of tartar into an enamelled saucepan. Heat slowly till boiling. Stir only until sugar is dissolved, and cook without stirring until it spins a good thread, then let it stand aside a moment only. Meanwhile beat the whites until very stiff. Add gradually the syrup and vanilla to flavour, and beat vigorously until cool enough to spread. Spread the lower layer with icing and sprinkle thickly with chopped raisins. Cover with the second layer, ice, and sprinkle with chopped almonds. Add the third layer, ice and cover with chopped figs, and put on fourth layer. To icing that remains add raisins, nuts and figs. Spread this mixture over the top and sides of cakes.

Bake in Gas Cooker at 350° F.
In an Electric Cooker bake at 375°.

DRIED APRICOT CAKE

Two eggs, their weight in butter and sugar, 6 oz. flour, 2 oz. dried apricots, half teaspoon baking powder.

Beat butter and sugar to a cream. Sift the flour; divide it in two portions. Break one egg into cake. Add one tablespoon flour. Beat well; stir in half flour. Repeat with other egg. Add fruit to mixture. Leave a little flour to mix with the baking powder, and add this last. Bake one and a half to two hours.

Prunes, pears, ginger may be added instead of apricots.

In an Electric Cooker bake at 375°.
Bake in Gas Cooker at 325° F.

"FAIRVIEW" CAKE

One pound sugar, ½ lb. butter, 6 oz. currants, 6 oz. raisins, five eggs, 1 lb. S.R. flour, lemon peel, 2 oz. almonds.

Cream butter and sugar. Add eggs one by one. Beat about 10 mins. Bake for 1½ hours in slow oven. — Mrs. J. Read, Kingswood.

In an Electric Cooker bake at 350°.
Bake in Gas Cooker at 300° F.

FEATHER CAKE

Beat ½ lb. butter to a cream. Add one and a half cups sugar. Break over butter and sugar four eggs. Add three cups self-raising flour, eight tablespoons of water. Mix well. Bake in a moderate oven for half an hour. — Mrs. F. G. Miller.

In an Electric Cooker bake 375°.
Bake in Gas Cooker at 325° F.

FRUIT CAKE

One and a half lb. flour, ¾ lb. sugar, ¾ lb. butter, two teaspoons cream of tartar, one teaspoon soda, half teaspoon salt, one teacup raisins, one teacup sultanas, one teacup currants, quarter packet mixed spice.

Melt butter, mix with milk. Just enough wanted to mix it. Sour milk is the best to use.

Icing.—Half cup icing sugar. Mix with a little milk. Add tablespoon of orange cream. —Daphne Milton, Willaston.

In an Electric Cooker bake at 375°.
Bake in Gas Cooker at 300° F.

Half lb. butter, 1½ cups sugar (brown), 3 cups S.R. flour, 3 eggs, ¼ lb. sultanas, ½ lb. mixed fruit, ¼ lb. chopped nuts, ¾ cup milk, 1 level teaspoon ground cinnamon, ½ teaspoon essence vanilla.

Cream butter and sugar, add gradually the well-beaten eggs, then the fruit and nuts and vanilla. Sift the flour with the spice, and add with the milk. Bake in moderate oven 1½ hours.

—Mrs. C. M. Dunstone, Alberton.

FRENCH CAKE

One and a quarter cups of flour, ½ lb. butter, two-thirds cup of milk, one cup of sugar.

Beat butter and sugar to a cream, then add eggs and flour, lastly milk. Beat all well for a quarter of an hour.

In an Electric Cooker bake at 375°.
Bake in Gas Cooker at 350° F.

GERMAN NUT CAKE

Half pound S.R. flour, ¼ lb. sugar, ¼ lb. butter, one egg.

Mix flour and sugar. Rub in butter, damp with egg. Roll out thin, spread with jam. Fold over. Brush with egg and sprinkle walnuts or almonds on top.

—Mrs. E. G. Harrison, Lower Mitcham.

In an Electric Cooker bake at 425°.
Bake in Gas Cooker at 325° F.

GENOESE SPONGE CAKE

Two eggs, 4 ozs. castor sugar, 2 oz. butter, 4 oz. S.R. flour, three dessertspoons milk, essence.

Cream butter and sugar. Add one tablespoon of the flour and half the beaten egg. Then add remainder of flour and rest of the egg, then milk and essence last. Bake in moderate oven for half an hour. Line the cake tins with greased paper.

—Mrs. George Prince.

In an Electric Cooker bake at 375°.
Bake in Gas Cooker at 350° F.

GINGERBREAD

Half cup golden syrup, 1½ cups plain flour, 1 egg, ½ cup milk, 1 oz. sugar, ½ teaspoon baking powder, 1 teaspoon ground ginger, 2 oz. lard.

Melt syrup, sugar, and lard, then add to well-beaten egg; mix baking powder in warm milk; add ginger, then flour. Bake for ¾ hour. — Miss M. F. Holmes, Pinnaroo.

In an Electric Cooker bake at 375°.

GOOD LUNCH CAKE

One pound butter or dripping, 1 lb. sugar (¾ lb. white, ¼ lb. brown), six eggs, one and a half cups milk (large), two cups currants, half packet spice and a little cinnamon, 2 lb. self-raising flour.

Bake in flat meat dish for one and a half to two hours.
— A. Evans, Kenilworth.

In an Electric Cooker bake at 375°.
Bake in Gas Cooker at 350° F.

GOOD CAKE

Half pound butter, two eggs, one cup milk, one and a quarter cups sugar, two and a half cups flour, lemon peel, half teaspoon carbonate soda, one teaspoon cream of tartar, one cup sultana raisins, one cup currants.

Method.—Beat butter and sugar to a cream. Add eggs and milk, peel and fruit, then flour and rising. Bake about two hours in moderate oven. — Mrs. Hill, St. Peters.

In an Electric Cooker bake at 375°.
Bake in Gas Cooker at 300° F.

GOOD PLAIN CAKE

Quarter pound butter, ½ lb. flour, 6 oz. sugar, half cup milk, two eggs, essence.

Method.—Cream butter and sugar. Add eggs and beat well. Then stir in flour, milk and essence. Ice with orange or passion fruit icing. — Miss Jean Dixon, Medindie.

In an Electric Cooker bake at 375°.
Bake in Gas Cooker at 325° F.

CORNFLOUR SWISS CAKE

Ingredients.—6 oz. cornflour, 3 oz. flour, 6 oz. sugar, 4 oz. butter, three eggs, one teaspoon baking powder.

Method.—Cream butter and sugar. Add all ingredients with two tablespoons of milk. Beat well for 10 minutes. Put a little candied peel on top. Bake in a hot oven.

In an Electric Cooker bake at 375°.
Bake in Gas Cooker at 400° F.

CUP CAKE

One cup butter, two cups sugar, three cups flour, one cup milk, four eggs, two teaspoons cream of tartar, one teaspoon carbonate of soda, cup currants, cup sultanas or raisins, little peel.

Method.—Beat butter and sugar to a cream. Add eggs and milk well beaten, then flour (sifted) and fruit. Mix well together until thickness of cream. Bake an hour and a half.

—Mrs. A. H. Kerr.

In an Electric Cooker bake at 450°.

Bake in Gas Cooker at 325° F.

CURRANT CAKE

Three-quarter pound flour, ¾ lb. currants, ½ lb. castor sugar, ½ lb. butter, two eggs, nutmeg to taste, half teaspoon mace, small teaspoon baking powder, a little candied peel, small cup milk.

Bake in a slow oven three hours.

—Mrs. C. Elfenbein, Port Elliot.

In an Electric Cooker bake at 375°.

Bake in Gas Cooker at 300° F.

CENTENARY CAKE

Ingredients.—1 cup brown sugar, 6 oz. butter, 3 eggs, ½ cup milk, ½ orange (juice and grated rind), 2 tablespoons cocoa, 1 cup self-raising flour, 1 cup plain flour, ½ teaspoon salt, 4 oz currants, 4 oz. raisins, 4 oz. sultanas.

Method.—Sift flour, salt and cocoa together. Add the fruits and orange rind. Cream the butter and sugar until light and beat in the eggs one at a time. Add the flour mixture alternately with the milk. Add the orange juice and beat until smooth. Put mixture in a well-greased deep cake tin and bake in a moderate to slow oven for 1½ hours When cake is cold ice with Chocolate Fruit Frosting.

In an Electric Cooker bake at 375°.

Bake in Gas Cooker at 325° F.

CHOCOLATE FRUIT FROSTING

Beat 2 tablespoons butter to a cream; add 1 tablespoon cocoa (dissolved in sufficient boiling water to make a smooth paste), pinch salt, ½ teaspoon vanilla essence. Add 2 cups sifted icing sugar, alternately with 2 tablespoons milk. Beat after each addition until smooth, adding more milk if required. Beat until the consistency of whipped cream. Lastly fold in ½ cup raisins (finely chopped). Spread immediately on to cake and decorate with whole raisins.

GRANDMOTHER'S CAKE

One pound butter, 1 lb. sugar, 1¼ lb. flour, two teaspoons cream of tartar, one teaspoon carbonate soda, 1 lb. currants, one packet mixed spice, nine eggs.

Beat butter and sugar to a cream. Add fruit and spice, then eggs, and lastly the flour. This mixture makes delightful little patty pan cakes; or if cooked in a large tin for three hours, in a slow oven, will keep for weeks.

—Mrs. M. Luck, Croydon Park.

In an Electric Cooker bake at 375°. for small cakes 475°.

Bake in Gas Cooker at 325° F. For small cakes bake at 400° F.

GRANDMA NORMAN'S YEAST SEED CAKE

Two pounds flour, one teaspoon salt, two tablespoons brewer's yeast, one pint lukewarm milk or water, one cup sugar, ½ lb. dripping well clarified, one tablespoon caraway seeds.

Mix yeast and liquid together and let it stand for a few minutes, then gradually work it into the flour with which the salt has been well mixed until it is a soft dough. Let this stand in a warm place until it rises and becomes quite light. Then thoroughly mix in the dripping, sugar, and lastly the caraway seeds. Let rise again for 20 minutes to half an hour, and then put into one or two well-greased cake tins and bake in moderate oven for an hour. If put into one large tin bake for 1½ to 2 hours.

—Mrs. C. R. Morris, Unley Park.

In an Electric Cooker bake at 400°.

Bake in Gas Cooker at 350° F.

GRANDMA NORMAN'S YEAST SEED CAKE, No. 2

Ingredients.—1 pint of good yeast, 5 ozs. of butter, 1 egg, 5 ozs. castor sugar, 1½ lb. of flour, 3 ozs. caraway seeds, ¾ pint milk.

Method.—Sift ¼ lb. flour into a large basin, with a pinch of salt. Strain in the yeast, mix to a smooth batter, cover basin and get to rise in warm place for about 1 hour. Sift remainder of flour into another basin, rub in the butter, add sugar and mix together well.

When the yeast mixture is ready, stir into the other prepared ingredients; add beaten egg and the milk made warm; mix all together; and beat well.

Put the mixture to rise in a warm place until it has risen to double its size—it will take about 2 hours. Then put into two well-greased cake tins, and bake till brown, about three-quarters of an hour.

—Mrs. C. R. Morris, Unley Park.

In an Electric Cooker bake at 400°.

Bake in Gas Cooker at 350° F.

JEWISH CAKE

Half cup butter, three-quarters cup sugar, half cup milk, a cup and a half S.R. flour, three eggs, one teaspoon cinnamon, two teaspoons chocolate or cocoa.

Cream butter and sugar. Add eggs one at a time. Beat well and add milk. Add flour and cinnamon and chocolate. Stir in lightly. Bake in fairly hot oven.

Icing.—Quarter pound icing sugar, small piece butter, one teaspoon cocoa or melted chocolate, half teaspoon cinnamon. Mix all together, moistening with little milk. Decorate with few chopped almonds. —W.G.T.

In an Electric Cooker bake at 375°.

Quarter pound butter, one cup sugar. Beat to a cream. Add three eggs well beaten, a cup and a half S.R. flour, with half teaspoon each cinnamon and ginger and two tablespoons sultanas. Stir in half a cup warm milk in which one tablespoon of treacle has been melted. Bake 20 minutes in a moderate oven. Cut through centre and fill with mock cream or jelly. Decorate top with chocolate icing and walnuts. — Mrs. Willshire.

In an Electric Cooker bake at 375°.

Bake in Gas Cooker at 350° F.

RICH COFFEE CAKE

Two and a half cups of butter and sugar, one cup of treacle and one large cup of strong coffee, five eggs well beaten, five cups of flour, two teaspoons carb. soda, 1 lb. each of currants and raisins, pinch salt, ¼ lb. mixed peel, two tablespoons each of ground cloves and cinnamon, one teaspoon each of allspice and nutmeg.

Mix in the usual way and bake two hours.

— M. Reynolds, Port Elliot

In an Electric Cooker bake at 375°.

Bake in Gas Cooker at 300° F.

LIGHT GINGERBREAD

One cup treacle, one cup butter, one cup milk, three cups flour, two cups sugar, four eggs, one tablespoon ginger, one teaspoon carbonate soda. Add a little cinnamon if liked.

Mix butter, sugar and eggs together, then add other ingredients, and bake in a moderate oven for about an hour and a half.

— A. Evans, Kenilworth.

Use one cup sugar. — Mrs. Mayfield, King's Park.

In an Electric Cooker bake at 375°.

Bake in Gas Cooker at 350° F.

MARBLE CAKE

Half a pound of butter, ½ lb. sugar, three eggs, one gill milk, ¾ lb. flour, one teaspoon baking powder, vanilla essence, a few drops cochineal, one heaped tablespoon cocoa.

Cream butter and sugar. Add gradually the well-beaten eggs, and essence. Sift flour and baking powder, and add alternately with the milk. Divide the mixture into 3 parts; leave one part plain, colour one pink, add cocoa to the other. Put small heaps from each into a prepared tin. Bake in a moderate oven for an hour to an hour and a quarter. — K. E. Sharman.

In an Electric Cooker bake at 375°.
Bake in Gas Cooker at 350° F.

ORANGE CAKE

Beat to a cream one cup sugar, half cup butter, three eggs one at a time (well beaten), the grated rind of orange, then half cup of milk and two cups S.R. flour. Frost over top with juice of orange thickened with icing sugar when cake has been taken from oven. — Mrs. J. Read, Kingswood.

Three cups flour, ½ lb. butter, two cups sugar, five eggs, one cup milk, one teaspoon soda, two teaspoons cream tartar, the grated rind and juice of one orange.

Filling.—Juice of two oranges and the rind of one, ½ lb. icing sugar. — Mrs. G. Bradley, Torrens Park.

In an Electric Cooker bake at 375°.
Bake in Gas Cooker at 350° F.

PLAIN CAKE

Half pound butter, one and a half cups sugar, four eggs, half cup milk, essence lemon, three cups flour.

Mix butter and sugar to a cream, then add eggs one by one, and beat well, then add flour. Bake three-quarters to one hour. — Mrs. Mackie.

In an Electric Cooker bake at 375°.
Bake in Gas Cooker at 325° F.

POVERTY CAKE

One cup milk, one cup sugar, tablespoon treacle or golden syrup, a piece of butter the size of an egg, 2¼ cups flour, one teaspoon carbonate of soda, one cup of raisins, one nutmeg (grated).

Beat sugar and butter well, then add treacle or golden syrup, then milk, to which the carbonate of soda has been added, then flour and lastly nutmeg and raisins. — M. Carmichael.

In an Electric Cooker bake at 375°.
Bake in Gas Cooker at 350° F.

POUND CAKE

Ingredients.—1 lb. butter, 1 lb. sugar (half dark, half white), eight eggs, 1 lb. currants, ½ lb. sultanas, ¼ lb. lemon peel, one small packet spice, three tablespoons treacle, three tablespoons milk, a little mace and vanilla, four cups S.R. flour.

Method.—Cream butter and sugar. Add eggs (well beaten) gradually, then milk and other ingredients, adding the fruit last. Mix together well, and bake in decreasing oven heat two to three hours. The heat for the first half-hour should be very hot.

—Vida A. Lushey.

In an Electric Cooker bake at 325°.
Bake in Gas Cooker at 300° F.

RED INDIAN CAKE

Half pound butter beaten to a cream, ½ lb. sugar added, three eggs well beaten, one-quarter pint milk, ¾ lb. plain flour, half teaspoon carb. soda.

Mix soda and half the flour well together, then stir into the butter, sugar, eggs and milk. Add to the rest of the flour ½ lb. sultanas, ½ lb. currants, ½ lb. almond kernels, ¼ lb. lemon peel and stir all together. Put in a greased tin and bake in a moderate oven for two hours. —Mrs. Ashton, Brighton.

One and a half pounds flour, 1 lb. butter, 1 lb. sugar, 1 lb. currants, 1 lb. raisins, four eggs, one pint milk, ½ lb. peel, two teaspoonfuls carb. soda. A little spirits added keeps it moist. Bake in a slow oven for two hours.

—Miss K. Shannon, Encounter Bay.

In an Electric Cooker bake at 350°.
Bake in Gas Cooker at 300° F.

SODA CAKE

One pound butter, 1 lb. sugar, four eggs, four cups flour, one pint milk, warmed, in which dissolve two teaspoons carbonate soda, 1 lb. currants, ½ peel. Add flour last. Put in two round cake tins. —Mrs. A. R. Reed, Cunningham.

In an Electric Cooker bake at 375°.
Bake in Gas Cooker at 300° F.

SNOW CAKE

Take half a teacup butter, one cup sugar, one and a half cups flour, half cup sweet milk, the whites of four eggs, one heaped teaspoon baking powder sifted with the flour; flavour with lemon. Bake in a moderate oven.

—Mrs. W. Simmons, Ardrossan.

In an Electric Cooker bake at 375°.
Bake in Gas Cooker at 350° F.

RUSSIAN CAKE

Quarter pound butter, 6 oz. sugar, three eggs, ½ lb. S.R. flour.

Method.—Cream butter and sugar. Add eggs one at a time. Beat well, sift in flour. When mixed, divide into two parts; leave one white, colour other with two tablespoons coffee essence. Bake in flat tin. When cold, spread raspberry jam between coloured and white till you make a square or oblong cake. Put only enough jam to make it stick. Ice all over, and sprinkle with coconut. Cake should look like a draught board when cut.

— Mrs. Gooding, Port Pirie.

In an Electric Cooker bake at 375°.
Bake in Gas Cooker at 325° F.

SCRIPTURE CAKE

Ingredients.—Three and a half cups flour, two tablespoons baking powder, three cups sugar, one cup butter, six eggs, one cup water, one tablespoon honey, two cups raisins, two cups figs, one cup almonds, spice to taste.

Method.—Beat sugar and butter to a cream. Add eggs well beaten, then water, dry ingredients (sifted together), and fruit.

Bake in a moderate oven for three hours.

— L. Grey, Railway Town, B.H.

In an Electric Cooker bake at 350°.
Bake in Gas Cooker at 3.25° F.

BIRTHDAY CAKE

Beat together ½ lb. butter, ½ lb. sugar, 4 eggs. Add 1 tablespoon treacle, ½ teaspoon spice, ½ lb. raisins, ½ lb. currants, 1 piece lemon peel, blanched almonds, ½ lb. flour, ½ teaspoon carb. soda in a little boiling water. Mix well. Bake 2½ hours in a slow oven. — Mrs. Walter E. Mounster.

In an Electric Cooker bake at 325°.
Bake in Gas Cooker at 300° F.

JUBILEE CAKE (To be eaten with butter)

A cup and a half S.R. flour, one dessertspoon butter, one tablespoon castor sugar, one cup sultanas and currants, lemon peel, one egg, half cup milk, pinch salt.

Method.—Mix dry ingredients together. Add egg and milk. Bake half an hour. While still hot, pour in two tablespoons icing sugar mixed with milk, and sprinkle with coconut.

— Miss Rennett. — J.M.A. — J.C.C.

In an Electric Cooker bake at 400°.
Bake in Gas Cooker at 375° F.

One and a half cups S.R. flour, one tablespoon butter rubbed into flour. Add one tablespoon castor sugar, pinch salt, one cup currants, one cup sultanas, lemon peel, one egg, ¾ cup milk. Put in small round tin with lid, and bake in a moderate oven.

— Mrs. E. J. McLachlan, Semaphore.

SEED CAKE

Four ounces butter, 6 oz. sugar, two eggs, 10 oz. flour, one dessertspoon caraway seeds, a teaspoon and a half of baking powder, one pinch salt, one gill milk.

Cream butter and sugar. Add eggs well beaten and seeds, and beat well. Stir in alternately the milk and flour, sifted with baking powder and salt. Bake in a moderate oven for an hour to an hour and a quarter.

In an Electric Cooker bake at 375°.

Bake in Gas Cooker at 325° F.

SPICE CAKE

Half pound butter, ½ lb. white sugar, two eggs, half pint warm milk, just about 1 lb. S.R. flour, ¾ lb. currants and raisins, 2 oz. mixed spice, two teaspoons cinnamon, a few almonds.

Bake in moderate oven from one to one and a half hours.

— A. L. Lillecrapp, Hill Ridge.

In an Electric Cooker bake at 375°.

Bake in Gas Cooker at 325° F.

SPONGE GINGERBREAD

Two large cups flour, ¼ lb. butter, one cup sugar, one cup milk, one cup treacle, one cup sultanas and lemon peel, one dessertspoon ground ginger, one dessertspoon spice, one heaped teaspoon carbonate soda.

Method. – Cream butter and sugar, warm the treacle, dissolve soda in milk. Mix and bake in a large high-sided cake tin in a moderate oven.

In an Electric Cooker bake at 400°.

Bake in Gas Cooker at 325° F.

SPONGE CAKE

Nine eggs, 1 lb. sugar, ½ lb. flour.

Beat yolks and sugar together. Beat whites well, with a little grated rind of a lemon, add to yolks and sugar; add flour. Do not beat after the flour has been added. — Mrs. W. Simmons.

In an Electric Cooker bake at 375°.

Bake in Gas Cooker at 350° F.

TENNIS CAKE

Six ounces butter, 6 oz. sugar, 10 oz. flour, four eggs, 6 oz. seeded and chopped lexias, ½ lb. currants, ½ lb. sultanas, 4 oz. mixed peel, 2 oz. almonds, one small teaspoonful of baking powder.

Method.—Beat butter and sugar to a cream, then break eggs in one at a time. Add the fruits, peel and almonds, and lastly sift in the flour and baking powder. Time to bake, two hours.

In an Electric Cooker bake at 325°.

Bake in Gas Cooker at 300° F.

SULTANA CAKE

Half pound butter, ½ lb. sugar, ¾ lb. flour, one teaspoon baking powder, three eggs, one gill milk, ½ lb. sultanas, half teaspoon essence lemon, big pinch of salt.

Cream butter and sugar. Add beaten eggs, then sultanas. Add sifted flour and baking powder in small quantities alternately with small quantities of milk. Add essence. Bake in decreasing heat for one and a half hours.

— Mrs. K. K. Ridgway, "Maradene," Wolseley.

One cup butter, one cup sugar, one cup milk, three cups flour, five eggs, two teaspoons cream of tartar and one of carbonate of soda, few drops essence of lemon and ½ lb. sultanas.

Cream butter and sugar. Add gradually the well-beaten eggs, then sultanas, essence. Sift flour with cream tartar, soda, add alternately with milk. Bake in moderate oven. — Anonymous.

In an Electric Cooker bake at 375°.
Bake in Gas Cooker at 325° F.

TEDDY BEAR CAKE

Required.—2 tablespoons butter, 1 cup sugar, half cup milk, 3 eggs, 2 cups flour, essence of vanilla or lemon.

Method.—Beat butter and sugar to cream. Add eggs and beat well. Then add milk and essence. Lastly add flour, and beat for ten minutes. Bake for a quarter of an hour in a hot oven.

This batter also makes nice Lamingtons, the ordinary icing for them being rather highly flavoured with vanilla.

In an Electric Cooker bake at 375°.
Bake in Gas Cooker at 350° F.

TENBY CAKE

Half pound flour, ½ lb. dates (chopped), 2 oz. butter, 2 oz. brown sugar, quarter pint milk, ½ teaspoon carbonate of soda.

Beat butter and sugar to cream. Add dates and then flour with soda in it. Lastly pour on milk, stirring all the time. Pour in greased tin, bake for about 1½ hours. — E. F. Benskin.

In an Electric Cooker bake at 375°.
Bake in Gas Cooker at 350° F.

VINEGAR CAKE

Half pound butter, one and a half cups sugar, three cups of flour, 1 lb. dates, one cup raisins, two eggs, two tablespoons vinegar, 1 teaspoon soda, 1 cup milk, candied peel, essence lemon.

Beat soda in milk to mix. Bake one hour.

— Mrs. Mayfield, King's Park.

In an Electric Cooker bake at 375°.
Bake in Gas Cooker at 325° F.

GRACE CAKE

Two cups flour, one cup sugar, three eggs, small cup of milk, heaped tablespoon butter. Cream butter and sugar, add eggs separately, then milk; flour last. Any flavouring desired. Bake 20 minutes in hot oven. Ice.

— Miss E. Hill, Black Forest.

In an Electric Cooker bake at 370°.
Bake in Gas Cooker at 375° F.

WALNUT CAKE

Two cups S.R. flour, one cup sugar, three eggs, ½ lb. butter, two dessertspoons of cocoa, one teaspoon of mixed spice, one small teaspoon vanilla, half cup of milk, ½ lb. walnuts chopped fine.

Method.—Beat butter and sugar to a cream, then add eggs one at a time, then cocoa, spice and vanilla, then flour. Add half the walnuts, leaving other for decorating the top with icing.

— Miss R. Burke, Maitland.
— Miss Lewis, Joslin.
— Mrs. Speers, Port Pirie.
— Mrs. Leslie Smith, Kensington Gardens.

One cup sugar, half cup butter, one cup walnuts, half cup milk, two eggs, two cups flour, half teaspoon carb. soda, one teaspoon cream tartar.

Beat butter and sugar together, add eggs and milk, lastly flour and rising. — E. M. Evans, Keyneton.

In an Electric Cooker bake at 375°.
Bake in Gas Cooker at 350° F.

WAR CAKE

Ingredients.—Three cups plain flour, two cups brown sugar, four tablespoons lard, one teaspoon salt, one teaspoon cinnamon, one cup raisins, two teaspoons carbonate soda.

Method.—Boil all ingredients together for five minutes after the mixture begins to boil. When cold, add three cups flour and the soda dissolved in one teaspoon hot water. Roll into two loaves. Bake in a moderate oven for an hour and a quarter.

In an Electric Cooker bake at 375°.
Bake in Gas Cooker at 350° F.

WEST INDIAN CAKE (Brown)

One and three-quarter pounds plain flour, 1 lb. butter, 1¼ lb. sugar, 1 lb. sultanas, 1½ lb. currants, grated nutmeg, ¼ lb. lemon peel, two cups milk, four eggs, two teaspoons carbonate of soda, three-quarters cup chopped almonds.

Cream butter and sugar, then add eggs well beaten. Mix soda in milk. Add fruit and flour. Bake in moderate oven from three to four hours.

— Miss Niehuus, King's Park.

In an Electric Cooker bake at 350°.
Bake in Gas Cooker at 300° F.

WHOLE MEAL LUNCH CAKE

One pound S.R. flour (whole meal), 6 oz. butter, 6 oz. sugar, 6 oz. raisins or dates, 3 eggs, pinch salt, milk to mix (1 cup).

Cream butter and sugar. Add beaten eggs. Mix to rather moist dough. Bake in meat dish in moderate oven. — W.G.T.

In an Electric Cooker bake at 375°.
Bake in Gas Cooker at 350° F.

WELSH CAKE

One pound flour, ½ lb. butter, ½ lb. sugar, 2 oz. peel, ½ lb. sultanas, ¼ lb. currants, one tablespoon treacle, one egg, one cup milk, one teaspoon carbonate soda, one tablespoon vinegar.

Mix all ingredients dry. Add soda in vinegar while fizzing, then beat egg and milk. Bake in two tins one hour.

— Mrs. E. H. Bakewell.

In an Electric Cooker bake at 375°
Bake in Gas Cooker at 325° F.

IMITATION POUND CAKE

1½ lb. plain flour, ½ lb. butter, ½ lb. currants, ½ lb. raisins, ½ lb. almonds, a little essence of lemon and lemon peel, a little salt, 1 cup of white sugar, 1 cup brown sugar, 4 eggs, 2 teaspoons of cream of tartar, 1 teaspoon carb. soda.

Beat butter and sugar together; add eggs one by one. Mix in other ingredients. Bake for several hours. — F. E. Manuel.

In an Electric Cooker bake at 325°.
Bake in Gas Cooker at 300° F.

IMITATION POUND CAKE No. 2

One pound flour, one cup white sugar, one cup brown sugar, one cup butter, ½ lb. currants, ½ lb. raisins, four eggs, lemon peel, one cup sour milk, one teaspoon soda.

Bake for one hour or a little more.

— Mrs. J. F. Farrow, Tea Tree Gully.

In an Electric Cooker bake at 325°.

Bake in Gas Cooker at 300° F.

GOOD CHRISTMAS CAKE

1 lb. butter, 1 lb. sugar, 1 lb. plain flour, 9 eggs, 2 lb. currants, 1 lb. raisins, ¼ lb. almonds, ¼ lb. peel, ½ nutmeg, ¼ oz. cinnamon, ½ oz. ginger, ½ pkt. allspice, ¼ oz. mace, ½ gill brandy.

Put butter in a warm place, then work into cream with hand; add the sugar with spices mixed in; break in the eggs one at a time, then beat for 20 minutes. Add brandy and flour gradually; then add all other ingredients. Bake in slow oven for 3 hours. This will make two nice sized cakes. — F. Horton, Largs.

In an Electric Cooker bake at 325°.

Bake in Gas Cooker at 300° F.

COCONUT CAKE

The weight of three eggs in butter, sugar and S.R. flour, and the weight of two eggs in coconut; cochineal.

Method.—Beat butter and sugar to a cream. Add three eggs well beaten; then add coconut and cochineal, lastly add flour. Bake in slow oven for ½ hour. — D. E. Norman, Kent Town.

In an Electric Cooker bake at 375°.

Bake in Gas Cooker at 325° F.

ROSEBERRY CAKE

Make the same as Dried Apricot Cake (see page 137), adding 2 oz. glace cherries.

BIRTHDAY CAKE

Half lb. butter, ½ lb. brown sugar, ¾ lb. plain flour, 1 teaspoon salt, 2 level teaspoons baking powder, 4-6 ozs. currants, sultanas, seeded raisins, 2 ozs. candied peel, 3 eggs, ¼ pint milk.

Beat butter and sugar to a cream, add beaten eggs, then milk (stirring in gradually), add flour sifted with rising and salt. Add fruit and mix all well together. Put in tin lined bottom and sides with brown paper. Bake 2-2½ hours.

Almond Icing: Mix 4 ozs. almond meal with 8 ozs. icing sugar. Add just enough egg yolk to make a very stiff paste. Roll out to exactly fit top of cake, and press on.

Sugar Icing: Sift 8 ozs. of icing sugar, stir in one tablespoon water and a teaspoon of lemon juice. Make sufficiently warm to pour over cake.

In an Electric Cooker bake at 325°.
Bake in Gas Cooker at 300° F.

FRUIT OR CHRISTMAS CAKE

A pound and a half plain flour, 1 lb. brown sugar, ¾ lb. currants, ¾ lb. butter, ¾ lb. stoned raisins, five or six eggs, ¼ lb. lemon or minced peel, one cup milk, nutmeg to taste, two small teaspoons carbonate of soda, one tablespoon golden syrup or treacle, 2 or 3 ozs. chopped almonds, pinch of salt.

Cream butter and sugar, then add eggs. Beat well. Mix soda in milk. Add the fruit and flour, then mix till stiff enough. Put in buttered tins and bake in slow oven for two and a half hours.

— Miss Niehuus, King's Park.

In an Electric Cooker bake at 325°.
Bake in Gas Cooker at 300° F.

LIGHT GINGER CAKE

Two cups flour, one cup sugar, 4 oz. butter, one egg, one cup milk, three teaspoons ground ginger, one teaspoon carbonate soda, two tablespoons golden syrup, 2 oz. lemon peel.

Beat sugar and butter to a cream, add the egg, put soda in milk, and then add flour and ginger, and last of all lemon peel. Bake in a slow oven about half an hour. — M. Carmichael.

In an Electric Cooker bake at 375°.
Bake in Gas Cooker at 325° F.

SPONGES AND LAYER CAKES

ICING AND CAKE FILLING

SPONGES AND LAYER CAKES

APPLE SHORTCAKE

Three eggs, their weight in sugar, butter and flour (self-raising), apples stewed fairly dry, whipped cream, flavoured vanilla.

Method.—Beat butter and sugar to a cream, add the eggs and beat well, then add flour slowly sifted in and spread in two sandwich tins and bake in a moderate oven. When cold spread one cake with the stewed apples, then put whipped cream on top and place other layer on top. —Mrs. R. E. Chapman, Naracoorte.

In an Electric Cooker bake at 375°.

Bake in Gas Cooker at 350° F.

CHOCOLATE SPONGE SANDWICH

One cup of sugar and three eggs beaten for 20 minutes, add one cup of self-raising flour, and lastly one tablespoon of butter in two tablespoons of boiling water, and mix with butter and water four tablespoons of cocoa, flavour with essence of vanilla.

—K. Hawkes, Kent Town.

In an Electric Cooker bake at 375°.

Bake in Gas Cooker at 350° F.

BUTTER SPONGE

Six ounces S.R. flour, 6 oz. sugar, 4 oz. butter, three eggs, three or four tablespoons milk, pinch of salt, few drops essence.

Cream butter and sugar. Add well-beaten eggs, and beat all well. Add ½ flour and ½ milk, rest of flour, then milk. Bake in moderate oven 20-30 mins. —Mrs. H. K. Ridgway, Wolseley.

In an Electric Cooker bake at 375°.

Bake in Gas Cooker at 350° F.

CINNAMON SPONGE

Three eggs, 1 cup sugar, 2 oz. butter beaten well together. Add ½ cup milk, 1 teaspoon cinnamon, enough flour to make a smooth batter.

Bake in sandwich tins. Put raspberry jam between.

—Mrs. F. W. Roediger, "Riverside," Gawler.

Half lb. flour, ¼ lb. butter, ½ lb. sugar, 3 eggs, 1 tablespoon cinnamon, ½ teaspoon carb. soda, 1 teaspoon cream tartar, cup of milk.

Method.—Cream butter and sugar together. Add eggs well beaten, sift soda, cream of tartar and cinnamon with flour. Mix all well together and bake in sandwich tins half an hour.

Filling.—One tablespoon of butter and three ounces of castor sugar, beat together to a cream. Spread on cakes when cold.

—Mrs. G. Bradley, Torrens Park. —May Kenny, Port Elliot.

In an Electric Cooker bake at 375°.

Bake in Gas Cooker at 350° F.

SHORTBREAD CAKES

Eight ozs. flour, 4 ozs. sugar, 5 ozs. butter. Mix butter into the flour and sugar; make into little cakes, and bake in moderate oven. — Mrs. K. W. Smith, King's College.

In an Electric Cooker bake at 400°.

Bake in Gas Cooker at 350° F.

SMALL CHOCOLATE CAKES

Four ounces butter, 4 oz. sugar, 4 oz. S.R. flour, two eggs, two tablespoons milk, 2 oz. cocoa.

Beat butter and sugar to a cream; add eggs and milk, then sift in flour and cocoa. Place in small paper cake containers and bake about 10 minutes.

Icing.—One tablespoon cocoa, two tablespoons icing sugar, piece of butter the size of a walnut, one tablespoon boiling water. Sprinkle iced cakes with coconut.

— Mrs. G. Rogers, Torrensville.

In an Electric Cooker bake at 475°.

Bake in Gas Cooker at 400° F.

CHOCOLATE CAKE

Three ounces butter, 6 oz. sugar, two eggs (beat whites and yolks separately), nearly half a cup of milk, 6 oz. flour, 2 oz. chocolate powder, one teaspoon cream of tartar, half teaspoon carbonate of soda. Bake 20 minutes.

Filling.—One tablespoon melted butter, three tablespoons icing sugar, vanilla.

Icing.—Quarter pound icing sugar, one dessertspoon chocolate powder, one tablespoon of boiling water.

— Mrs. E. H. Bakewell.

In an Electric Cooker bake at 375°.

Bake in Gas Cooker at 350° F.

COLD OVEN SPONGE

Beat 2 tablespoons butter and ¾ cup sugar to a cream. Add 3 eggs and pinch of salt, and beat well. Add about 3 tablespoons of milk. Sift a cup of S.R. flour and add lightly to mixture. Put in cold oven and light to half flame. Bake 15 to 20 minutes.

— Mrs. S. C. Lawrence. North Adelaide.

CHOCOLATE SPONGE SANDWICH

Three-quarters cup sugar, one cup flour, three eggs, one tablespoon chocolate, one tablespoon boiling water. Bake in moderate oven for ten to fifteen minutes. When cool coat with chocolate icing and almonds. Fill with whipped cream.

—H. Morphett, Torrens Park.

In an Electric Cooker bake at 375°.
Bake in Gas Cooker at 350° F.

CHOCOLATE LAYER CAKE

Four ozs. butter, 6 ozs. castor sugar, 3 eggs, 2 tablespoons cocoa, ½ cup milk, 8 ozs. plain flour, 2 level teaspoons cream of tartar, 1 level teaspoon carb. soda, vanilla.

Blend the cocoa with the milk. Sift the flour with the rising and salt. Cream the butter and sugar, add gradually the well-beaten eggs, then the blended cocoa and vanilla. Add gradually the sifted flour; stirring till a smooth, soft batter is formed. Put into two well-greased sandwich tins and bake in a slow oven (325 deg. 3) till done. When cold join together with raspberry jam or whipped cream. Cover top with chocolate icing.

For the Icing

One oz. unsweetened chocolate, 1 teaspoon butter, 3 dessertspoons hot water, sifted icing sugar, vanilla essence.

Break up the chocolate then place it in a bowl and stand over boiling water till melted. Add the butter and hot water and beat well. Allow the mixture to cool a little, then add enough sifted icing sugar to give a spreading consistency. Add vanilla and beat well. Spread over the cake and mark with the prongs of a fork.

—A. L. Sharman.

Take one cup granulated sugar, half cup of butter, two eggs, two-thirds cup milk, one and three-quarters cups flour, two teaspoons baking powder, and essence of vanilla to taste. Add cocoa or grated chocolate to make it the colour you wish. Place chocolate in a cup and stand in hot water till melted.

This is a standby for all occasions, and will keep moist for about a week. To have it as a layer cake, put half in two or one-third in each of three layer cake pans, and bake.

In an Electric Cooker bake at 375°.
Bake in Gas Cooker at 350° F.

BUTTER ICING FOR CHOCOLATE LAYER CAKE

Put a piece of butter the size of a walnut in a bowl and warm slightly. Add about 6 oz. of icing sugar, a little milk, and a few drops of vanilla essence. Beat till smooth and creamy. Spread between layers and on top.

COFFEE SANDWICH

Three eggs, one cup flour (S.R.), one cup sugar, one table spoon butter melted in four tablespoons boiling water.

Method.—Beat eggs and sugar for a quarter of an hour, then mix the flour, lastly add the butter melted in boiling water. Stir but do not beat. Put in sandwich tins and bake in a moderate oven.

Icing for same.—One tablespoon strong coffee, as much icing sugar as it will take up, one teaspoon butter. Beat together and put between cake. —Mrs. Butterfield, Ki Ki.

In an Electric Cooker bake at 375°.
Bake in Gas Cooker at 350° F.

DOLLY VARDEN CAKE

One half cup butter, one cup sugar, 1½ cups flour, two eggs. three-quarter cup milk, two small teaspoons cream tartar, and one teaspoon carb. soda. Self-raising flour may be used instead of plain flour, with cream tartar, soda, etc., added.

Make three layers, two plain and make the third one brown by adding spice, peel and currants. When cold, whip cream flavoured with vanilla and icing sugar and place together, the spiced layer in centre and ice the top and sprinkle with coconut coloured with a little cochineal. Add a little drop of cochineal to cream for the filling when whipped.

—Miss Rehn, W.C.T.U., Adelaide.

In an Electric Cooker bake at 375°.
Bake in Gas Cooker at 325° F

Half cup butter, one small cup sugar, 1½ cups S.R. flour, three eggs, three-quarters cup milk.

Divide the mixture into two parts. Into one put half cup sultanas, little lemon peel, three-quarters of a teaspoon vanilla and enough mixed spice to make it dark. Flavour the other half with essence of lemon. Bake separately in sandwich tins. Fill with icing sugar, mixed with melted butter and a squeeze of lemon. —E. Norman, Kadina.

EGYPTIAN CAKE

Beat two eggs with three-quarter cup sugar for about 10 minutes. Add quarter cup water. Mix two teaspoons of spice with one cup of S.R. flour and stir in lightly. Bake in hot oven in sandwich tins. Make chocolate icing and put between the cakes and on top. —Mrs. Arbon, Brighton.

In an Electric Cooker bake at 375°.
Bake in Gas Cooker at 350° F.

PASSION FRUIT LAYER CAKE

Beat ¼ lb. butter and ½ lb. sugar (bare) to a cream; add three well-beaten eggs gradually, 3 or 4 drops essence of lemon. Sift ½ lb. flour, 1 teaspoon cream of tartar, ½ teaspoon carb. soda, a pinch of salt, and add alternately with a small cup of milk.

Bake in two sandwich tins in moderate oven 20 to 30 minutes.

Filling.—Cream 1 oz. butter and 1 oz. icing sugar. Add the pulp of two or three passion fruit and sufficient sifted icing sugar to make a soft creamy mixture.

Icing.—Strain juice of 3 passion fruit, add 6 oz. icing sugar, few drops cochineal, beat well. If too dry add water. — A. Sharman.

In an Electric Cooker bake at 375

Bake in Gas Cooker at 350° F.

GEM CAKE

One cup sugar, ¼ lb. butter, three eggs well beaten, and tour tablespoons milk, 1½ cups flour, two teaspoons cream of tartar, one teaspoon soda, three teaspoons cinnamon, a few currants, and a few drops essence lemon. Bake in sandwich tins, turn cakes out carefully and put jam or a good cream filling between and ice the top with pink icing.

— Miss Branson, Brighton.

In an Electric Cooker bake at 375°.

Bake in Gas Cooker at 350° F.

GINGER SANDWICH

One tablespoon butter, three-quarters cup sugar, halt cup milk, one egg, half cup treacle, two teaspoons ginger, one teaspoon spice, half teaspoon carbonate soda, one and a half cups flour.

Cream butter and sugar; add the beaten egg and treacle. Sift in spice, ground ginger and flour. Stir in soda dissolved in a little boiling water. — Daphne Milton, Willaston.

In an Electric Cooker bake at 375°.

Bake in Gas Cooker at 350° F.

FRUIT SANDWICH

Half lb. butter, two cups sugar, one cup milk, three cups flour, two teaspoons cream tartar, one teaspoon carbonate of soda.

Take half the butter and sugar, beat to a cream; then add the yolk of five eggs, half milk, flour and rising. Mix the other half in the same way, adding the whites of eggs, and divide this mixture in half and bake. When cold, place the first half between the latter, spreading a layer of banana between each. Ice top layer, decorate with jelly. — M. Carmichael.

In an Electric Cooker bake at 375°.

Bake in Gas Cooker at 350° F.

GINGER SPONGE SANDWICH

Ingredients.—Three eggs, 3 oz. sugar, 4 oz. plain flour, half level teaspoon carbonate of soda, two tablespoons treacle, one heaped teaspoon of ground ginger, three tablespoons boiling water, one dessertspoon butter (heaped).

Method.—Beat eggs and sugar until thick and frothy. Dissolve butter and treacle in boiling water. Add sifted flour, soda and ginger to eggs and sugar. Note.—Stir, but do not beat. Add treacle, water, butter, and stir. Cook for 20 minutes.

In an Electric Cooker bake at 375°.

Bake in Gas Cooker at 350° F.

LEMON SPONGE

Four eggs, one cup sugar, one cup sifted flour, two tablespoons water, and one tablespoon cream.

Beat eggs and sugar for 20 minutes. Stir in lightly sifted flour, water and cream. Bake in a moderate oven for 20 minutes. When cooked, add a filling made with one cup sugar, the juice and rind of a lemon, and one tablespoon of cornflour boiled together. — Anonymous.

In an Electric Cooker bake at 375°.

Bake in Gas Cooker at 350° F.

MILK CAKE

One and a half cups flour, two eggs, 2 oz. butter, three-quarter cup sugar, half pint milk, one teaspoon cream tartar, half teaspoon carbonate soda, pinch salt.

Cream butter and sugar, beat eggs and add and go on beating for 10 minutes. Sift flour, tartar, and salt and add alternately with milk. Lastly add soda dissolved in a little milk. Pour into well-greased sandwich tins, bake in moderate oven 10 minutes.

Filling for Cake.—Half a cup water, half cup sugar, one tablespoon cornflour, and rind of one lemon. Boil sugar, water, and rind of lemon. Mix cornflour to a smooth paste with juice of lemon, boil for few minutes.—Miss H. Spencer, Wayville.

In an Electric Cooker bake at 375°.

Bake in Gas Cooker at 350° F.

MILK CAKE

Half cup butter beaten to a cream, one cup sugar added, half cup milk, two eggs well beaten, two cups S.R. flour.

This mixture may be baked in sandwich tins for 25 minutes and spread with raspberry jam, or it may be baked in a deeper tin for 40-45 minutes and iced with chocolate icing.

—Mrs. Noble, Brighton.

In an Electric Cooker bake at 375°.
Bake in Gas Cooker at 350° F.

ORANGE CAKE

Five eggs (leaving out white of one), two cups flour, two cups sugar, two oranges, half cup cold water, half teaspoon soda, one teaspoon cream tartar.

Beat eggs and sugar for half hour, add water and grated rind and juice of one orange. Sift in flour gradually. Bake 20 minutes in sandwich tins.

Icing.—Beat white of egg to stiff froth, then add rind and juice of other orange. Add about half a pound icing sugar. Put between and on top of cake. —Anon.

In an Electric Cooker bake at 375°.
Bake in Gas Cooker at 350° F.

SPONGE SANDWICH

Four eggs, one cup sugar, one cup plain flour, one teaspoon cream of tartar, half teaspoon carbonate soda, two tablespoons cold water, essence.

Method.—Beat eggs and sugar to a stiff froth from 20 to 30 minutes. Sift in flour and cream of tartar and mix. Add carbonate soda dissolved in two tablespoons cold water. Bake fifteen to twenty minutes.

—Mrs. Harry Arbon, 2 Birkdale Avenue, Clarence Park.
—Mrs. E. Coliver, Torrens Park. —M. McRae, Goodwood Park
—Miss E. Cooper, Farrell's Flat. —Selma Bowering.

Six eggs, the weight of four in flour and five in sugar, two teaspoons cream tartar and one of soda.

Beat whites and yolks separately with a tablespoon of cold water with the yolks. Bake in papered tins without grease; place together with jam or any other filling. —Miss J. Stribling.

In an Electric Cooker bake at 375°.
Bake in Gas Cooker at 350° F.

Five eggs well beaten with one cup of sugar. Add one cup flour with half teaspoon soda and one teaspoon cream of tartar. Bake about 10 minutes in a hot oven in sandwich tins. Two tablespoons of cocoa added to the flour will give it a nice chocolate flavour. Whipped cream is used for the filling, passion fruit added if liked. —Miss E. Lawrie, Hobart.

ROYAL SPONGE CAKE

Beat separately the whites and yolks of three eggs till very stiff. Boil one cup of sugar with four tablespoons of cold water until it strings or thickens. Put whites and yolks together, pour in hot syrup, beat till lukewarm. Sift in cup of flour, flavour, and bake in layers. Put together with jelly, frost, sprinkle over desiccated coconut. — Mrs. Bungey, Woodville.

In an Electric Cooker bake at 375°.
Bake in Gas Cooker at 350° F.

RIBBON CAKE

Two cups S.R. flour, 1 cup sugar, 6 eggs, ¼ lb. butter, pinch salt.

Beat butter to a cream, then add sugar, eggs, and flour. When well mixed divide in three parts; colour one with cochineal, one with cocoa, and leave one as it is. Bake in moderate oven; put jam or icing sugar filling between each layer and ice top.

— Mrs. Pearl Bowering, "Wheatley," Peterborough.

Half pound butter, ½ lb. sugar, three eggs, ¾ lb. flour, heaped teaspoon baking powder, half teaspoon vanilla essence, one gill milk, one tablespoon cocoa, half teaspoon cochineal.

Cream the butter and sugar and add yolks of three eggs and white of one. Add flour and milk and flavouring. Divide mixture into three parts. To one part add cocoa, and to another cochineal. Pour mixtures into three greased sandwich tins and bake in a moderate oven for 20 minutes to half an hour. Spread jam between layers and sprinkle top with icing sugar.

— Mrs. George Prince. — Miss Jean Leslie, Mitcham.

Use ¼ lb. butter. — Mrs. E. Morris, Torrensville.

In an Electric Cooker bake at 375°.
Bake in Gas Cooker at 350° F.

SPONGE SANDWICH

Three eggs, 1 breakfast cup S.R. flour, 1 cup sugar, 2 tablespoons cold water.

Beat eggs, sugar together for ¼ hour, sift in flour and mix well, add water. Use 2 sandwich tins. Bake in moderate oven for 20 mins.; orange or lemon filling. — Mrs. C. M. Dunstone, Alberton.

In an Electric Cooker bake at 375°.
Bake in Gas Cooker at 350° F.

THREE-MINUTE CAKE

One large cup flour, ¾ cup sugar, 3 eggs, 3 tablespoons milk, 2 tablespoons butter, 1 teaspoon carb. soda, 2 teaspoons cream of tartar. Put all ingredients together in basin, beat well for 3 mins. Bake in sandwich tins 15-20 mins. Mrs. S. C. Lawrence, Nth. Adel.

In an Electric Cooker bake at 375°.
Bake in Gas Cooker at 350° F.

SPONGE ROLL

Four eggs, 1 cup sugar, 1 cup flour, 2 teaspoons baking powder.

Put in baking dish and bake 10 minutes. Put out on damp cloth and roll, then unroll and spread jam and roll again on paper sprinkled with icing sugar. — A. L. Lillecrapp, Hill Ridge.

— Mrs. Campbell, Brisbane.

One cup flour, three-quarter cup sugar, three eggs, one teaspoon cream of tartar, half teaspoon carbonate soda, one teaspoon butter melted in four teaspoons boiling water.

Beat eggs and sugar 10 minutes. Stir flour, soda, tartar and pinch salt, and add. Lastly add butter dissolved in the water. Bake in hot oven quarter of an hour. Turn out and roll in a towel, and leave for a few minutes. Unroll, spread with jam and roll up again. — Miss H. Spencer, Wayville.

In an Electric Cooker bake at 400°.

Bake in Gas Cooker at 400° F.

VANILLA CAKE

One cup flour, three-quarters cup sugar, 3 oz. butter, three eggs, one tablespoon cornflour.

Beat butter to cream. Add sugar. Break eggs in one by one, mix. Add flour, lastly cornflour. Bake in sandwich tins. Fill and ice.

In an Electric Cooker bake at 375°.

Bake in Gas Cooker at 350° F.

WALNUT SANDWICH CAKE

Four eggs, two cups sugar, one cup butter, one dessertspoon spice, one dessertspoon cinnamon, six or eight walnuts chopped, one cup milk, three cups self-raising flour.

Cream sugar and butter well. Add eggs one at a time. Add spice, walnuts, flour and milk. Cook either in three tins or two very large ones. — B. L. Rowley.

In an Electric Cooker bake at 375°.

Bake in Gas Cooker at 350° F.

WALNUT CAKE

Three ounces butter, one cup flour, half cup milk, pinch of salt, one cup brown sugar, two eggs, one teaspoon cream tartar, half teaspoon soda, dessertspoon spice and cinnamon mixed with 12 chopped walnuts. Beat butter and sugar to cream, add eggs, flour, spice, cinnamon and cream tartar. Put soda in little hot water, add milk, mix in cake while warm.

Bake in sandwich tins and put together with jam. Ice with a plain icing and place walnuts on top. Improves with keeping.

— Mrs. G. H. Lang, Gawler South.

In an Electric Cooker bake at 375°.

Bake in Gas Cooker at 350° F.

ICINGS AND CAKE FILLINGS

ALMOND ICING

One lb. icing sugar, 6-8 ozs., almond meal, yolks of eggs, 1 tablespoon sherry or orange flower water, 2 tablespoons strained orange or lemon juice.

Sift the icing sugar and add to it the almond meal. When well mixed add the yolks of the eggs, the orange flower water, or sherry, and sufficient of the fruit juice to form a firm paste. Turn on to a board well sprinkled with icing sugar and knead it thoroughly.

To cover the cake with almond icing.—If necessary trim the cake and make it flat on the top. Cut off sufficient paste to cover the top of the cake and roll it out to the required size. Brush over the top of the cake with a lightly beaten egg white or the thin part of apricot jam. Lift on the paste and press it on to the cake. Roll the paste into a strip as long as the circumference of the cake and as wide as its depth. Brush the sides of the cake with icing. If the cake is very large, it will be best to do the sides of the cake in 3 or 4 strips. Make all the joins carefully and allow the paste to dry thoroughly before applying the icing.

— A. L. Sharman, Black Forest.

FRUIT FILLING

Beat together 1 oz. of butter and 1 oz. icing sugar; add the juice of half a large orange or lemon and sufficient sifted icing sugar to form a soft creamy mixture when beaten together.

FRUIT ICING

Six ounces sifted icing sugar, 2 tablespoons strained fruit juice. Beat well together; pour over cake and smooth with a knife dipped in hot water.

MOCK CREAM FILLING

Beat together 1 oz. butter and 1 oz. sifted icing sugar; add a few drops of vanilla essence, 2 oz. icing sugar, and enough milk to make a soft creamy mixture. Beat well and spread between cakes.

CHOCOLATE ICING

One oz. unsweetened chocolate, 1 small teaspoon butter, vanilla essence, sifted icing sugar.

Break up the chocolate, then place it in a basin and stand over boiling water till melted. Add the butter and hot water and beat well. Allow the mixture to cool a little, then add enough sifted icing sugaı to give a spreading consistency. Add vanilla and beat well. — A. L. Sharman, Black Forest.

CHOCOLATE ICING FOR LOAF CAKE

Take some icing sugar (sifted), add milk till it will spread without running, add cocoa to make it a nice brown. When the cake is covered, smooth over with a knife dipped in cold water, and dot over with halved shelled walnuts or with coconut.

ICING

One cup sugar, one teaspoon butter, one-quarter cup milk, half teaspoon cream tartar, essence according to taste, and boil five minutes. — Miss A. Stinson, Clarence Park.

Put 2 oz. loaf sugar in a pan with one tablespoon cold water and juice of quarter lemon. Stir till boiling, then pour out, and keep stirring until thick. Put on the cake and dry in the air.

LEMON FILLING FOR CAKES

One cup sugar, one tablespoon arrowroot, one cup boiling water, grated rind and the juice of one lemon.

Mix arrowroot and sugar together with the lemon, which should be strained. Add the boiling water and boil until stiff.

A little cochineal may be added if desired.

— J. Treasure, Georgetown.

MOCK CREAM FOR CAKE FILLING

Boil one cup milk, thicken with one tablespoon cornflour, and allow to cool. Beat 2 oz. butter and 2 oz. icing sugar to a cream. Add first mixture a little at a time till used up, beating well all the time. Flavour with vanilla.

— Miss D. Cochrane, Auburn, Victoria.
— Miss K. Shannon.
— F. Laub, Solomontown.

ORANGE FILLING FOR SPONGE CAKE

One orange, half a lemon, half teacup sugar, one dessertspoon cornflour, half teacup water.

Grate rind of orange and lemon, strain juice. Mix cornflour and water. Add sugar, rind and juice, and boil for a few minutes, stirring well. Let cool before placing between sponge sandwich. — Mrs. E. Haselgrove, Unley Park.

BISCUIT AND SHORTBREADS

BISCUITS AND SHORTBREADS

AFTERNOON TEA BISCUITS

One pound self-raising flour, ¾ lb. sugar, ½ lb. butter, two eggs.

Mix butter and sugar to a cream, add eggs previously beaten, lastly flour. Roll out and bake on a floured slide in a hot oven.

— Mrs. Cross, Kadina. — Mrs. W. Simmons.

In an Electric Cooker bake at 400° 12 minutes.

One cup butter, one cup sugar, one egg, pinch salt, half packet desiccated coconut, juice of half a lemon, as much S.R. flour as you can knead into mixture.

Put through mincer and twist into fancy shapes. Trim with almonds, sugar, dates, etc. — J.M.A.

In an Electric Cooker bake at 425° 15 minutes.

Bake in Gas Cooker at 350° F.

ALMOND CREAM BISCUITS

Two eggs (yolks only), one cup S.R. flour, three tablespoons sugar, ¼ lb. butter, blanched almonds.

Beat butter and sugar, add beaten yolks, then flour. Mix to a very stiff paste, roll out, and spread with beaten white of egg and chopped almonds. Cut into shapes, and bake a golden brown. This mixture will do for date shells.

Two eggs (yolks only), ¼ lb. butter, four tablespoons cream (fresh or sour), one cup flour, three tablespoons sugar, almond essence, blanched almonds.

Mix into a stiff paste. Roll out, cut into shapes, brush with egg, sprinkle with coarse sugar and chopped almonds. Bake a light brown.

In an Electric Cooker bake at 400° 15 minutes.

Bake in Gas Cooker at 350° F.

AMMONIA BISCUITS

Ingredients.—Half pound butter, 1 lb. sugar, 4 eggs, 1 oz. rock ammonia, one cup milk.

Method.—Beat butter and sugar to a cream. Add eggs, powder the ammonia, dissolve in hot water (just a little), and mix in the milk. Use enough plain flour to make a nice dough. Roll very thinly, cut and bake in a hot oven.

In an Electric Cooker bake at 400° 15 minutes.

Bake in Gas Cooker at 350° F.

ALMOND FINGERS

Take ½ lb. flour, ¼ lb. butter, 1 oz. sugar, one teaspoon baking powder, one egg yolk, sufficient milk to make a stiff paste.

Rub the butter in the flour, sugar and baking powder. Then add egg yolk and milk. Roll out thinly, spread with icing, and cut into fingers, and bake a pale brown.

Icing.—White of an egg, ¼ lb. icing sugar, chopped almonds, and almond essence. — Mrs. G. Bradley, Torrens Park.

One teaspoon cream of tartar and half teaspoon carbonate soda may be substituted for baking powder.

— R. Jackman, Royston Park.

In an Electric Cooker at 400° 15 minutes.
Bake in Gas Cooker at 350° F.

ANZAC CRISPS

Two cups rolled oats, half cup sugar, one cup flour, one teaspoon cream tartar, half teaspoon of soda, half cup melted butter, one tablespoon golden syrup, four tablespoons boiling water.

Dissolve soda in water. Mix dry ingredients, then add syrup, then water and soda. — Miss K. Shannon, Encounter Bay.

In an Electric Cooker bake at 325° 20 minutes.
Bake in Gas Cooker at 350° F.

BACHELOR BUTTONS

One pound flour, ½ lb. butter, ½ lb. sugar, two eggs, two teaspoons of baking powder, flavour to taste.

Method.—Rub butter into flour. Add powder. Beat sugar and eggs together, then mix all together. Roll in hands like marbles, then roll in sugar. Bake in moderate oven.

— Mrs. Mayfield, King's Park.

In an Electric Cooker bake at 375° 12-15 minutes.
Bake in Gas Cooker at 350° F.

BANANA BISCUITS

Four ounces flour, 1 oz. castor sugar, 2 oz. butter, and one large banana.

Mix sugar and butter together, add banana; mix well and then add flour. Drop on cold slide (greased), and bake till crisp.

In an Electric Cooker bake at 425° 15 minutes.
Bake in Gas Cooker at 350° F.

BATH BISCUITS

Two pounds of flour, 1 lb. sugar, ¼ lb. butter, 1 oz. ammonia, one pint milk.

Mix ammonia (crushed free of lumps) in flour, rub in butter and sugar. Mix with milk (warm). Roll out thinly as possible. Bake in hot oven.

In an Electric Cooker bake at 400° 12-15 minutes.
Bake in Gas Cooker at 375° F.

BISCUITS

One pound flour, 1 lb. butter, 1 lb. sugar, two-thirds of an ounce of ammonia, two and a half cups warm milk.

— Mrs. D. Easson, Port Pirie.

One and a half pounds flour, ½ lb. butter, two eggs, ½ lb. sugar, few drops essence of lemon, three-quarters of a cup of milk.

Beat sugar and butter to a cream, add eggs one at a time, essence and milk. Beat well, add flour, roll out thin, and cut. Bake to a nice golden brown.

In an Electric Cooker bake at 400° 12-15 minutes.
Bake in Gas Cooker at 350° F.

BRANDY SNAPS

Two pounds of flour, ½ lb. butter, 2 lb. sugar, 2 lb. treacle, teaspoon ginger. Bake in slow oven. — Daphne Milton, Willaston.

In an Electric Cooker bake at 325° 20 minutes.
Bake in Gas Cooker at 325° F.

BROWN BISCUITS

Half cup flour, two cups rolled oats, three-quarters cup sugar, cinnamon to taste. Put into a saucepan and warm ¼ lb. butter or dripping, one tablespoon treacle, one teaspoon carbonate soda, two tablespoons boiling water.

When melted, let cool, then mix with dry ingredients. Put on baking tray in small lumps. Care is needed in watching they do not burn. — Mrs. C. Cheetham, Brighton.

Two tablespoons butter, 2 tablespoons treacle; melt together, then add 1 cup sugar, 1 cup coconut, 1 cup S.R. flour, 2 cups flaked oats, half teaspoon soda in 3 tablespoons boiling water.

Drop on sheet and bake in hot oven.

— Mrs. Leslie Smith, Kensington Gardens.

In an Electric Cooker bake at 400° 20 minutes.
Bake in Gas Cooker at 350° F.

CHAMPAGNE BISCUITS

Two cups sugar, 4 cups flour, 1 cup butter, 1 teaspoon soda, 2 teaspoons cream tartar, 2 eggs.

Flavour with lemon or vanilla, mix with sweet milk, cut with biscuit cutter and bake in quick oven. — M. McRae.

In an Electric Cooker bake at 400° 12-15 minutes.
Bake in Gas Cooker at 350° F.

CHOCOLATE FINGERS

Stir together till thick and smooth 3 oz. each of butter and castor sugar. Then sprinkle in ½ oz. of cocoa and beat in 2 eggs. With 6 oz. of flour mix just a little salt and ½ teaspoon of baking powder. Stir it in lightly, adding a little milk if too stiff to spread easily, and a slight flavouring of vanilla. Bake in a thin layer in an oblong or square tin lined with greased paper. When slightly cool coat with chocolate icing and cut into fingers.

— Daphne Milton, Willaston.

In an Electric Cooker bake at 425° 15 minutes.
Bake in Gas Cooker at 350° F.

COCKLES

Take quarter lb. flour, quarter lb. cornflour, quarter lb. sugar, quarter lb. butter, 2 eggs, 1 level teaspoon baking powder, a pinch of salt.

Beat butter and sugar together; break in 2 eggs, one by one; mix well, and add other ingredients. Drop in small teaspoons on a buttered tin, and bake in quick oven. Sandwich together with jam. — Jessie Vandepeer, Waringa, Ardrossan.

— E. Slater, Port Pirie. — T.A.

— Miss K. Shannon.

Use 2 oz. cornflour. — Mrs. W. Mawby.

In an Electric Cooker bake at 425° 12 minutes.
Bake in Gas Cooker at 400° F.

COCONUT OR ALMOND FINGERS

Half pound plain flour, one pinch salt, 1 teaspoon baking powder, ¼ lb. butter, 2 oz. sugar, 1 egg, 2 tablespoons milk, ¼ lb. icing sugar, essence of vanilla, 3 or 4 tablespoons coconut or 2 oz. almonds.

Cream butter and sugar and add yolk of egg beaten up with milk. Sift flour, salt and baking powder and work in with flavouring. Knead well and roll out about ¼ in. thick. Beat white of egg lightly, add sifted icing sugar, spread over mixture and sprinkle with almonds or coconut. Cut in fingers. Bake in hot oven till light brown. — Miss Jean Leslie, Mitcham.

— Mrs. F. Hazelgrove.

In an Electric Cooker bake at 400° 12-15 minutes.
Bake in Gas Cooker at 350° F.

COCONUT BISCUITS

Two and a half cups of flour (self-raising), one cup sugar, one cup butter, three eggs, one cup coconut.

Roll thin. Bake in hot oven.

In an Electric Cooker bake at 400° 12 minutes.

Three and half cups flour, three eggs, ½ lb. butter, two teaspoons cream tartar, one teaspoon carb. soda, one-quarter cup milk, one-half packet coconut, 1½ cups sugar.

Mix dry ingredients, then add butter, eggs and milk. Bake in moderate oven from seven to 10 minutes.

— Miss K. Shannon, Encounter Bay.

In an Electric Cooker bake at 400°.

Half pound each of S.R. flour, cornflour, sugar and butter, desiccated coconut, and four eggs.

Beat butter and sugar to a cream, add the beaten eggs, then flour, cornflour, and lastly the coconut. Put dessertspoonfuls on to a cold greased tray, and bake in a brisk oven. They may be rolled out and cut into shapes.

— Mrs. W. Greenwood, "Todmorden," Gawler.

In an Electric Cooker bake at 400°.

Bake in Gas Cooker at 350°F.

Half lb. dripping, I dessertspoon lemon juice, and ½ teaspoon carb. soda mixed well together. Add ½ cup milk, 1½ cups sugar, 2 cups coconut, and 4 cups S.R. flour. Mix well, roll out and cut into shapes. Bake in fairly hot oven till brown. 400°.

These are also delicious if two are joined together with jam or icing. If using jam, they should be eaten immediately, otherwise they become soft.

— Mrs. T. Reynolds, Cremorne, N.S.W.

COCONUT MACAROONS

Three whites of eggs, one cup sugar, two cups desiccated coconut, one teaspoon cornflour, 2 oz. almonds (blanched and chopped), essence of vanilla.

Method.—Beat whites of eggs in basin to stiff broth. Add sugar, and beat over hot water till it forms a crust on the bottom. Remove from the hot water, add essence, cornflour, and coconut. Put in small quantities on greased paper, and bake in a slow oven for 20 to 30 minutes. Half an almond may be put aside for the top of each macaroon.

In an Electric Cooker bake at 325°.

Whisk the whites of three eggs till very light, then add 8 oz. castor sugar and 6 oz. of grated coconut. Roll into pyramids, bake on greased paper in rather a cool oven till just coloured. Flavour to taste.

— Miss K. Shannon, Encounter Bay.

In an Electric Cooker bake at 325°.

Bake in Gas Cooker at 350° F.

CREAM BISCUITS

One cup cream, one cup sugar, two eggs, enough S.R. flour to stiffen (about three cups).

Mix cream and sugar and eggs together for about five minutes, then add flour and roll out thin. Cut into shapes, and bake in moderate oven. —Mrs. J. P. Peterson, Ardrossan.

In an Electric Cooker bake at 400° 12 minutes.

Bake in Gas Cooker at 350° F.

CRANBROOK BISCUITS

Four cups sugar, 1 lb. butter, eight eggs, three-quarters cup of milk, three teaspoons cream of tartar, one and a half teaspoons carbonate of soda, flour enough to be able to roll the mixture, flavour with lemon to taste.

Method.—Beat butter and sugar to a cream. Add eggs and milk, then flavouring, lastly flour, with cream of tartar and carbonate of soda. Roll, cut into shapes. Bake in a hot oven for about 10 minutes. If packed in an air-tight tin will last three months. Above quantity will fill ordinary small sized biscuit tin.

—Mrs. Hill, St. Peters.

In an Electric Cooker bake at 400°.

Bake in Gas Cooker at 350° F.

DATE DROPS

Half pound butter, half cup sugar, one egg, one teaspoon cinnamon, three-quarter cup almonds (chopped), three-quarter cup dates (stoned), a cup and a half flour, half teaspoon carbonate soda.

Beat butter and sugar to a cream. Add well-beaten egg, then flour with cinnamon mixed in. Add dates and nuts. Dissolve soda in a tablespoon or more of boiling water. Stir well into mixture. Drop teaspoonfuls of mixture on cold shelf and bake 10 to 15 minutes. They should be pale brown.

—A. M. Carter, Port Elliot.

In an Electric Cooker bake at 425°.

Bake in Gas Cooker at 350° F.

DATE SQUARES

Three cups flour, one teaspoon cream tartar, half teaspoon soda, half cup sugar, one cup butter, three eggs. Add a little milk if required.

Roll out, spread half with dates, cover with other half, cut into squares and bake. Ice the top and sprinkle with coconut. Jam can be used instead of dates. —Mrs. W. Wise, Prospect.

In an Electric Cooker bake at 375°.

Bake in Gas Cooker at 350° F.

BISCUITS WITHOUT EGGS

Three cups flour, one cup sugar, one cup butter, half cup milk, two teaspoons cream of tartar, one teaspoon soda.

Melt butter and sugar in the milk. Add flour, flavour with ground ginger or any other flavouring that is preferred.

— Mrs. C. Elfenbein, Port Elliot.

In an Electric Cooker bake at 400° 15 minutes.
Bake in Gas Cooker at 350° F.

DAINTY BISCUITS

Two eggs, half cup sugar, two tablespoons of milk, one tablespoon butter, half teaspoon cream tartar, quarter teaspoon carbonate soda, enough flour to make stiff paste. Roll out thin and bake in a hot oven. — Mrs. A. C. Ellis, Port Elliot.

In an Electric Cooker bake at 400° 15 minutes.
Bake in Gas Cooker at 350° F.

EGG BISCUITS

Two tablespoons butter creamed with one cup of sugar. Add two eggs well beaten, then two full cups of self-raising flour and a few drops of essence of lemon.

Roll out thinly, cut into shapes, and bake in a hot oven.

— Mrs. J. Greenwood, Algate.

In an Electric Cooker bake at 400° 15 minutes.
Bake in Gas Cooker at 350° F.

SULTANA OR CURRANT COOKIES

Half lb. sugar, ½ lb. butter, 1 lb. flour, salt, 4 level teaspoons cream of tartar, 2 level teaspoons soda, 2 eggs, 4 tablespoons milk, ½ lb. currants. Rub butter and sugar into the flour, sifted, with cream of tartar. Add currants and mix in well-beaten eggs and milk. Roll into balls, and bake in a hot oven 20 minutes.

In an Electric Cooker bake at 425°.
Bake in Gas Cooker at 375° F.

CAIRO CAKES

Cream 6 oz. of butter in a basin. Add 2 oz. of castor sugar. Mix until creamy with wooden spoon. Add 8 oz. of flour, flavouring any essence. Mix until the paste leaves the sides of basin. Turn out on board, and with the hands form into a roll about 1½ in. thick, then with floured knife cut into slanting slices about 1 in. thick. Bake till light brown. — Mrs. Beasley, Gawler.

In an Electric Cooker bake at 425° 15-20 minutes.
Bake in Gas Cooker at 350° F.

DOUGHNUTS

Two eggs, two tablespoons melted butter, 4 to 6 oz. castor sugar, quarter teaspoon salt, half pint milk, quarter teaspoon ground cinnamon, one teaspoon baking powder, flour to make soft dough.

Sift sugar into basin. Add eggs and beat well together. Add butter, cinnamon, salt, baking powder and milk. Sieve in by degrees enough flour to make soft dough. Knead and roll out ½ in. thick. Cut into small circles. Put together with jam, moistening edges with egg. Fry in hot fat until golden brown—about five minutes. Drain and roll in powdered sugar.

— Mrs. E. G. Harrison.

Half pound flour, one teaspoon baking powder, 2 oz. butter, one egg, a little milk, jam, one pinch salt.

Sift the flour, salt and baking powder in a basin, rub in butter and add sugar. Make into a soft dough with egg and milk. Knead lightly, and roll out ¼ in. thick. Cut with a round cutter. Put a small teaspoon of jam on half the pieces; brush over the others with beaten egg. Place two together and press edges well. Cook in a saucepan of smoking hot fat, three or four at a time. Lift out and drain on paper. Sprinkle with sugar.

Doughnuts are best when quite fresh. — A. Sharman.

EVE'S BISCUITS

Half cup butter, half cup sugar, two small eggs, enough S.R. flour (about one and a half or two cups) to make a stiff paste. Roll out thinly and cut. Mix about three-quarters of a cup of icing sugar with a tiny drop of milk to stiff paste. Ice each biscuit (before baking). Sprinkle each one with desiccated coconut. Bake in hot oven about 10 minutes.

— Mrs. Chas. Coote, Port Elliot.

In an Electric Cooker bake at 400°.
Bake in Gas Cooker at 350° F.

THE FIFE BISCUITS

Quarter pound butter creamed with ¼ lb. sugar. Beat in one egg and add ½ lb. S.R. flour. Bake in hot oven for about 20 minutes.

In an Electric Cooker bake at 400°.
Bake in Gas Cooker at 350° F.

WALNUT BISCUITS

Beat together 1 egg and 1 cup of sugar, add ¼ lb. melted butter, beat well, add 1 cup S.R. flour, 2 teaspoons cocoa and 1 cup walnuts. Place on greased tray in teaspoonfuls in hot oven. 350° F. gas. 400° electric.

GINGER NUTS

Three pounds flour, ¾ oz. soda, ¾ lb. butter, 1 lb. treacle, 2 lb. brown sugar, 1 oz. ginger, ½ oz. spice, three-eighths pint milk.

Mix dry ingredients, then add treacle and milk. Bake in a moderate oven from seven to 10 minutes.

— Miss K. Shannon, Encounter Bay.

One pound of flour, one pinch salt, one teaspoon carbonate soda, 1 oz. ginger, one teaspoon mixed spice, ½ lb. treacle, ¼ lb. clarified dripping, 3 oz. brown sugar, two tablespoons milk.

Sift the flour, salt, soda, ginger and mixed spice. Melt the dripping, sugar and treacle, and pour on to sifted flour, etc., and add the milk. Knead well and roll out ¼ in. thick. Cut with a round cutter and bake in a moderate oven for 15 to 20 minutes.

— Mrs. T. C. Sharman, Black Forest.

In an Electric Cooker bake at 375°.
Bake in Gas Cooker at 350° F.

IDEAL BISCUITS

Half a pound butter or lard, ¾ lb. sugar, 1½ lb. flour (S.R.), half cup sweet milk, two eggs, pinch of salt.

Beat butter to a cream, add sugar and eggs. Beat all together, then add flour and milk. Bake in a fairly hot oven.

Use plain flour, three-quarter teaspoon carbonate soda, one teaspoon and a half cream tartar. — C. Finn, Keyneton.

In an Electric Cooker bake at 425° for 10 minutes.
Bake in Gas Cooker at 375° F.

ISABEL BISCUITS

Three pounds flour, 1 lb. butter, 1 lb. sugar, 4 eggs, one cup milk, one teaspoon soda, two teaspoons cream tartar.

Method.—Beat butter to a cream, add sugar and eggs well beaten, the soda in the milk, cream of tartar in flour. Work all together, roll thin and bake in a hot oven. — M. McRae.

In an Electric Cooker bake at 400° 10 minutes.
Bake in Gas Cooker at 375° F.

LIGHT BISCUITS

A pound and a half flour, ½ lb. butter, ½ lb. sugar, three eggs, half teaspoon soda, one teaspoon cream of tartar.

Rub butter well into flour. Beat eggs and sugar, and mix with little milk. Bake until brown in hot oven.

— Mrs. S. P. Bond.

In an Electric Cooker bake at 400°.
Bake in Gas Cooker at 350° F.

"LUCKY THOUGHT" BISCUITS

Half cup oatmeal, one and a half cups self-raising flour, half cup sugar, two tablespoons dripping, half teaspoon ground cinnamon, half teaspoon ground cloves, good pinch salt.

Rub together and mix stiff with two tablespoons treacle. Take a lump of this mixture and roll out on board, by hand, until a long sausage. Cut into 1 in. long pieces.

In an Electric Cooker bake at 400° 15-20 minutes.
Bake in Gas Cooker at 350° F.

HONEY CAKES

One pound dark brown sugar, 1 lb. treacle, 6 oz. dripping, one packet mixed spice, one heaped teaspoon ground ginger, three eggs.

Bring treacle.and sugar to a good heat, then pour over the dripping in a good-sized basin with spice and eggs; then keep on adding S.R. flour until it is nice stiff dough and clear from the hands. Cut in shapes and bake in hot oven. Do not roll them too thinly. — L. C. Weber.

In an Electric Cooker bake at 425° 15 minutes.
Bake in Gas Cooker at 350° F.

MACAROONS

The whites of two eggs beaten to a stiff froth, one spare breakfast cup of fine sugar. Beat till very firm, then add three tablespoons coconut. Drop on paper strewn with sugar and bake in slow oven till firm and lightly browned.

— M. Theim, Beulah Park.

In an Electric Cooker bake at 275° 30 minutes.
Bake in Gas Cooker at 350° F.

MERINGUES

Whites of three eggs and half a pound of sugar.

Beat whites of eggs with pinch of salt. Add sugar in teaspoons. Bake in very slow oven. Probable time to cook, half an hour or longer. — Mrs. A. W. Piper.

In an Electric Cooker bake at 275°.
Bake in Gas Cooker at 200° F.

MIDDLETON BISCUITS

A pound and a half of flour, 12 oz. sugar, 6 oz. butter, ¼ oz. rock ammonia.

Grate ammonia on the sugar. Mix with the flour. Add milk sufficient to make as stiff as pastry. Stand one hour or more before baking. Use plenty of flour in rolling out. Do not eat while hot. — Mrs. David Williams.

In an Electric Cooker bake at 400° 12-15 minutes.
Bake in Gas Cooker at 350° F.

BROWNIES, OR MUNCHERS

Two cups flaked oats, one cup butter, one cup coconut, one cup sugar, two tablespoons treacle or golden syrup, three-quarters cup flour, ½ teaspoon carb. soda, 1 tablespoon boiling water.

Mix dry ingredients in a separate bowl. Melt the golden syrup and butter and add to dry ingredients, and put boiling water on soda and add last of all. Cook in a moderate oven till a light brown. — M. Carmichael.

In an Electric Cooker bake at 325° 20-30 minutes.
Bake in Gas Cooker at 350° F.

NICE PLAIN BISCUITS

Two cups flour, two teaspoons cream tartar, one of carbonate soda, one cup sugar, ¼ lb. butter, two eggs, and a few drops of essence lemon.

Mix flour, powder and sugar together in a bowl, then rub butter into the flour and mix with beaten-up eggs. Roll out thin and cut into shapes and bake. — E. Blucher, Ki Ki.

In an Electric Cooker bake at 400° 12-15 minutes.
Bake in Gas Cooker at 350° F.

LADY'S FINGERS

One cup sugar and butter, two eggs, four tablespoons milk, teaspoon baking powder, two cups flour, to mix.

Make into stiff paste. Cut into 4-in. finger lengths. Bake in hot oven.

In an Electric Cooker bake at 425° 10 minutes.
Bake in Gas Cooker at 350° F.

NUTTIES

Take two cups flaked oats, three-quarter cup of plain flour, one-half cup sugar, one-quarter cup chopped almonds, one-half cup butter, one-half teaspoon carb. soda, one dessertspoon treacle, two tablespoons boiling water.

Mix oats, flour, sugar and almonds together, then add treacle and butter melted. Dissolve soda in boiling water. Bake in moderate oven. — Thelma J. Batchelor, Prospect Gardens.
— A. Lillecrapp, "Hill Ridge."

In an Electric Cooker bake at 325° 20-30 minutes.
Bake in Gas Cooker at 350° F.

A quarter pound butter, ½ cup sugar, ¾ cup chopped walnuts, ¾ cup chopped dates, 1 egg, 1 teaspoon ground cinnamon, 1½ cups flour, ½ teaspoon carb. soda dissolved in 1 tablespoon boiling water.

Beat butter and sugar to a cream, add well-beaten egg, then walnuts and dates and flour sifted with cinnamon; add carb. soda in water, and stir well into the mixture. Drop from teaspoon on slide and bake 15 to 20 minutes in a moderate oven.

OATMEAL BISCUITS

Two cups flour, one cup oatmeal, three-quarters of a cup sugar, 5 oz. butter, one teaspoon cream of tartar, half teaspoon soda, two eggs well beaten.

Rub butter into flour, add other ingredients, and lastly mix with the eggs. Roll out fairly thick, and bake in a hot oven.

— Edith E. Rutt.

In an Electric Cooker bake at 375° 10-15 minutes.

Two cups flour, two cups Quaker oats or oatmeal, one cup sugar, one cup raisins chopped finely, one cup butter, one teaspoon carbonate soda dissolved in one tablespoon of cold water, one pinch salt. Cut and bake in a moderate oven.

—Mrs. Murray Anderson, Hawthorn.

In an Electric Cooker bake at 375° 10-15 minutes.
Bake in Gas Cooker at 375°

OATMEAL KISSES

One cup castor sugar, one egg, three-quarter cup oatmeal, three-quarter cup S.R. flour, vanilla flavouring.

Beat egg and sugar together, add oatmeal, and lastly flour. Drop on buttered paper and bake in a hot oven. — J.M.A.

In an Electric Cooker bake at 400° 20-30 minutes.
Bake in Gas Cooker at 350° F.

OATMEAL MACAROONS

Mix together two and a half cups of rolled oats, one cup of sugar, two eggs (yolks and whites beaten separately), one tablespoon melted butter, two teaspoons baking powder, one teaspoon vanilla.

Drop on greased baking tins and cook in a hot oven. A few almonds are an improvement. — J.C.C.

In an Electric Cooker bake at 400° 20-30 minutes.
Bake in Gas Cooker at 350° F.

COCONUT BISCUITS

A quarter pound butter, one cup sugar, beat to a cream; add 2 eggs, $1\frac{1}{2}$ cups S.R. flour, and one cup coconut.

Turn out of teaspoon on to a hot slide and bake in quick oven 15 to 20 minutes. Currants or sultanas may be added if liked.

— Eleanor M. Abbott, Port Elliot, S.A.

In an Electric Cooker bake at 425°.
Bake in Gas Cooker at 375° F.

ORANGE JUMBLES

Quarter pound flour, two teaspoons baking powder, half teaspoon salt, 1 oz. butter, a little milk, 2 oz. sugar, and an orange.

Wipe the orange, grate off rind, and work into the sugar until of a uniform yellow colour. Add enough orange juice to make it the consistency of jam. Sieve flour, salt and baking powder into a bowl. Rub in butter, form into a dough with a little milk, and roll out to ¼ in. thick. Spread with the orange mixture, and roll up. Cut in ¾ in. slices, place on a greased tin, and bake in a hot oven for about 15 minutes. Brush over with orange juice and sprinkle with sugar. — Miss D. Cochrane, Auburn, Victoria.

In an Electric Cooker bake at 425°.
Bake in Gas Cooker at 350° F.

PLAIN BISCUITS

Two cups S.R. flour, small cup of sugar, ¼ lb. butter, one or two eggs, beaten with a little milk.

Mix, roll out and bake 10 minutes in a brisk oven.

— Miss Morphett, Torrens Park.

In an Electric Cooker bake at 400°.
Bake in Gas Cooker at 350° F.

RATAFIA BISCUITS

Four eggs, ½ lb. butter, 1¼ lb. S.R. flour, ¾ lb. sugar, two small teaspoons essence ratafia.

Melt butter and pour when warm on the well-beaten eggs. Add dry ingredients, mix well, break in small pieces and roll in sugar, and place chopped almonds on each. Bake 15 minutes.

— M.B., St. Peters.

In an Electric Cooker bake at 425°.
Bake in Gas Cooker at 350° F.

ROLLED OATS BISCUITS

Two cups rolled oats, three-quarters cup S.R. flour, half cup sugar, half cup butter, one teaspoon treacle, half teaspoon carb. soda.

Method.—Mix all dry ingredients together. Dissolve butter with two tablespoons of boiling water and one teaspoon treacle. Mix all together and place out on a cool slide in suitable quantities, with an almond in each centre. Bake in hot oven until brown.

— Miss A. C. Ellis, Port Elliot.
— Miss E. Prince, Avenel Gardens, Medindie.
— Mrs. W. B. Mawby, St. Peters.

Use one cup sugar. — Miss Rehn, W.C.T.U., Adelaide.

In an Electric Cooker bake at 400° 20-30 minutes.
Bake in Gas Cooker at 350° F.

ROSALA BISCUITS

Two cups S.R. flour, half cup sugar, ¼ lb. butter, one egg, and yolk of another.

Method.—Mix all dry ingredients, then make into a stiff paste with one egg and yolk and little milk if needed. Roll out thin. Beat white of egg to a stiff froth, then add enough icing sugar to make firm. Spread over rolled dough and sprinkle with coconut. Cut into fingers and bake 15 minutes.

— Mrs. W. B. Mawby, St. Peters.

Use the yolk of one egg and a little milk.

— Mrs. F. J. Wright.
— Mrs. H. D. Blenkiron. — T.A.
— K. Shannon.

Two large cups S.R. flour, and work well in ½ lb. butter; then separate one egg and mix the yolk with one small cup of sugar. Beat this well, then mix with flour and butter, also pinch of salt and a few drops of essence (any sort). Then work well together, and if too dry add a little milk. Roll very thin, and cut in strips. Spread with icing and bake a light brown.

— Mrs. H. E. R. Dinham, Ardrossan.

In an Electric Cooker bake at 400°.
Bake in Gas Cooker at 350° F.

SAND TARTS

Two cups flour and sugar, one of butter, or beef dripping, two eggs (reserve white of one).

Mix, roll out, cut and brush with white of egg, sprinkle with sugar, cinnamon. Put a blanched almond or raisin on top in the centre of each. — M Higginbottom.

In an Electric Cooker bake at 400 15-20 minutes.
Bake in Gas Cooker at 350° F.

SOLDIERS' BISCUITS

Half cup flour, one cup brown sugar, two cups rolled oats, half cup melted butter, one teaspoon carbonate of soda, one good tablespoon treacle, two tablespoons boiling water.

Method.—Melt butter, treacle and boiling water in a saucepan and bring to the boil. Add soda just before pouring into dry ingredients. Mix dry ingredients, make a well in the middle and pour in boiling mixture, stirring well. Drop small pieces on oven tray and bake in a slow oven from ten to fifteen minutes. When cooked, leave on tray for a few minutes to harden, then take off. When cold they should be brittle. If still soft, put back into oven again. — B. W. Brice, High Street, Unley Park.

— Mrs. Walter Hurn, Angaston.

Use one cup of flour. — E. L. Pledge, Laura.

In an Electric Cooker bake at 375°.
Bake in Gas Cooker at 350° F.

SPONGE KISSES

Two ounces butter, 4 oz. sugar. Beat to a cream. Add two eggs, essence to taste. Mix well, then stir in 6 oz. flour with one heaped teaspoon of baking powder. Make into light dough. Add a little more flour if necessary. Roll out, cut into shapes, sprinkle with sugar, and bake in good oven. When cold, fasten together with jam. If difficult to roll out, a good plan is to break off small pieces and roll between fingers into a small ball. Sprinkle slide of oven with flour. —Mrs. Beasley, Gawler.

In an Electric Cooker bake at 425° 10 minutes.
Bake in Gas Cooker at 350° F.

SPINSTER'S BUTTONS

Five ounces self-raising flour, 2 oz. butter, 2 oz. sugar, one egg.

Method.—Rub butter into flour, beat egg and sugar together. Take pieces size of walnut and roll in hands and flatten. Dip in sugar and bake in moderate oven 10 minutes. —E. Lane.

Two cups flour, two tablespoons butter, two eggs, half cup sugar, one teaspoon cream tartar, half teaspoon carb. soda. Rub flour and butter together, then mix. Drop on tins and sprinkle top with sugar.

—Miss K. Shannon, Encounter Bay.

In an Electric Cooker bake at 375°.
Bake in Gas Cooker at 375° F.

STUFFED MONKEYS

Two cups brown sugar, 1 lb. butter, 1½ lb. flour, little cinnamon, two eggs.

Mix together, roll out into little cakes ½ in. thick.

Filling.—Chopped almonds, fig jam, preserved ginger, and mixed peel chopped fine. Mix together, and put a little on each cake. Fold over like a pasty.

In an Electric Cooker bake at 425° 12-15 minutes.
Bake in Gas Cooker at 375° F.

SULTANA BISCUITS

Ingredients.—4 oz. self-raising flour, pinch salt, 2 oz. butter, 1 oz. sugar, 4 oz. sultanas (seeded), rind one lemon, juice half lemon, one egg.

Method.—Cream butter and sugar. Add egg whole. Add sifted flour and salt. Knead on a floured board, and roll into a thin sheet. Add rind and juice of lemon to sultanas and stir over fire until a mash. Add a little water if necessary. Spread on one half of pastry and fold the other half over, making a sandwich. Cut into oblong lengths about 3 in. long. Bake in a hot oven for 12 minutes. Dates may be done the same way.

In an Electric Cooker bake at 400°.
Bake in Gas Cooker at 350° F.

SUNBEAMS (BISCUITS)

Two and a half cups flour, half cup sugar, half cup butter, half teaspoon carbonate soda, one teaspoon cream tartar, two eggs. Add flour and rising last, then roll out very thinly. Spread with raspberry jam and roll up as for roly-poly, then cut in narrow strips and bake. — L. Carmichael, Tiparra West.

In an Electric Cooker bake at 375° 10-15 minutes.
Bake in Gas Cooker at 350° F.

TEA KISSES

Ingredients.—One cup of butter, one cup of sugar, two cups of S.R. flour, the yolks of two eggs, and two tablespoons of milk.

Method.—Cream butter and sugar together. Add the yolks of the eggs and milk. When this is well mixed add by degrees the flour, and lastly the well-beaten whites of two eggs. Grease a tin and drop the dough on it from a teaspoon. Scatter sugar over them, and bake from five to ten minutes in hot oven.

— Daisy E. L. Evans, Keyneton.

In an Electric Cooker bake at 425°.
Bake in Gas Cooker at 350° F.

SWEETHEARTS (BISCUITS)

One pound flour, ½ lb. butter, ½ lb. sugar, three eggs.

Mix well, cut into various shapes. Brush over with egg and sprinkle with chopped almonds, sugar and cinnamon. Bake in moderate oven. — M. F. Williamson, Port Elliot.

In an Electric Cooker bake at 375° 10-15 minutes.
Bake in Gas Cooker at 350° F.

TUMBLES

Six ounces flour, 6 oz. sugar, 4 oz. butter, one egg and rind of one lemon grated.

Keep back half the sugar to roll them in. Cut in shapes.

— Mrs. S. P. Bond.

In an Electric Cooker bake at 375° 10-15 minutes.
Bake in Gas Cooker at 350° F.

UNCLE TOBY MACAROONS

One egg, half cup sugar, two-thirds tablespoon of butter melted, two-thirds cup of rolled oats, one-third cup of desiccated coconut.

Method.—Beat eggs very lightly, add sugar and beat again. Add butter, rolled oats and desiccated coconut and pinch of salt. Flavour with vanilla. Drop from teaspoon on to buttered slide and bake in hot oven for ½ hour. — Mrs. D. Stribling, Brighton.

In an Electric Cooker bake at 400°.
Bake in Gas Cooker at 350° F.

TWIST FINGERS

Four eggs, ½ lb. sugar, ¼ lb. S.R. flour. Beat eggs and sugar together for 10 minutes, then add flour, flavour with ratafia. Place dessertspoonfuls on a slide widely apart, and turn envelope shape while warm. When cold, fill with cream and jelly made from jelly crystals. — E. Norman, Kadina.

In an Electric Cooker bake at 400°.

Bake in Gas Cooker at 350° F.

VANILLA BISCUITS

Mix ¼ lb. butter, ½ lb. sugar together. Add 2 well-beaten eggs, ¾ lb. flour (S.R.). Flavour with essence vanilla. Drop spoonfuls on oven shelf, bake till brown. — Mrs. W. Greenwood, Gawler.

Quarter lb. butter, ½ lb. sugar, ½ lb. S.R. flour, 2 eggs, 3 oz. currants.

Method.—Mix butter and sugar to a cream. Add currants, flavouring, then the flour. Mix with the eggs well beaten. Drop from spoon on buttered slide, and bake in hot oven about 10 minutes. — Mrs. D. Stribling, Brighton.

In an Electric Cooker bake at 400° 10 minutes.

Bake in Gas Cooker at 350° F.

VANILLA WAFERS

Four ounces cornflour, 4 oz. self-raising flour, 4 oz. butter, two eggs, 4 oz. sugar, and vanilla essence.

Beat butter and sugar to a cream. Add eggs (beaten), vanilla and flour. Roll out about an ⅛th in. cut into fingers, sprinkle with castor sugar, bake for few minutes. — M. Collett, Port Elliot.

In an Electric Cooker bake at 400° 10 minutes.

Bake in Gas Cooker 375° F.

VIENNA BISCUITS

One pound S.R. flour, ½ lb. sugar, ½ lb. butter, one egg, one dessertspoon cinnamon.

Rub butter into flour and sugar, mix with egg and a little milk. When cooked they can be split open (while hot), spread with jam and iced. Are nice plain.

Use two eggs. — V. A. Lushey.

In an Electric Cooker bake at 400° 12-15 minutes.

Bake in Gas Cooker at 350° F.

SHORTBREAD

One pound flour, ½ lb. butter, ¼ lb. sugar.

Directions.—Place all ingredients on paste board and gradually work in. Cook in moderate oven. — Mrs. Campbell, Brisbane.

Add one teaspoon cream tartar, half teaspoon carbonate soda. — Mrs. Stanley Haskard, Jamestown.

In Electric Cooker bake at 350°.

Bake in Gas Cooker at 325° F.

ROLLED OATS SHORTBREAD

Five ounces sugar, 6 ozs. butter, 10 ozs. rolled oats, vanilla.

Press together on butter paper in small meat dish, and mark into squares. — J.M.A.

In an Electric Cooker bake at 400°.

1 lb. flour, ½ lb. butter, 3 tablespoons crushed sugar rubbed in. Roll and bake in moderate oven.

— Mrs. Murray Anderson, Hawthorn.

In an Electric Cooker bake at 350°.
Bake in Gas Cooker at 350° F.

SHORTBREAD SANDWICH

Half pound S.R. flour, ¼ lb. butter, ¼ lb. sugar, two eggs, essence lemon. Beat butter, sugar and flour together till like bread crumbs, add lemon and eggs beaten, work to a stiff paste with hands, divide into 4 pieces. Have two tins ready, well buttered, roll out thinly, lay on tins, spread with jam, cover with remaining piece, trim edges, brush with beaten egg, sprinkle with almonds. When cold cut into squares. — F. Jackman, Royston Park.

In an Electric Cooker bake at 350°.
Bake in Gas Cooker at 325° F.

SCOTTISH SHORTBREAD

One lb. butter, 1½ lb. plain flour, ¼ lb. rice flour, ½ lb. castor sugar.

Mix the ingredients together until the dough is smooth. Break pieces off. Knead into flat cakes. Prick with a fork. Place on greased paper, and bake half hour in moderate oven.

— Mrs. M. A. Luck, Croydon Park.

In an Electric Cooker bake at 350°.

Two pounds flour, 1 lb. butter, ½ lb. sugar, one egg.

Cream butter, sugar and egg together, and then knead in flour with the wrists. Bake half an hour in moderate oven. Make in flat cakes, pinch the edges, and prick all over. Decorate.

In an Electric Cooker bake at 350°.
Bake in Gas Cooker at 325° F.

VIENNESE TARTLETS

Beat 4 oz. butter until slightly creamy. Add 3 oz. castor sugar, ½ lb. flour, a few drops of vanilla, and a pinch of salt. Add the beaten yolk of one egg, and beat to a soft paste. Well grease patty pans. Fill three parts with the mixture; rough it with a fork, make a little dent in centre of each. Bake in moderate oven to pale biscuit tint. Remove from tins when cold. Put dot of jam on each. — S. R. Smith, Congregational Manse, Kadina.

In an Electric Cooker bake at 400° 15 minutes.
Bake in Gas Cooker at 350° F.

BREAD, SCONES, ROLLS

BREAD, SCONES, ROLLS

BILLY LOAF

One cup wholemeal, one cup plain flour, one teaspoon cream tartar, half teaspoon carb. soda, one tablespoon sugar (if liked sweet), one tablespoon treacle in cup milk.

Mix as for scones, making a wet dough. Bake in greased nut-loaf tins (with the lids on) for about one hour in hot oven.

— Mrs. M. A. Luck, Croydon Park.

In an Electric Cooker bake at 400°.
Bake in Gas Cooker at 400° F.

BROWNIES

Four cups wheatmeal, 2 teaspoons cream tartar, 1 teaspoon soda, 1 teaspoon salt, 4 or more tablespoons golden syrup, 2 cups milk.

Mix. Half fill greased nut-loaf tins. Place lids on, bake in hot oven 1½ hours.

— L. Good, Unley Park.

In an Electric Cooker bake at 400°.
Bake in Gas Cooker at 350° F.

BREAD

Two pounds of flour, one teaspoon of salt, half a pint of milk, and half a pint of water (fairly warm).

Make hole in middle of flour and pour in about half a cup of yeast. Mix with hot milk and water. Knead well until spongy. Cover and wrap warmly, and set to rise overnight. When risen, knead lightly into loaves and about half fill the tins. Put to rise in warm place about one or two hours. Bake in oven.

In an Electric Cooker bake at 525°. Put in bread and reset at 450°.

Bake in Gas Cooker at 400° F.

TEA BUNS

Use the above mixture with the addition of sugar.

In Electric Cooker bake at 450°.
Bake in Gas Cooker at 400° F.

YEAST BUNS

Add raisins, currants, etc., to the above mixture.

In an Electric Cooker bake as for Tea Buns.
Bake in Gas Cooker at 375° F. Regulo & Adjusto Setting No. 5.

NUT BREAD

Two and a half cups S.R. flour, one small cup brown sugar, **nearly a cup of milk, one egg, ½ lb. chopped walnuts.**

Beat sugar and egg five minutes. Add milk, flour and nuts. Bake half an hour in closed (greased) tins in hot oven.

—M.B., St. Peters. —M. Thiem.

In Electric Cooker bake at 400°.
Bake in Gas Cooker at 400° F.

NUT BREAD

Two cups of flour (self-raising), one cup milk, half cup sugar, one egg, piece of butter size of walnut, 12 almonds or 16 walnuts chopped finely.

Cream sugar and butter, add beaten egg, then milk, flour and nuts. Grease tins and only half fill them and bake in hot oven for one hour. — M. Wilks.

In an Electric Cooker bake at 400°, top off, bottom low $\frac{3}{4}$ hour.

Two cups self-raising flour, half cup sugar, three-quarters cup chopped walnuts or other nuts, or sultanas, one egg, one tablespoon butter, pinch of salt.

Rub butter into dry ingredients, and egg beaten with milk. Bake in nut-loaf tins in hot oven for three-quarters of an hour. This quantity makes two.

Use one cup sugar and omit butter.

In Electric Cooker bake at 400°.

Take two cups of flour, two teaspoons of baking powder, half a cup of sugar, one egg, half a cup of nuts chopped finely, a pinch of salt, a small cup of milk.

Mix all well together. Let rise for 20 minutes in warm place, then bake in slow oven. This is delicious served in thin slices with butter for afternoon tea. — M. Miller, Renmark.

In Electric Cooker bake at 400°.
Bake in Gas Cooker at 400° F.

MALT BREAD

Half lb. S.R. flour, 1 egg, 1 tablespoon extract malt, little milk.

Mix the beaten egg with malt, and add milk. Then mix with flour to consistency of fairly soft scone. Half fill nut-loaf tin which has been greased. Put on lid, bake for 50 minutes. — M.A.

In an Electric Cooker bake at 400°.
Bake in Gas Cooker at 400° F.

One cup of self-raising flour, one cup wholemeal, one dessert-spoon treacle, a pinch of salt, a little milk (half a cup).

Bake in a deep tin, with lid greased, for one hour. — R. Scott.

In an Electric Cooker bake at 400°.

WALNUT LOAF

Half lb. walnuts shelled and cut up. Beat one egg, one table-spoon sugar, one tablespoon of golden syrup, pinch salt, and half cup milk together, then add nuts, and lastly two cups of S.R. flour. Put into two well-greased loaf tins and cook from half to three-quarters of an hour. — E. Dobbie, Kadina.

In an Electric Cooker bake at 400°.
Bake in Gas Cooker at 400° F.

WAR BREAD

Three cups wholemeal S.R. flour, one teaspoon salt, one tablespoon treacle dissolved in three-quarter cup of hot water, three-quarters cup milk. Butter a tin and half fill with mixture.

— Mrs. A. S. Adamson, Unley.

In an Electric Cooker bake at 400°.
Bake in Gas Cooker at 400° F.

WHOLEMEAL NUT BREAD

One packet wholemeal S.R. flour, 2 tablespoons treacle, 1 teaspoon salt, 2 large cups milk; 1 egg can be added; nuts to taste.

Mix thin; put in well-greased tin with lid. Bake in hot oven for three-quarters of an hour. — Mrs. G. McRitchie.

In an Electric Cooker bake at 400°.
Bake in Gas Cooker at 400° F.

SCONES

Half pound S.R. flour, one pinch salt, one teaspoon butter, quarter pint milk.

Sift flour and salt. Rub in butter with tips of fingers. Mix to a soft dough. Knead and roll out 1 in. thick. Cut, put on a floured slide, glaze and bake in a very hot oven for eight to ten minutes.

In an Electric Cooker bake at 550°.
Bake in Gas Cooker at 450° F.

CHEESE SCONES

A cup and a half flour, 2 oz. grated cheese, butter the size of a walnut, half teaspoon carbonate soda, one teaspoon cream of tartar, one egg and milk. Mix and roll out in the usual way.

— Miss D. Cochrane, Auburn, Victoria.

In an Electric Cooker bake at 550° 7-8 minutes.
Bake in Gas Cooker at 450° F.

DROP SCONES

One egg, 1 scant cup of S.R. flour, ¼ cup milk, 2 oz. sugar.

Beat egg well with sugar. Add milk. Sift flour into a basin. Add egg and milk gradually to the flour. Heat gem trays and grease them. Put a teaspoon of mixture in each. Bake in hot oven for 10 minutes. — Miss Ruth Stacy.

One heaped cup of flour, one egg, one cup of milk, one-quarter teaspoon salt, half teaspoon carbonate of soda, one-quarter teaspoon tartaric acid, two teaspoons sugar.

Method.—Sift flour, salt, carb. soda, acid and sugar into a basin. Mix with the milk and take up in spoonful and drop on to a hot greased griddle. When cooked one side turn over (if possible use one cup buttermilk instead of an egg).

In an Electric Cooker bake at 500°.
Bake in Gas Cooker at 425° F.

COUNTRY SCONES (Very Good)

Two ounces butter, ¾ lb. of flour, two teaspoons of baking powder, 1½ oz. castor sugar, 1½ oz. sultanas, half pint sour milk (juice small lemon will curdle milk), two eggs.

Method.—Sift flour and powder. Add sugar and butter, mixing well. Add sultanas. Mix with egg and milk. Make about eight large-sized scones or little round ones. The large size bake for 10 to 15 minutes; small size, eight minutes. — A.G.A.

In an Electric Cooker bake at 550°.
Bake in Gas Cooker at 450° F.

EDINBURGH SCONES

One pound flour, three teaspoons baking powder, quarter teaspoon salt, 1 oz. butter, 1 oz. castor sugar, 1 oz. lard, 1½ oz. currants (if liked), one egg, half pint milk or buttermilk.

Mix salt, flour, baking powder, etc. Beat egg and add milk. Mix to rather wet dough. Form into rough cakes and bake for about 20 minutes. — E. F. Benskin.

In an Electric Cooker bake at 550°.
Bake in Gas Cooker at 450° F.

GEM SCONES

Two tablespoons butter, two tablespoons castor sugar, two eggs, 7 oz. flour (self-raising), enough milk to make mixture like a thick cream.

Have gem irons very hot. Put piece of butter size of pea in each iron cup. Oven must be very hot. Bake for six minutes.
— A.G.A.

One and a half cups S.R. flour, one egg, one tablespoon butter, one tablespoon sugar, one cup milk, and pinch salt.

Method.—Mix butter and sugar to a cream, pour milk into whipped egg and mix all well together. Use gem scone trays very hot and almost fill with mixture.

— A. G. Vandepeer, "Waringa," Ardrossan.
— Mrs. Cockington.

In an Electric Cooker bake at 500°.
Bake in Gas Cooker at 425° F.

FRIED SCONES

Useful when short of bread and a substitute needed in a hurry.

Mix two cups S.R. flour with one cup of milk (the mixture should then be just thin enough to drop from the spoon nicely). Drop tablespoonful into deep hot fat and fry for a few moments. Turn if fat is not deep enough to cover. These quantities should make enough for five. They are nice fried in bacon fat and served with bacon, but are delicious if fried in lard or good dripping, drained well, and eaten with honey or maple syrup and butter.

FRUIT SCONES

Half pound S.R. flour, one pinch salt, 1 oz. butter, 1 or 2 oz. sugar, 2 oz. currants, sultanas or dates, 1 egg, less than ½ pint milk

Sift flour and salt. Rub in butter. Add fruit and sugar. Mix with egg and milk. Knead well, roll out 1 in. thick. Cut out and put on a prepared slide, glaze and bake in a hot oven.

In an Electric Cooker bake at 550°.
Bake in Gas Cooker at 450° F.

BREAKFAST ROLLS

Make the dough used for bread into small balls and set to rise for a few minutes. Bake in oven for about 10 or 15 minutes. These are much improved by adding a little butter to milk and a beaten egg when adding the yeast.

In an Electric Cooker bake at 450°.
Bake in Gas Cooker at 375° F.

MILK ROLLS

Two ounces butter, 1 lb. S.R. flour, half pint milk, pinch salt.

Mix into dough. Make into small pieces. Brush over with milk. Bake about 15 minutes. Brush over again just before taking out from oven. — M. Higginbottom.

In an Electric Cooker bake at 550°.
Bake in Gas Cooker at 425° F.

COFFEE ROLLS

Two oz. butter, 2 oz. sugar, 1 egg, 1 cup milk, 1 lb. S.R. flour

Rub the butter into the sugar and flour, add egg well beaten. Stir in gradually the flour and the milk. Roll out, cut in rounds, fold each round over and bake in hot oven for about 10 minutes.
— Mrs. Thatcher.

Use 3 oz. butter. — E. Lane. — Miss R. Burke, Maitland.

In an Electric Cooker bake at 525°.
Bake in Gas Cooker at 425° F.

TEA CAKE OR FLUFFY SCONE

Rub one tablespoon of butter into two cups of self-raising flour, add a pinch of salt and one tablespoon of sugar and mix in the flour. Beat up one egg, add to it one cup of milk, stir together and mix in flour, etc. Pour the mixture into a well-buttered tin (a sandwich tin or tin plate) and bake from 20 to 25 or even 30 minutes in the same heat as for scones.

The mixture is rather thin when you put it in the oven. It is a nice brown when cooked.

In an Electric Cooker bake at 500°.
Bake in Gas Cooker at 425° F.

SAVOURIES

FILLINGS FOR SANDWICHES

SAVOURIES

CHEESE BISCUITS

Four ounces flour, one pinch salt, half teaspoon baking powder, 2 oz. butter, 2 oz. grated cheese, half teaspoon dry mustard, squeeze lemon juice, one pinch cayenne, yolk of one egg.

Sift flour, salt and powder. Rub in butter. Add cheese, mustard, cayenne and lemon juice. Moisten with egg yolk and a little water. Roll out and cut in rounds. Bake in a hot oven for 10 to 15 minutes.

In an Electric Cooker bake at 400°.

Bake in Gas Cooker at 350°F.

CHEESE STRAWS

Six ounces flour, one pinch salt, one pinch cayenne, 4 oz. butter, 4 oz. grated cheese, yolk of egg, a little water.

Rub butter into flour. Add the cheese and seasoning. Make into a stiff paste and work till free from cracks. Roll out thinly on a floured board. Cut in strips 4 in. by $\frac{1}{4}$ in. Roll out trimmings, and cut 10 or 12 rings. Put on a greased tin and bake in a hot oven till a pale brown. Put five or six straws in each ring, and serve on a paper doyley on a dish.

In an Electric Cooker bake at 400°.

Bake in Gas Cooker at 350° F.

ITALIAN RISSOLES

Half pound rice, 3 tablespoons chopped onion, 1 oz. butter, $1\frac{1}{2}$ pints stock or milk, 4 oz. grated Parmesan cheese.

Brown the onion in the butter, add rice and boiling stock. Stew for 40 minutes, season with salt and pepper, then add grated cheese and a tablespoon butter. Mix well; serve very hot.

— Miss Gwen Scammell.

MACARONI CHEESE

Four ounces macaroni, half teaspoon salt, 3 oz. grated cheese, half pint milk, 1 oz. butter, 1 oz. (bare) flour, one pinch cayenne, half teaspoon made mustard, three large tomatoes.

Cook the macaroni in fast boiling salted water for 20 minutes. Strain and put into a greased pie-dish. Melt the butter in a saucepan, stir in smoothly the flour. Add the milk gradually, and boil for three minutes. Stir in two-thirds of the cheese and the tomatoes (peeled and sliced thinly). Season well. Pour over the macaroni, sprinkle with remaining cheese, brown in oven.

OYSTER SAVOURY

One dozen oysters, put in saucepan in their own liquor, pepper and salt, 1 teaspoon butter, heat thoroughly but do not boil. Add 2 tablespoons very thick white sauce, and a little cream is a great improvement. Serve on slices fried bread.

— Mrs. R. J. Nosworthy, Killara, N.S.W.

SARDINE CANAPES, SAVOURY

Sardines, 1 teaspoon mustard, ½ teaspoon pepper, ½ teaspoon anchovy paste, ½ teaspoon French mustard, 1½ dessertspoons vinegar, fried croutons, small pinch cayenne, 3 oz. butter, yolks of 2 hard-boiled eggs.

Cut the sardines in two, split tails in half and take out bones; skin the top apart, and take out the bones also. Put in a bowl with the yolks of the eggs, mustard, French mustard, vinegar, anchovy paste, butter, and pound well, and pass through a wire sieve. Put a little of the mixture on each crouton, crimp round the edge with a knife dipped in cold water; put half a sardine on each one. Serve cold.

— Mrs. J. G. Thompson, Turramurra, N.S.W.

MACARONI CROQUETTES

One ounce well-cooked macaroni, ½ oz. grated cheese, cayenne pepper, salt, egg and bread crumbs for frying.

Ingredient for panada.—Half ounce flour and butter, half gill of milk, make same as white sauce.

Boil the macaroni and chop, make panada, and add the macaroni with the cheese. When the mixture is cool, add the yolk of eggs and let it stand to cool on the plate. Shape into pear-shaped forms, egg and crumb, and fry in deep fat. Put little fine pices of macaroni at each end and garnish with parsley.

CHEESE SOUFFLE

Beat two eggs, whites and yolks separately. Add to the yolks 2 oz. grated cheese, 1 oz. flour, a cup of milk, pepper and salt to taste. Mix well, then add stifly-beaten whites of eggs. Pour into buttered pie-dish, and bake in hot oven till golden brown—about 30 minutes. Serve immediately.

In an Electric Cooker bake at 375°.

Bake in Gas Cooker at 350° F.

ANCHOVY AND EGG

Cut a round of bread and butter, place on it a slice of hard-boiled egg, then an anchovy and piece of parsley.

— Mrs. J. G. Thompson, Turramurra, N.S.W.

SALTED ALMONDS

Quarter pound almonds, half tablespoon salad oil or clarified butter, fine salt.

Blanch and dry almonds, and place in a clean baking tin with the fat. Put in a moderate oven. Turn frequently till a pale brown. Turn on to kitchen paper and sprinkle liberally with salt. When cold, shake off loose salt. Keep air-tight.

Any nuts may be done this way. — A. Sharman.

PARMESAN CROUTES

Fried Croutons, ½ pint cream, 1 dessertspoon Worcester sauce, 1½ ozs. grated parmesan cheese, little salt; dust cayenne pepper, minced parsley, tomato.

Cut croutons out with a round cutter, fry in boiling fat. Whip cream, add Worcester sauce, cheese, salt and pepper. Stir gently together; put a slice of tomato on each crouton, then put the parmesan mixture roughly on with a fork. Sprinkle a little finely minced parsley over the top of each one; garnish with fresh parsley. Serve cold.

— Mrs. J. G. Thompson, Turramurra, N.S.W.

SARDINE SAVOURIES

One small tin sardines, 1 egg, salt and pepper to taste, 1 teaspoon finely chopped parsley, 3 dessertspoons milk.

Remove bones from sardines (back bone) and mash sardines. Flavour with pepper and salt, whip up eggs, add 3 dessertspoons milk, add parsley. Stir in mashed sardines. Use oil from sardines to grease dish for baking mixture. Bake in dish of water. When mixture is set, cut into squares and place them on buttered biscuits. — Mrs. O. F. Patison, Mosman, N.S.W.

CELERY AND NUT SAVOURIES

Ingredients.—Cheese pastry, 3 sticks celery, 3 tablespoons chopped walnuts.

Method.—1. Make the cheese straw pastry. Fit it into small patty tins. Press the pastry well on to the tins with the fingers, bake like biscuits.

2. Prepare the celery and cut into small dice, also cut the walnuts finely and mix the two together.

3. Put a little cream cheese into the bottom of each case, fill with celery and nuts and sprinkle with salt and pepper.

4. Decorate round the edge with cream cheese.

— Mrs. J. T. Sutcliffe, Bondi, N.S.W.

CHEESE SAVOURY

Yolks of 3 eggs (hard boiled), dessertspoon melted butter, 2 heaped tablespoons grated cheese, 3 dessertspoons tomato sauce; mix all to paste. Place one teaspoon of mixture on a buttered cheese biscuit.

Trim with parsley and strips of the whites of the eggs.

Mrs. O. F. Patison, Mosman, N.S.W.

SAVOURY RICE

Quarter pound rice, one pint boiling water, one pinch salt (good), 2 oz. grated cheese, one teaspoon chopped parsley, one teaspoon butter.

Cook the rice in the boiling water till soft. Add cheese, parsley and lemon rind. Put into a greased pie-dish; put butter on top and bake in oven till golden brown. Tomatoes may be added. Put alternate layers of rice and tomatoes in the dish.

CHEESE SAVOURY

Whip ½ cup cream, season with salt and cayenne. Mince 1 cup of crisp celery, add 2 oz. grated cheese, and mix with the cream.

Place one spoonful on a cheese biscuit, and decorate with a slice of stuffed olive. —Mrs. R. J. Nosworthy, Killara, N.S.W.

MUSHROOM SAVOURIES

Ingredients.—Small cases from puff pastry, small button mushrooms, 1 oz. butter, 1 oz. flour, ¾ cup mushroom liquid, 1 yolk of egg, salt and cayenne, 1 tablespoon cream.

Method.—Filling: 1. Prepare the mushrooms and put them to cook in a little milk from 10 to 15 minutes till quite tender. Drain off the liquid and make it up to ¾ cup with milk if necessary. Melt the butter, add flour, then the liquid, and boil.

2. Add salt and cayenne, also yolk of egg and cream. Reheat without boiling and return the mushrooms to it. Fill the cases with this mixture and serve hot or cold.

—Mrs. J. T. Sutcliffe, Bondi, N.S.W.

CHEESE AND CAPSICUM SAVOURY

One dessertspoon melted butter, ¼ teaspoon salt, pinch of cayenne pepper, 1 tablespoon plain flour, 1 dessertspoon sugar; mix well together; add 3 dessertspoons water and juice of 1 lemon. Bring to boiling point stirring constantly. Remove from fire, add 2 tablespoons grated cheese, 1½ tablespoons finely chopped capsicum. Mix all together. Add ½ tablespoon cream. Spread on cheese biscuits; trim with capsicum.

—Mrs. O. F. Patison, Mosman, N.S.W.

LOBSTER SAVOURY

Make a fairly stiff white sauce, add a little fresh cream, salt and pepper. Chop some cooked lobster or crayfish and mix with the white sauce, fill some boat-shaped cases of puff pastry, and decorate with parsley.

—Mrs. R. J. Nosworthy, Killara, N.S.W.

CHEESE SAVOURIES

One cup grated cheese, pinch cayenne pepper, dash of Worcestershire sauce, 1 egg, 1 tablespoon butter (melted).

Beat all together, spread thickly on thick slices of bread; then cut in finger lengths, put a piece of bacon on each. Bake on scone tray in a moderate oven for about half an hour until bread is quite crisp. Serve hot.

— Mrs. Harry Arbon, Clarence Park.

GHERKIN AND EGG

One dessertspoon melted butter, stir in 1 tablespoon flour and 1 pinch salt, 1 teaspoon sugar; add 1½ tablespoons milk, stir constantly till cooked. Remove from fire. Add whites of 2 finely chopped hard-boiled eggs. Add 4 finely chopped gherkins (small), juice of half lemon. Mix well together. Spread on biscuits and garnish with pieces of gherkin.

— Mrs. O. F. Patison, Mosman, N.S.W.

BOMBAY TOAST

One oz. butter, 2 eggs, 1 teaspoon anchovy essence, 10 chopped capers, cayenne pepper, small rounds of buttered toast.

Put butter in double saucepan and stir till it melts, then stir in the eggs and other ingredients and continue stirring until the mixture begins to set. Have ready some small rounds of hot buttered toast, spread the mixture on, and serve at once very hot.

— Mrs. R. H. Shorter, Warrawee, N.S.W.

HAM TOAST

Half lb. chopped lean ham cooked, ¾ oz. butter, 1 egg, pepper, slices of toast.

Melt the butter in a saucepan, add ham and pepper, and when this is hot add the well-beaten egg, stir until it sets lightly, then spread on slices of hot buttered toast, and serve. Care must be taken that the egg does not harden too much.

— Mrs. R. H. Shorter, Warrawee, N.S.W.

DAVENTRY TOAST

Ingredients.—Six rounds of toasted or fried bread, 6 olives, 1 dessertspoon anchovy paste, 1 dessertspoon butter, 1 hard-boiled egg, 1 teaspoon lemon juice, cayenne.

Method.—1. Toast the bread and cut into rounds, or cut the rounds of bread and fry them in a little butter till a golden brown.

2. Mix the anchovy paste, butter, yolk of egg, lemon juice and cayenne into a paste

3. Stone the olives and fill them with some of the paste.

4. Pipe a rose of paste on each croute and stand an olive in the centre of the rose.

5. Decorate with small shreds of white of egg. Serve as a cold savoury.

— Mrs. J. T. Sutcliffe, Bondi, N.S.W.

EGG SAVOURY

Boil hard six eggs, peel while hot, cut in halves. Remove yolks carefully (do not break whites). Place yolks in bowl and crumb with fork. Add tablespoon melted butter; flavour with salt and pepper; 1 heaped teaspoon curry powder. Mix all to paste. Should mixture be too dry, bind with little cream. Then put this mixture into the whites of eggs.

Fry in butter small squares of bread to golden brown. Place half of egg on each square.

Trim with small pieces of parsley, and place a dice of red capsicum in centre of egg.

—Mrs. O. F. Patison, Mosman, N.S.W.

TOMATO AND EGG

On a round cheese biscuit place a slice of tomato and pile upon this some hard-boiled egg—which has been mashed with a fork, and decorate with capers.

—Mrs. R. J. Nosworthy, Killara, N.S.W.

ASPARAGUS LOGS

Ingredients.—Pastry.—Mix the flour, cheese and salt, rub in the butter, and mix into a dough with the water.

Two oz. flour, ¼ teaspoon salt, 1 teaspoon grated cheese, 1 teaspoon butter, cayenne, water, some cooked asparagus, egg, bread crumbs.

Methods.—1. Roll the pastry very thinly, and cut into pieces one inch by three inches.

2. Brush with egg and sprinkle with cheese, salt and cayenne. Place piece of asparagus on each.

3. Roll pastry round asparagus.

4. Dip in flour, egg and bread crumbs, then fry. Serve either hot or cold.

ANCHOVY PUREE

Ingredients.—1 dessertspoon Anchovy paste, 1 hard-boiled egg, squeeze lemon juice, 1 oz. butter.

Method.—1. Blend yolk and anchovy paste together. Add the butter, cayenne and lemon juice and beat into a very smooth paste.

2. This may be made ready and put away for use. Keep in a cool place. —Mrs. J. T. Sutcliffe, Bondi, N.S.W.

SALT STICK

Make a stiff dough of flour, water, and a little butter, salt to taste. Roll to required size with the hand. Bake in a hot oven till pale brown.

—Mrs. J. A. Haslam, King's College, Kensington Park.

In an Electric Cooker bake at 425° 15 minutes.
Bake in Gas Cooker at 350° F.

DEVILLED ALMONDS

Prepare as for salted almonds, using cayenne pepper as well as salt. Devilled almonds should be served hot.

SPAGHETTI

Five large tomatoes, skin and place in a saucepan with dessertspoonful butter, pepper and salt, cook till mashed small.

In another saucepan boil until tender (about 20 minutes) one large cup macaroni in salted water, drain and mix with tomatoes, add one large saucer grated cheese and a little cayenne pepper.

Serve very hot on toast, if liked.

WELSH RAREBIT

Into a cold pan put half a pound of cheese, cut up rather fine, and good-sized lump butter, and one teacup milk in which two level teaspoons maizena have been mixed. Set over fire and stir as the mixture begins to cook. Put in a little salt just before taking from the fire. Made in this way you will have a delicious Welsh rarebit with no lumps in it. — M. McRae.

AN ATTRACTIVE CHEESE SAVOURY

Spread a large cheese biscuit lightly with butter, and place on it a thin slice of cheese cut out with a small, round, fluted cutter. Whip up three tablespoons of cream, seasoned with salt, cayenne and celery salt, and place in a forcing bag. Force a rose of cream on to the cheese and decorate with thin strips of chilli and tiny sprigs of parsley.

BENGAL SAVOURY

Quarter lb. ham, 3 tablespoons cream, 1 tablespoon grated cheese, pinch cayenne, little chutney, cheese biscuits (large).

Chop the ham very finely, mix with the cream, spread the cheese biscuits with this, then a layer of chutney on top of the ham. Sprinkle lightly with the grated cheese, then a little paprika or finely chopped parsley. Place in oven for a few minutes to heat before serving.

CHEESE AND MAYONNAISE SANDWICH

Two hard-boiled eggs, 1 tablespoon melted butter, ¼ lb. dry cheese (grated), teaspoon made mustard, ¼ teaspoon salt, 1 tablespoon vinegar, little cayenne.

Mix the hard-boiled yolks of eggs in basin till smooth. Add the grated cheese and the mustard; mix thoroughly; stir in the vinegar, salt and cayenne to taste; spread mixture between biscuits.

FILLINGS FOR SANDWICHES

ANCHOVY PASTE

Cut up ½ lb. ham and 1 lb. beefsteak (free from fat and gristle), ¼ lb. butter, two tablespoons anchovy sauce, one teaspoon salt, one-quarter each of cayenne and white pepper and ground mace. Put all together into an enamelled can and stand in boiling water; boil for six hours. Take from the fire and beat with a fork; put through mincer twice while hot. Anchovy sauce and mace may be omitted. — Mrs. Chas. Coote, Port Elliot.

BLOATER PASTE

Six red herrings, ¼ lb. butter, two tablespoons of cream, half teaspoon cayenne pepper.

Mince herrings and boil all together for 15 minutes.

— Anonymous.
— J.C.C.

CHEESE AND ASPARAGUS SANDWICHES

Mix some grated cheese with sufficient butter to form a paste; season it with salt, pepper, a little curry powder and two or three drops of vinegar. Spread it rather thickly on to buttered bread, and on the top put a layer of small cooked asparagus heads. If these are not procurable, some coarsely chopped beetroot, lightly seasoned with oil and vinegar, will be found very nice.

EGG AND CHEESE SANDWICHES

Pass a hard-boiled egg through a sieve or gravy strainer into a bowl and add a large teaspoon of butter, a heaped tablespoon of grated cheese and some salt and pepper. Beat the mixture until it is soft and creamy, spread on buttered bread, and put some thin slices of cucumber, if liked, between before closing the sandwiches.

FEDERAL CHEESE

Half pound cheese, two tablespoons cream, one tablespoon butter, one teaspoon mixed mustard, one teaspoon salt, cayenne to taste.

Put cheese through the mincer. Put all into double saucepan. Boil 15 minutes (stirring). — J.M.A.

FRENCH CHEESE

One pound tomatoes, 2 oz. grated cheese, one egg, a few bread crumbs, thyme, salt, 1 oz. butter.

Method.—(1) Skin the tomatoes, slice and fry them in butter. (2) Strain off the liquor and add to the pulp the cheese, thyme and salt. (3) Fry all together for a few minutes till cheese is cooked. Add well-beaten egg and cook till pan is left clear. If not thick enough, add the bread crumbs or a second egg. (4) Serve on toast or, when cold, use for sandwiches.

— E.M.D.

Two ounces cheese, one egg, one teaspoon butter, two teaspoons thyme, two tablespoons tomato sauce, and pinch of cayenne pepper.

Method.—Shred cheese very small, beat up egg, and other ingredients in order given. Put all in saucepan and stir over fire until dissolved to a paste. — Miss E. Hill, St. Peters.

MAYONNAISE FOR SANDWICHES

Yolks of two eggs, one tablespoon flour, 1½ tablespoons sugar, one teaspoon mustard, few grains cayenne pepper, a little salt, 1½ tablespoons melted butter, and three-quarters of a cup of milk.

Mix dry ingredients and add yolks only slightly beaten, butter and milk and a quarter cup of white wine vinegar. Cook very slowly until it thickens.

MEAT SAVOURY

One pound mutton (lean only to be used), two level teaspoons salt, one-half level teaspoon pepper, one teaspoon nutmeg (grated).

Method.—Cut meat up into small pieces about 1½ in., sprinkle with ingredients, put into a jug or small billycan (something with a lid is advisable). Stand this in a saucepan of cold water and boil until quite tender. When cool pass through a fine mincer and use with bread and butter as a savoury.

— Miss R. Burke, Maitland.
— M. F. Holmes, Pinnaroo.

POTTED MEAT PASTE

One pound topside beef, ¼ lb. butter, two tablespoons anchovy sauce, one teaspoon salt, quarter teaspoon cayenne pepper, nutmeg to taste.

Boil four hours. Leave jar uncovered. Lid on pan. When cooked, stir into a paste. Will keep about a week.

— Mrs. H. R. Adamson.

MINCE FOR SANDWICHES

One pound steak, one tablespoon Worcestershire sauce, nutmeg to taste, $\frac{1}{4}$ lb. butter, one teaspoon pepper, two teaspoons salt.

Cut the meat into squares and put into a jar with the other ingredients. Cover and stand in a saucepan of boiling water. Cook for four hours. Take out meat, mince and mix well with its own gravy. Put in jars, pour over melted butter, and cover.

Anchovy sauce may be used instead of Worcestershire.

— Miss J. Colliver.

SCRAMBLED EGG SANDWICHES

Beat a new-laid egg until it becomes a thick, frothy mass, and pour it into a small saucepan containing about a dessertspoon of melted butter, season it with pepper and a little nutmeg, and flavour with dessertspoon of grated cheese, a teaspoon or two of tomato sauce or a few drops of anchovy essence, and stir until the egg is cooked, taking care to remove it from the stove while it is still creamy without being too soft. When cold, spread on buttered bread and make into sandwiches.

SUGGESTIONS FOR SANDWICHES

Slice thinly and butter white or brown bread. Fill with any of the following:—

Celery and cheese.

Chopped boiled bacon and eggs, green peppers.

Lettuce, chopped apple and nuts.

Dates and peanuts or almonds.

Chopped corn beef, celery and gherkins.

Chopped dates and cream cheese.

Chopped ham and raisins.

Chopped pineapple, cream cheese and nuts.

Chopped tongue and horseradish.

Peanut butter and ginger.

Sardines, chopped egg and mayonnaise.

Salmon, celery and mayonnaise.

German sausage and capers.

— Mrs. A. C. Hill, Killara, N.S.W.

SANDWICH FILLINGS

CHOCOLATE CREAM.—Equal quantities of whipped cream and chocolate powder mixed with a few drops of vanilla essence and spread between slices of bread.

HONEY AND WALNUT.—Pound shelled walnuts together with sufficient honey to make a smooth paste, and spread on bread and butter.

BANANA CREAM SANDWICHES.—Take 3 bananas, 2 tablespoons apple or raspberry jelly, a few drops lemon juice, and some white and brown bread. Thinly slice the bread and butter it, mash the bananas with the jelly and lemon juice. For each sandwich take a slice of white bread and one of brown, spread the mixture between, and press together.

KIPPER AND EGG.—Mash together some raw kipper and minced hard-boiled egg, and spread on bread and butter.

APPLE AND CELERY.—Peel, core, and chop two apples, wash and chop four sticks celery; mix them with two tablespoons of mayonnaise sauce, and spread on thin bread and butter.

CREAM CHEESE AND BANANA.—Slice some bananas, cover with mayonnaise, and place between slices of bread spread with cream cheese.

CHOCOLATE AND GINGER.—Grate a bar of chocolate, mix with grated preserved ginger and a little cream, also a squeeze of lemon juice, and spread between thin slices of buttered bread.

MOCK CRAB.—Skin two tomatoes and pound together with a chopped hard-boiled egg and 2 oz. of grated cheese. When a smooth paste, add half teaspoon of made mustard and a teaspoon of vegetable extract.

HAM AND HORSERADISH.—Add 1 tablespoon of pickled horseradish to 2 tablespoons of well-creamed butter. Mix well and spread on bread. Lay thin slivers of cold boiled ham between two slices of bread.

COOKED FISH.—Flaked and mixed with lemon juice.

GRATED CARROTS.—Mixed with a very little salt and sugar.

MEAT EXTRACT.—Mixed with a little of the beaten butter.

ONE HARD-BOILED EGG.—Chopped finely and mixed with one tomato, skinned and beaten to a pulp with a fork, then seasoned to taste.

POUNDED SARDINES.—Mixed with chopped hard-boiled egg.

POUNDED SARDINES.—Mixed with a little lemon juice and a few chopped hazel nuts.

CREAM CHEESE.—Beaten with finely-chopped walnuts.

GROUND ALMONDS.—Beaten with the butter.

GRATED APPLES and chopped nuts beaten with the butter.

BANANAS squashed with a fork and mixed with lemon juice.

CHOPPED DATES, figs or raisins.

SANDWICHES FOR SCHOOL LUNCHEONS

Wholemeal bread, cut thinly and buttered; fill with chopped nuts and chopped parsley.

Brown bread, buttered and filled with chopped nuts, banana, and a little chopped dried apricot.

White bread and butter filled with a little salmon beaten up with tomato pulp, and on this slices of cucumber which have lain a moment in vinegar. — Mrs. Walter E. Mounster.

DRINKS

DRINKS

LEMONADE

One gallon of water, three lemons cut in halves. Boil lemons in water, and while boiling add one pound of sugar and stir till dissolved. Pour over two teaspoons of cream tartar. Stir well. When cold bottle and cork tightly. Keep for two weeks, then ready for drinking. — W. H. Chard.

BOSTON CREAM

Two cups sugar, four cups water, one ounce tartaric acid, one teaspoon essence lemon, the white of one egg.

Dissolve sugar in hot water, and when cold add acid and essence of lemon and the white of egg beaten stiffly. Put a small quantity in glass, add cold water, and stir in a quarter teaspoon of carbonate soda. — Mrs. Thatcher.

CHILLI WINE

Two small cups white sugar, one heaped teaspoon citric acid, 14 chillies, one dessertspoon essence of lemon.

Put in a large dish and pour on two quarts boiling water. Add a little burnt sugar to give it colour. Essence of lemon and burnt sugar to be added when nearly cold.

— Mrs. J. A. Haslam, King's College, Kensington Park.

GINGER ALE SYRUP

Four pounds sugar, 2 oz. white ginger, one tablespoon cream tartar, one teaspoon citric acid, about 36 bird's eye chillies, two quarts water.

Boil all together for 20 minutes and colour with burnt sugar.

GINGERETTE

Two teaspoons essence of lemon, three teaspoons essence of ginger, three teaspoons essence of citric acid, 1¼ lb. of sugar.

Put all ingredients into a basin and pour on one pint of boiling water. Stir till all is dissolved, then bottle. Put two tablespoons of gingerette in a tumbler of water or soda water.

— N. Newman, Wayville.

HOP BEER

One kerosene tin of water, 3 lb. sugar, quarter packet of hops, 2 oz. whole ginger, half cup of clean wheat.

Boil all together for 15 minutes, then stand till cold. Bottle and leave standing for 24 hours, then cork and tie down corks.

— Anonymous.

HOME-MADE HOP BEER

Quarter pound hops, 4 oz. raisins, ¼ lb. ginger, 4 oz. wheat, 4 lb. sugar, four gallons water.

Boil all together for about one hour. Strain until cool. Add beaten whites of two eggs. Stand for 12 hours. Bottle and cork well.

PINEAPPLE LEMONADE

Take a tin of pineapple, cut in small pieces, and turn into a bowl with own juice and that of four lemons. Pour over two and a half quarts boiling water with sugar sufficient to sweeten. Cover vessel tightly, and in three hours strain, it is then ready for use. — Miss B. Skewes, Victor Harbour.

RASPBERRY BALM

Two cups sugar, four cups water (to be boiled). Remove from fire and add acid crystals to taste. When cold add essence of raspberry and roseine colouring, and just a little vinegar.

— Miss E. Norman.

RASPBERRY SYRUP

Two pounds raspberries (mashed), one pint water. Let it remain till next day, then drain through bag, and to every pint of juice add one pound sugar and half teaspoon tartaric acid. Boil 20 minutes. Add quarter cup of vinegar just before removing from fire. Serve diluted with water.

— Mrs. A. S. Adamson, Unley.

OATMEAL DRINK
ALSO SUITABLE FOR INVALIDS

One ounce oatmeal, ½ lemon, 1 quart water, 1½ ozs. sugar.

Mix the oatmeal to a thin, smooth batter with cold water. Add the thinly peeled lemon rind and the strained juice. Boil together the sugar and the water, then pour it over the batter, stirring all the time. Leave till cold, then strain and serve.

— A. L. Sharman, Black Forest.

LEMON SYRUP

Six pounds of sugar into one gallon of water, with the white of an egg. Boil for one hour. Mix a little of it in a jug with a quarter pound of citric acid and 45 drops of essence of lemon. Mix together, stand till cold, then boil and bottle.

— Mrs. J. E. Creswell, College Park.

Two pounds sugar, three teaspoons tartaric acid, one teaspoon and a half cream of tartar, one quart water.

Boil for 20 minutes, and when cool add one teaspoon essence of lemon, and bottle when cold. — D. Pearson.

Two pounds sugar, two ounces citric acid, one quart boiling water, two teaspoons essence of lemon.

Mix acid, sugar and essence in a bowl, and pour on boiling water. Bottle when cool. — Mrs. T. C. Sharman, Black Forest.

Six pounds sugar dissolved in 6 pints warm to hot water. When cold add 2 oz. tartaric acid, 1 dessertspoon of essence of lemon; bottle.

LEMON SQUASH

Two lb. of sugar, 1 oz. citric acid crystals, 1 large dessertspoon epsom salts. Pour over these 1½ pints boiling water; when cool add grated rind of 2 lemons (or oranges) and juice of six. Bottle; will keep for some time.

RASPBERRY VINEGAR

Six pounds sugar, six pints water, one bottle vinegar. Boil till sugar is dissolved. When cool, add one bottle raspberry essence and enough cochineal to colour nicely. This makes about six bottles. — Mrs. F. W. Roediger, "Riverside," Gawler.

One quart of boiling water, over six pounds sugar, one dessertspoon tartaric acid, one bottle cochineal, one bottle essence raspberry, one pint vinegar.

Stir all together, then add another quart of boiling water.

— Mrs. J. F. Farrow, Tea Tree Gully.

Nine pounds raspberries to half gallon vinegar. Let them stand two or three days, then strain. To every pint of juice add a pound and a half of sugar. Let it just come to boil, bottle, but do not cork till cool.

—Mrs. J. A. Haslam, King's College, Kensington Park.

Boil a pound and a half sugar with one pint of water for five minutes. When cool add two small cups vinegar, three teaspoons essence of raspberry, and one teaspoon cochineal. Strain and bottle. This quantity makes two large bottles.

— Mrs. Stanley Haskard, Jamestown.

Three-quarters bottle brown vinegar, two quarts water, 2½ lb. sugar, one bottle raspberry essence, one bottle cochineal.

Boil the sugar, water and vinegar for one hour. When cold, add the essence and cochineal. Stir well and bottle.

— Miss E. Cooper, Farrell's Flat.

PASSION FRUIT DRINK

Nine passion fruit, 2 teaspoons citric acid, 2 cups sugar, 2 cups water.

Method.—Bring to boil sugar and water. While boiling pour over passion fruit pulp and acid; stir well, let stand till cold. Strain and bottle. Use as cordial.

— Mrs. Harry Arbon, Clarence Park.

LEMON CORDIAL

Juice of 6 lemons, 5 cups water, rind of 4 lemons, 2 lbs. sugar, 1 oz. citric acid.

Put water, sugar, acid and rind in saucepan and bring to the boil. Take off and add juice. If preferred, this may be strained.

— M.B.

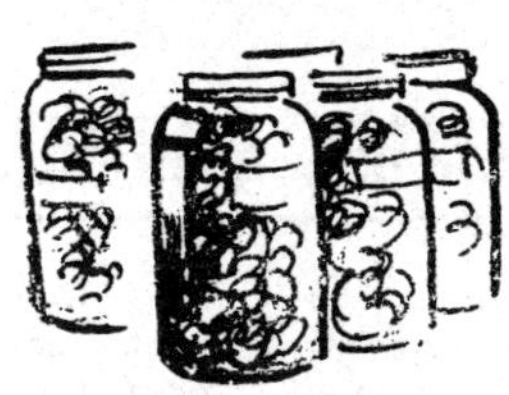

JAMS, JELLIES, MARMALADES

PRESERVES

JAMS, JELLIES, MARMALADES

The fruit should be firm and sound. Over-ripe fruit will not set; it is apt to candy, ferment, or go mouldy, because there is too much sugar and not enough jelly in the fruit.

The sugar acts as a preservative. The usual proportions are ¾ lb. sugar to 1 lb. fruit.

The preserving pan should be shallow, as it allows evaporation to take place freely.

COOKING.—Insufficient cooking often causes failure, and mould on jam is the result. The object in cooking is to evaporate water in fruit. If insufficiently cooked the jam will not set; if over cooked the jellying properties are destroyed and colour is spoiled. The jam should boil quickly—usually one hour after adding sugar. Bottle when warm, cover and label, and store in a cool dry place.

AN ACID HINT

When apples or quinces are tasteless, it is a good plan to add tartartic acid to the fruit. Use half a teaspoon of acid to 10 lb. of fruit for jam. For pies just a pinch is required.

— Mrs. Huish, Brighton.

To cover jam, dip tissue paper in milk and press down carefully, when dry it is stiff like parchment and will keep for 12 months or more.

— Mrs. J. E. McGrath, St. Peters.

MAKING JAM

It is a good plan to put a couple of forks or some marbles on the bottom of the pan; this prevents the jam from "catching," and stirring is not required so constantly.

— Mrs. C. Cheetham, Brighton.

TO TEST IF JAM OR JELLY IS DONE

Always test jams before bottling. Put a little jam on a cold saucer or plate, and stand in a cool place for a few minutes. If a thin skin has formed the jam is done.

WHOLE FRUIT JAM

For berries of any kind, well butter bottom of pan. Leave fruit in overnight with 1 lb. sugar. Do not stir, and put rest of sugar in by degrees. When boiling apricots, cut in halves, and melon in dice cooked this way is a great improvement on stirred jam.

APPLE GINGER JAM

Peel, halve and core the apples. To each pound of apples allow 1 lb. of sugar, half a pint of water, and 1 oz. best white ginger. Put them into preserving pan in layers, adding the water afterwards. Let stand all night. The following morning strain the fluid off, and boil it for half an hour. Put the fruit into the boiling liquid and continue to boil till the apples are clear. If desired, this preparation can at this stage be made in a conserve, and for this purpose should be left in the syrup and put into glass jars. In this form it is a tasty and dainty preparation. If desired, it may be crystallised, and for this the syrup must be strained off and the fruit dried in the sun, when it takes the form of preserved ginger. — Mrs. Beasley, Gawler.

Two lbs. apples, 1½ lbs. sugar, 1 lemon, 1 oz. ginger. Peel, core and quarter the apples, then put them in a pan with alternate layers of sugar and ginger, add barely a pint of water, and allow them to soak 12 hours. Boil 1 hour, after which the fruit and syrup should appear transparent. Keep the apple as whole as possible, then add the grated rind of the lemon, and the juice. When it has set it is ready for use.

— Mrs. C. Hoskin, Aldgate, S.A.

APRICOT JAM

Eight pounds apricots, six pounds sugar.

Wipe apricots, cut in halves, cover with all the sugar, and let stand overnight. Bring slowly to the boil and boil rapidly for about an hour.

APRICOT AND PINEAPPLE JAM

One pound dried apricots, one large tin pineapple, 3 lb. sugar. Pour apricots and water in which they are soaked into a preserving pan and boil about 15 minutes, then add pineapple, sliced small, and juice, also the sugar. Boil one hour.

— S. R. Smith, Congregational Manse, Kadina.

BLACKBERRY AND APPLE JAM

Six pounds blackberries, 6 lb. apples (weighed after paring and coring), 9 lb. sugar.

Put apples in a preserving pan and barely cover with water. Cook till soft. Pick over blackberries and add with sugar and cook till done. If liked, plums may be used instead of apples.

— E.O.S.

BLACK CURRANT JAM

Two pounds fruit, two cups of rain water, 4 lb. sugar.
— Mrs. Williams.

To every pound of currants, add two pounds sugar and three pints of water. Boil three hours. Boil half an hour before adding sugar. —Mrs. A. S. Adamson, Unley.

BLACK CURRANT AND APRICOT JAM

Six pounds apricots peeled and stoned, 6 lb. sugar, 2 lb. black currants, topped and tailed.

Cut up the apricots and sprinkle with 2 lb. sugar, and let stand all night. Next morning put currants on to boil with one pint of water, and boil till soft, then add apricots and bring to boil, then add rest of sugar and boil for one hour. To every pound of apricots allow one pound sugar.

—Mrs. M. L. Evans, Ivanhoe, Keyneton.

Four pounds apricots, five pounds prepared black currant pulp, seven pounds sugar.

Bring apricots and half sugar to the boil, and boil for 30 minutes. Add black currant pulp and rest of sugar. Bring to the boil and boil for about 30 minutes. — F.M.S.

DAMSON JAM

To each pound of damsons allow $\frac{3}{4}$ lb. sugar. Remove the stalks from the damsons, then wash and drain them. Put the damsons into a preserving pan and heat slowly till most of the juice is extracted. Bring to the boil, then add the sugar; stir till boiling, and boil till the jam sets. During the cooking remove as many stones as possible.

DRIED APRICOT JAM

Two pounds fruit, wash quite clean, pour on four quarts boiling water. Leave overnight. Simmer gently for an hour and a quarter. Add 7 lb. sugar. Boil again for one hour. Do not break the fruit when stirring. (Any dried fruit may be used in the same way.) — Mrs. J. A. Parkes, Malvern.

QUINCE JELLY

Wipe 6 lbs. quinces (do not cut them), place in a pan and pour over them 6 lb. sugar, six pints of water. Boil gently for four hours. Gently lift out fruit whole, which can be used as preserve. Put jelly in jars.

— D.H.D.
— Mrs. S. P. Bond.
— Mrs. G. Barnes.

Use 5 lb. sugar. — Edith E. Rutt.

EGG PLUM AND PINEAPPLE JAM

Seven lbs. egg plums (stone and halve them), 4 lb. pineapple cut into dice, $\frac{3}{4}$ lb. sugar to every pound of fruit, two cups water.

Boil very quickly for 20 minutes or half an hour. (Use preserved pineapple if wished and the syrup instead of water.)

— Miss E. Hill, Black Forest.

FIG JAM

To every pound of fruit add half pound of sugar. Cut off green stems, open figs, and cover with the sugar, and allow to stand all night. Next day boil together for three-quarters of an hour with a little ground ginger, and add blanched almonds a few minutes before taking off the fire. No water to be used. Lemons may be added. — Mrs. E. R. Ingham, Highgate.

GOOSEBERRY AND CHERRY JAM

Six pounds ripe gooseberries, six pounds dark cherries.

Place in stewpan and add about two or three cups of water. Boil for about half an hour, then add twelve pounds sugar, and boil until it jellies. — Mrs. M. A. Luck, Croydon.

GRAPE JAM

Six pounds of grapes, four and a half pounds of sugar.

Wash and pick grape stems off, and drain overnight. Next day boil with the sugar for two to two and a half hours. Skim the pips as they rise after boiling for some time. This jam is greatly improved by adding a jar of fig jam or figs and a little acid.

— Mrs. E. R. Ingham, Highgate.

KING'S JAM

Take two pounds ripe grapes, one cup water. Boil to a pulp, strain, and to the liquid add two pounds ripe pears, peeled and sliced. Reduce to half by boiling, sweeten to taste, and bottle. Place in a warm oven, let cool off all night. A larger quantity may be made in same proportion.

— Mrs. A. J. Ridgway, Dunalbyn, Wolseley.

LOGANBERRY JAM

Allow 1 lb. fruit to 1 lb. sugar. Bruise the berries to create moisture. Sprinkle a little sugar over the fruit and let it stand in a moderately hot place until a lot of juice has formed. Boil the fruit half an hour, then add sugar. Boil quickly for about 20 minutes.

— L. Horton, Kew.

FIG JAM

Twelve pounds figs, three lemons, nine pounds sugar.

Cut figs up night before, and put on half the sugar. Put the rest of the sugar on when boiling. Put no water on the figs and it will keep longer as there will be a syrup after lying all night in sugar. Put in a few drops of essence of lemon before taking up.

— A. Evans, Rockville, Keyneton.

GREEN FIG JAM

Wipe figs with damp cloth and cut in slices, and to every pound of fruit allow three-quarters of a pound sugar, juice of half a lemon, and quarter pint of water.

Boil sugar, water and lemon juice together for five minutes. Remove the scum, then add the fruit, and boil steadily until it looks clear. Figs may be peeled, if preferred.

— Mrs. A. J. Ridgway, Dunalbyn, Wolseley.

GOOSEBERRY AND RASPBERRY JAM

Six pounds gooseberries, 1 lb. raspberries, 9 lb. sugar, 14 cups water.

Mince fruit, add water, and boil for 1½ hours. Add sugar and boil for 40 minutes.

— Mrs. G. McRitchie.

GOOSEBERRY JAM

To six pounds fruit, topped and tailed, allow six pints of water and 12 lb. sugar. Boil till it jells, usually three hours or more.
—Mrs. R. G. Abbott, Port Elliot.
—Mrs. R. F. Goode.

Three pounds gooseberries, six pounds sugar, six cups water. Boil gooseberries and water for 10 minutes until soft. Then add sugar and boil until it jells. —Miss H. Spencer, Wayville.

Six pounds gooseberries, four and a half pints water. Boil to a pulp, then add a pound and a half sugar to each pound of fruit. Boil till a little will set. Boil quickly and not too long. Keep well stirred. —Mrs. R. E. Chapman, Naracoorte.

To every pound of gooseberries add one pint of water and one and a half pounds of sugar. Boil until very red—about three hours. —Mrs. A. J. Ridgway, "Dunalbyn," Wolseley.

MELON JAM

Two pounds melon, seven pounds sugar, three lemons, eight cups of water to each pound of melon, half a pound preserved ginger.

Cut melon and lemons overnight, and put all the water over it. Boil next morning, and when the melon begins to look transparent add the sugar; then boil until the mixture responds to the jelly test. —Mrs. H. Benfield, Croydon.

Two pounds melon, 7 lb. sugar, seven cups water, six lemons, two small oranges.

Cut melon small as dice; cut lemons and oranges fine. Boil for an hour and a quarter. —Mrs. S. P. Bond.

Cut the melon into inch cubes. To each pound of fruit add three-quarters of a pound of sugar and stand overnight. To ten pounds of fruit add four ounces ginger, six lemons cut up, and six ounces preserved ginger. Boil gently three to four hours. Bruise ginger and tie in a muslin bag.
—Mrs. W. Greenwood, "Todmorden," Gawler.

STRAWBERRY JAM

Exactly the same as raspberry, but boil for about an hour or until the syrup becomes rather thick.
—Mrs. E. R. Ingham, Highgate.

MELON AND PASSION FRUIT JAM

Fifteen or sixteen pounds of melon cut into dice, 12 lb. sugar, the juice of three lemons. Let the sugar and melon stand over night. Next day add the lemon juice, and boil for four hours, or until the melon is soft and clear. When nearly done, add the strained juice of three or three and a half dozen passion fruit. When the jam is cooked take off the fire and let it stand for a quarter of an hour. Then add the passion fruit seeds, stirring them well in. If the seeds are boiled in the jam they get hard and black.

MULBERRY AND APPLE JAM

Five pounds mulberries, one pound apples, four and a half pounds sugar, half cup water.

Put mulberries and apples through mincer, then boil 20 minutes. Add sugar and boil 1 hour and 20 minutes.

—Mrs. Pulford, Adelaide.

PEACH JAM

One pound dried peaches, four pints water, 3 lb. sugar, two lemons, 1 oz. blanched almonds. Wash peaches thoroughly in cold water for five minutes. Place in preserving pan and cover with four pints boiling water. Soak for 24 hours. Cut peaches into four pieces. Boil for 20 minutes, adding the juice of two lemons and the rinds. Add 3 lb. sugar, 1 oz. almonds, and boil quickly for 30 minutes or till jam sets when tested. Remove lemon rinds after boiling for a quarter of an hour with the sugar. This makes 6 to 6½ lb. of jam of remarkable quality and flavour.

PEAR JAM

Twelve lbs. pears cut into large pieces, 9 lb. sugar, 4½ pints water, 1 tablespoon cloves, 1 teaspoon citric or tartaric acid. Boil sugar and water together for quarter of an hour; add fruit, and boil for 4 or 5 hours, or until it turns red. (Tie cloves in muslin, and boil with jam.) Add acid about 20 minutes before it is done.

PLUM JAM

To each pound of plums, weighed after washing, stemming and stoning, allow ¾ lb. sugar.

First Method.—Put the prepared plums into a preserving pan with some cold water (a teacup to each 4 lb.). Heat very slowly till a generous amount of juice is extracted, then boil quickly for 15 to 20 minutes. Add the sugar, stir till it is dissolved, then bring to the boil and boil quickly till the jam is done.

Second Method.—Put the prepared plums into a preserving pan and sprinkle over them the sugar. Leave overnight. Next morning heat very slowly and when the sugar is all dissolved bring to the boil and boil quickly till done.

QUINCE HONEY

Take five quinces, four lemons, five cups of water, 5 lb. sugar.

Method.—Mince the quinces and the rind of two lemons. After mincing, add the juice of four lemons. Put five cups of water and 5 lb. of sugar in the pan and boil for 20 minutes. Add quinces and lemons, and boil for 35 minutes.

Take five large quinces, four pounds sugar, one pint water.

Method.—Take seeds only from quinces and put through mincing machine. Bring sugar and water to the boil and stir in quinces. Boil quickly for half an hour, stirring occasionally.

— Mrs. Rea, Adelaide.

— F. Laughton.

Ingredients.—Six large quinces, 4 lb. sugar, one pint water, one large tin preserved pineapple.

Method.—Boil sugar and water for 15 minutes, and mince the quinces and pineapple together. Add fruit to syrup and simmer for 40 minutes.

QUINCE SNIPS

Cut quinces into small dice. Weigh them; to every pound of fruit add one pound of sugar and half a pint of water. Boil peels and cores in water; strain, pour liquid on sugar, and boil for 20 minutes. Add quinces and simmer till deep red in colour.

— Mrs. E. H. Green, Port Pirie.

RASPBERRY JAM

Six pounds raspberries, six pounds sugar.

Method.—First day, beat fruit and sugar together with wooden spoon 15 minutes; let stand. Second day, exactly the same. Third day, again, then boil for five minutes. Skim and bottle.

— Miss Lewis, Lambert Road, Joslin.

To every pound of fruit, three-quarters of a pound of crystallised sugar. Put sugar on raspberries and allow to stand all night. Next day boil briskly for 25 minutes and put into small jars. No water should be used. Jam should be used fresh, as it loses its colour if kept too long.

RHUBARB JAM

Seven pounds rhubarb, three lemons, 6 lb. sugar.

Wipe the stalks, cut them into small pieces, and put in a preserving pan with sugar and lemon rind. Cover and leave for 12 hours. Strain off the juice and simmer for an hour. Add the rhubarb and strained lemon juice and simmer for an hour and a half to two hours. Bottle carefully.

ECONOMICAL JAMS AND JELLIES

BLACKBERRY.—12 lb. of berries, cover with water. Bring to boil for 15 minutes. Take out about 15 cups of juice to make jelly without breaking the berries more than possible. To the fruit for jam add 12 lb. sugar, also 3 lb. of apples which have been cooked to mash first. Boil together for 40 minutes.

JELLY.—To the 15 cups of juice add equal quantity of sugar. Boil for about 20 minutes. Test a small quantity in a saucer to see if it sets; if not, boil a few minutes longer.

Black currants can be done in the same way, using apricots instead of apples. Same quantities, same time for cooking.

HOW TO MAKE RASPBERRY JAM

Bring fruit to boil without sugar (15 minutes), then beat it till each grain is separate. Add the sugar, and boil for 30 minutes.

— A.G.A.

APPLE JELLY

Cut into thin slices the whole of the apple, and barely cover with water. Boil a full hour. Cut them up overnight if possible, and let them soak in the water. Strain through colander first and then through jelly bag. To one good cup of juice allow one spare cup of sugar. Boil juice one-half hour. Add sugar, and boil another half-hour. — M. R. Keynes.

To each pint of apple juice 1 lb. sugar, one large lemon to 12 lb. apples.

Wash and cut apples into quarters without removing skin or core. Place in preserving pan and add just enough water to cover. Add lemon rind very thinly pared, showing no white pith. Bring to boil and boil gently without stirring, keeping fruit unbroken, for about an hour and a half. Strain through piece of butter-muslin. Measure, and return to saucepan with the lemon juice. Bring to boil, add sugar, and boil for 20 to 30 minutes or till jelly will set when tested on a plate.

Note.—The apple pulp may be used for tarts or pies. Remove cores with spoon and fork. Add sugar and nutmeg. — W.G.T.

LOQUAT JELLY

Fruit must be unripe. Just cover with water and boil till quite tender. Strain and add one cup of sugar to each cup of syrup. Boil quickly about 25 minutes. Remove half the stones or it will be too bitter. — Mrs. Geo. Heath, Keyneton.

Slice three quarts of loquats and cover with water. Simmer gently for two hours. Strain through a jelly bag. To each pint of juice add 12 oz. sugar and one tablespoon of lemon juice. Boil gently until it jellies—about an hour and a half.

— L. Horton, Kew.

CITRON PRESERVE

Twelve pounds fruit (before boiling), 18 lb. sugar, eight pints water.

Boil the citrons in plenty of water till quite soft. Take them out and cool. Cut them in square pieces. Remove pulp and pips. Put sugar and water in pan. Allow it to boil 20 minutes, then put in peel and pulp carefully strained through a colander. Boil an hour and a half. — Mrs. R. H. Adamson.

PINEAPPLE AND PASSION FRUIT JAM

Four pounds passion fruit, one large pineapple, sugar.

Peel and shred pineapple and put in saucepan with sufficient water to cover. Cook slowly till tender, then add passion fruit (pulp and seeds only), and boil 10 minutes. Weigh and add an equal amount of sugar. Bring to the boil and boil quickly for 35 minutes. Pour into heated jars, and when cold cover and label.

MELON JELLY

Cut up eight pounds melon, leaving in seeds and rind on. Add a pound and a half of sugar, and let it stand all night. In another bowl cut seven fresh lemons. Cover with six pints cold water, and let stand all night. Next day mix together and boil until soft. Strain, and to every pint of juice add one pound sugar. Boil quickly for about two hours, and test a little in a saucer.

— Mrs. Pearl Bowering, "Wheatley," Peterborough.
— Mrs. G. M. Wright, "Barossa," Norwood.
— Miss M. A. Adams, Port Elliot.

PIEMELON JELLY

Cut up 16 lb. melon very thinly (peel and seed) and sprinkle 6 lb. sugar over. Stand all night. Cut up 12 large lemons (skin and seed) and cover with boiling water. Let stand all night. Then put all together in a preserving pan and boil till all is quite soft. Strain through jelly bag, and to each pint of juice add ¾ lb. sugar. Boil for an hour and a half or till it jellies.

— Mrs. Rice, Gawler.

GRAPE JELLY

Wash grapes and free them from stems. Mash them in a pan till broken. Heat slowly and cook until juice is well drawn out. Strain through cheesecloth. Measure the juice, and allow an equal measure of sugar. Boil until surface looks wrinkled and the liquid jellies on the edge. Skim well and turn into glasses.

— Mrs. A. V. Morris.

LEMON JELLY

Six pounds fresh lemons cut into thin slices. Pour over it five quarts of water and let stand for 24 hours. Then boil 10 minutes and strain through cheesecloth. Add one cup of sugar to each cup of water and boil half an hour. — R. Belcher.

CITRON MARMALADE

Four pounds citrons, four quarts water, 12 pounds sugar.

First Day.—Slice the citrons very thinly, add the water, and leave 24 hours.

Second Day.—Bring to boil and boil quarter of an hour.

Third Day.—Bring to the boil, add the sugar, and boil half an hour. Bottle when cool. — Mrs. T. C. Sharman.

GRAPE-FRUIT MARMALADE

Slice finely 4 lb. of fruit. Allow to stand overnight in eight pints of water, then boil one hour. Add 12 lb. of sugar, and boil for three-quarters of an hour.

If grape-fruit is not procurable, "Poor Man" orange will do.

— Mrs. J. A. Parkes, Malvern.

LEMON MARMALADE

To each lemon allow one pint of water and 1 lb. sugar. Cut lemons very thin, removing pips. Add the water and soak for 12 hours. Boil till tender, then add sugar and boil for half an hour.

– Mrs. S. P. Bond.
– Mrs. G. Barnes.

MARMALADE

Sixteen oranges, six lemons, 10 lb. sugar, four and a half quarts of water.

Cut the fruit into fine rings. Remove the pips, soak in water for 24 hours. Boil quickly one hour, then add sugar, and boil for one hour longer. — L. Horton, Kew.

MARMALADE (Scotch Recipe)

Four pounds Seville oranges, one gallon water. Cut up oranges very fine, removing pips. Soak in the water for 24 hours. Boil without sugar for half an hour, put in 12 lb. sugar, then boil for three-quarters of an hour. —Mrs. S. P. Bond.

POOR MAN'S ORANGE MARMALADE

Cut oranges in halves, slice fruit and skin together very thinly. To every pound of fruit add one quart of water; let it stand 24 hours.

Second day boil for 20 minutes, let stand again for 24 hours.

Third day weigh it and to every pound of pulp put 1¼ lb. of sugar, boil for 20 minutes quickly and stir and skim well.

—Mrs. A. H. Kerr, Mitcham.
—Mrs. G. M. Wright, Norwood.

Six pounds poor man's oranges, 12 pounds sugar, one dipper of cold water.

Cut oranges into thin slices and let stand overnight with one cup of sugar and the water on them. Boil next day until tender, then add the sugar, and boil until it thickens, which will take about 20 minutes. Bottle while hot.

— Mrs. A. Treasure, Georgetown.

QUINCE MARMALADE

One pound of sugar and one pint of water to every quince. Wipe quinces, cut in fine slices and core in centre (which may be removed if preferred). Boil fruit and water 20 minutes. Add sugar and boil slowly till mixture jellies. — M. Wilks.

ROYAL MARMALADE

Six pounds Seville oranges (not too ripe), 18 pounds sugar, six quarts water.

Cut oranges very thin. Let stand 24 hours. Boil one hour. Add sugar and boil quickly till it jells—about one hour.

APPLE MARMALADE

Take 6 lb. apples (when cored and peeled), 6 lb. sugar, six lemons. Cut lemons as for marmalade, pour over two quarts of water, and leave till next day. Then add the apples, and let boil one hour. Add sugar and boil until sufficiently firm. Do not splice apples until the day of boiling.

— Mrs. Beasley, Gawler.

MELON MARMALADE

Two pounds melon, 3 lemons, 3 oranges. Cut up overnight with 8 cups of water. In morning, boil till tender, then add 6 lb. sugar; then boil until it jellies.

— Mrs. E. B. Spry, Westbourne Park.

PRESERVES

PRESERVED FRUIT
(For Screw-top Jars)

THE FRUIT

should be firm, not too ripe, of one size. If fruit has to be peeled, drop in cold water to prevent it discolouring.

THE BOTTLES

should be thoroughly sterilised, and rubber rings and caps should fit tightly. Rubber rings should only be used once.

THE SYRUP

To every quart of water allow ½ lb. of best cane sugar. Bring to the boil and boil for half an hour, skimming when necessary

TO BOTTLE

Pack the fruit tightly into the sterilised bottles and make as attractive as possible. Fill up with cold syrup. Do not cap at once, as syrup sinks; if so, add more syrup. Dip rubber rings in hot water and fasten securely on bottles. If wished, water may be used in place of syrup.

TO STERILISE

Place bottles in a steriliser—a preserving pan or kerosene tin will do, provided plenty of packing is placed at the bottom and around the bottles. Add sufficient water to come two-thirds high up bottles. Bring slowly to 160 deg. F., and keep at that temperature for given time. The water should at least be allowed to reach 160 deg. F. If heated too quickly, the skin on the fruit breaks. Take from steriliser, tighten caps, and turn the steriliser to test for leaks. If leaking, re-sterilise. Next day put on the label, and store in a cool place.

TIME TO ALLOW FOR COOKING

Plums, 25 minutes; rhubarb, 20 minutes; apricots and peaches, 45 minutes; pears, one hour; berries, 30 minutes.

TO BOTTLE TOMATOES

Small tomatoes are best to use. Pack tightly in sterilised bottles, and cover with water. Put in steriliser and bring slowly to 170 deg. F. Take out and leave 24 hours. Repeat next day; leave two or three days, and sterilise again. Tomatoes done this way will keep indefinitely.

FIG PRESERVE

Twenty-four pounds ripe sugar figs, 18 lbs. of sugar, two and a half pints of water. Boil sugar and water a few minutes. Add figs, also 1 lb. of preserved ginger, six sliced lemons, one saltspoon cayenne pepper. Boil gently for three hours. Add 1 lb. of walnuts and boil for three-quarters of an hour.

— Mrs. J. A. Parkes, Malvern.

MINCEMEAT FOR CHRISTMAS PIES

Boil ½ lb. of lean beef till tender, chop fine and add ½ lb. of chopped apples, 1 lb. each of seeded raisins and currants, suet, ½ lb. mixed peel cut fine, half a packet of mixed spice, 1 lb. sugar, and one teaspoonful of salt.

Mix all ingredients together, add enough water to moisten, also the liquor the beef was boiled in, and boil about one hour, stirring occasionally. Put mincemeat in a stone jar and keep in a cool place. This will keep sweet for about a fortnight. Make into little pies in the ordinary way. — M. Reynolds, Port Elliot.

MOCK GINGER

Cut twelve pounds melon into squares about half an inch, and let stand in limewater overnight. Three-quarters of a pound of lime is enough to cover melon. Let stand for about 10 minutes, then strain and pour on melon. Put one gallon of water and twelve pounds sugar in your pan and let boil for five minutes, then drain melon and put in. Bruise three-quarters of a pound of dry ginger, put in a bag and soak all night. Throw in and let boil for six hours. Add five or six lemons. If you think it is boiling too dry, add little more water. — Miss A. Stinson.

LEMON CHEESE

One-half pound sugar, three eggs, the juice of 1½ lemons, the rind of one grated, one-eighth of pound of butter. Put these into a pan, stew gently till it becomes the consistency of honey, then pour into a jar. Keep in a cool place.

— Mrs. J. E. Creswell, College Park.

LEMON CREAM

Half pound good butter, yolks of four eggs, one nutmeg, ½ lb. sugar, juice of about three lemons, to taste.

Put butter, sugar and eggs in a cool oven till it is a thick cream. When cool, add lemon and nutmeg. This will keep for months if put in air-tight jars. — M. Thiem, Beulah Park.

LEMON CONSERVE

Quarter pound butter, 1 lb. white sugar, six eggs, three large lemons.

Put the butter in a double boiler. When melted, add sugar and eggs (well beaten), grated rind and juice of lemons. Stir the mixture over fire until thick as good cream. If put in jars and pasted down will keep for months.

— Mrs. Harry Arbon, Clarence Park.

Omit the whites of two eggs.

— Mrs. Agnes Bowering, Prospect.

PRESERVED FIGS

Peel and cut into small pieces ½ lb. green ginger, 6 lb brewer's crystal sugar, two pints of water.

Make into syrup by boiling for about three-quarters of an hour, then drop 6 lb. of figs into the boiling syrup. Boil gently for about four hours. Care must be taken to have the stalks on each fig. Slices of finely-cut lemon may be added, if liked.

— Mrs. E. R. Ingham, Highgate.

Fifteen pounds figs, seven cups water, 9 lbs. sugar, ½ lb. preserved ginger.

Boil sugar and water for one hour, then put in figs and ginger, and boil five to six hours. — V. A. Lushey.

TO CANDY PEEL

Put lemon, orange or citron peel into salt and water for four days (change water), then boil peel till soft, and drain; make a thin syrup with 1 lb. sugar and one quart water. Boil peel till clear. Make a thick syrup. Boil slowly till syrup candies. Dust the peel with castor sugar and leave in a warm oven all night.

— Mrs. H. R. Adamson.

TO DRY RAISINS

Have boiling four gallons water. Add two dessertspoons caustic soda. Have a second boiler with one gallon water, also boiling, and add two dessertspoons of oil. Keep both lots of water boiling all the time you are dipping the grapes. Dip the grapes into caustic soda first three times in and out, then once in the oil. Put in the sun to dry, covering every night.

— Mrs. H. R. Adamson.

MINCEMEAT

Half lb. each of seeded raisins, currants, sultanas, apples, and sugar, ¼ lb. suet, and 2 oz. each of lemon, orange, and citron peel and 2 oz. almonds.

Put all through a fine mincer, and add ½ teaspoon each of nutmeg, cinnamon, ginger, and allspice. A small wineglass of brandy helps to keep it. Mix well. Put in jars and tie down.

— Mrs. R. F. Slattery, Welland.

CHUTNEYS

SAUCES

PICKLES

CHUTNEYS

APPLE CHUTNEY

Two pounds apples, 2 lb. tomatoes, 1 lb. onions, ½ lb. figs, ½ lb. raisins, ½ lb. sugar, 1 teaspoon salt, 2 oz. ground ginger, 2 oz. mustard seed, ½ oz. tumeric, quarter teaspoon cayenne pepper, one quart vinegar.

Peel and core apples. Cut into pieces apples and onions. Add ingredients and boil for one hour to an hour and a half.

— Mrs. J. P. Peterson, Ardrossan.

Four pounds apples, 1 lb. sultanas, 1 lb. currants, 1 lb. seeded raisins, 2 lb. brown sugar, 3 oz. garlic, ½ oz. cloves, ¼ lb. bruised ginger (three tied in a muslin bag), ½ oz. mustard, quarter teaspoon cayenne, one tablespoon salt, one bottle and a half of brown vinegar.

Put apples through large mincer. Stew all slowly together for two hours. Bottle and seal. This will keep for two years.

— Mrs. H. R. Adamson.

APRICOT CHUTNEY

Two pounds apricots (pared and stoned), ¾ lb. brown sugar, ¼ lb. raisins (stoned and chopped), 1 lb. onions, one dessertspoon salt, one dessertspoon mustard, a teaspoon and a quarter cloves, quarter teaspoon ground ginger, a little cayenne pepper, enough vinegar to cover. Cook an hour and a quarter.

— Mrs. R. J. Lampe, St. Peters.

CASHMERE CHUTNEY

Three pounds green gooseberries or apples, 2 lb. light brown sugar, 1 lb. raisins, 1 lb. dates, ½ oz. garlic, two teaspoons red pepper, 4 oz. ginger chopped and powdered, 2 oz. salt, a bottle and a half of vinegar.

Have all ingredients well chopped except the dates. Top and tail gooseberries, but do not peel apples if used. Boil the fruit in enough vinegar to cover it. When soft add everything else (the dates being cut in small pieces). Boil for half an hour.

— E. Ferrier.

CHUTNEY

Three and a half pounds of apples (pared, cored and finely chopped), and 1½ lb. of raisins, 2 lb. of dates, 2 lb. onions, 1 lb. of crystallised ginger, 1 tablespoon of salt, 4 lb. of white sugar, one pint of red or green chillies, 7 lb. tomatoes, two quarts of vinegar, rind of half a lemon, all to be chopped finely, especially the apples.

Boil all together in an enamel saucepan till as thick as jam.

— Mrs. J. Hawkes, Kent Town.

FRUIT CHUTNEY

Six pounds ripe tomatoes, 2 lb. apples, 2 lb. peaches, 2 lb. figs, 2 lb. raisins, 2 lb. dates, 2 lb. currants, 2 lb. brown sugar, 2 lb. onions, 2 lb. raspberry jam.

Method. — Prepare fruit, cut into small pieces, and put in preserving pan with other ingredients. Add 1 tablespoon salt, 1 oz. cloves, 1 oz. whole ginger, 1 oz. peppercorns, ½ oz. mace, small teaspoon cayenne pepper. Put all spices into a muslin bag. Nearly cover with vinegar and boil for two hours.

PLUM CHUTNEY

Twelve pounds plums, 4 oz. whole ginger (bruised), two teaspoons cayenne, 3 teaspoons salt, 1 oz. cloves, 5 lb. sugar, four pints vinegar, 1 oz. whole pepper, 1 oz. whole allspice.

Boil all ingredients for four and a half hours. Rub through a colander, and bottle.

— Mrs. R. G. Abbott, Port Elliot.

QUICKLY-MADE CHUTNEY

Take one bottle of piccalilli pickles and mince it. Add one tin of plum jam. Mix well and boil for a few minutes. Bottle and cork tightly.

MUSHROOM KETCHUP

Any quantity of well-ripened mushrooms broken up and well salted. Let stand overnight; drain well, add a little water, and press till all possible liquid is extracted. Put all liquid in saucepan, adding 1 tablespoon ground ginger, 1 teaspoon allspice, salt and pepper to taste. Boil well, strain, bottle, and seal.

—Mrs. Walter E. Mounster.

CHUTNEY

Two pounds sugar, ¼ lb. dried chillies, 2 teaspoons salt, ¼ lb. garlic, ½ lb. onions, ¼ lb. ground ginger, 2 lbs. raisins, 1 lb. currants, two bottles vinegar, 8 lbs. tomatoes (green) or gooseberries.

Mince and boil till sufficiently thick. —M. Wilks.

MELON CHUTNEY

Eight pounds melon, 2 lb. onions, 2 lb. apples, ¾ oz. pepper, 3 oz. salt, ¾ oz. cloves, 1 oz. ground ginger, 1 oz. spice, three pints vinegar, half pint treacle, 2 lb. sugar and currants.

Boil all together for an hour and a half.

—Miss E. Stribling.

TOMATO CHUTNEY

Twelve pounds tomatoes, 4 lb. apples, 2 lb. sultanas, 2 lb. treacle, 1 lb. brown sugar, 2 teaspoons salt, 4 oz. shallots, 1 oz. cayenne, 1 oz. cloves, 1 oz. allspice (whole), 1 oz. white pepper, 1 oz. garlic, one quart vinegar.

Tie pieces in a muslin bag. Cut up tomatoes and apples. Chop or mince garlic and shallots. Put all ingredients in a pan and boil for two hours.

—Mrs. T. C. Sharman, Black Forest.

Twelve pounds tomatoes, 2 lbs. sugar, ¼ oz. cayenne pepper, two tablespoons of salt, two pints vinegar, ½ oz. cloves, 4 oz. garlic, 3 oz. white ginger, eight large apples.

Roughly chop garlic, tie in a bag with cloves and ginger. Pour boiling water on tomatoes and peel. Peel and core apples. Boil for three hours, or till thick, in a preserving pan. Strain through a colander. —A. Evans, "Rockville," Keyneton.

—Mrs. A. H. Kerr.

Eighteen pounds tomatoes (boil to a pulp and strain), then add 6 lb. onions, 6 lb. cooking apples, one head celery, one large bunch carrots, 3 oz. garlic, 2 lemons. Mince all together, and add 1 oz. dried chillies, 1 oz. ground ginger, 2 oz. cloves, 2 oz. white pepper, 2 tablespoons salt, 2 lb. sugar, 4 bottles vinegar. Boil all together for three hours.

—L. Carmichael, Tiparra West.

TOMATO AND APPLE CHUTNEY

Six pounds of tomatoes, 1 lb. sugar, four large apples, one pint vinegar, one tablespoon salt, ½ oz. cayenne pepper, 2 oz. garlic, ¼ oz. cloves, 1½ oz. white ginger.

Roughly chop garlic, tie in bag with cloves and ginger. Pour boiling water on tomatoes and peel; also peel and core the apples and slice. Boil all together for three hours or until thick.

— E. C. Honeyman, Ki Ki.

"OAKDENE" CHUTNEY

Four pounds rhubarb, five large onions, 1 lb. seeded raisins. Chop these ingredients finely. Put in enamel pan with two pounds brown sugar, three pints vinegar, one tablespoon each mustard, salt, black pepper, one teaspoon each cayenne and ground ginger. Boil for two hours. — Miss Kemp, Brighton.

QUINCE CHUTNEY

Four pounds of quinces (peeled, cored and sliced), 2 lb. stoned raisins, two large onions chopped, 1½ lb. of brown sugar, two teaspoons of salt, one teaspoon of allspice. Put ½ oz. of whole ginger, bruised, one teaspoon of pepper and one teaspoon of mace into a muslin bag. Add this to the other ingredients. Cover the whole with vinegar, and boil slowly for four hours. Take out bag of spice, and bottle chutney when cold.

— Mrs. F. Blucher, Ki Ki.

Three pounds quinces, 1 lb. apples, 2 lb. onions, 2 lb. white sugar, 1½ oz. salt, nine cloves or garlic, one teaspoon of ground ginger, one teaspoon cayenne pepper, one teaspoon allspice, half teaspoon of mace.

Method.—Peel and mince quinces, put in all ingredients, cover with two bottles of Seppelt's vinegar, and boil four hours.

— M. Wilks.

RHUBARB CHUTNEY

Two pounds rhubarb, two onions, 1 lb. dates, ½ lb. brown sugar, 1 oz. root ginger crushed, ½ oz. each capsicums and mustard seed (tie last three in a muslin bag).

Place all ingredients in a pan with a pint and a half of Seppelt's vinegar, and boil together for an hour and a half. Stir to prevent burning.

— Mrs. H. R. Adamson, Malvern.

TOMATO CHUTNEY

Twenty pounds tomatoes, 5 lbs. onions, 5 lbs. apples, 3 lbs. sugar, 2 lb. raisins, 2 tablespoons salt, 2 oz. cloves, 2 oz. ground ginger, ½ oz. cayenne pepper, 2½ pints vinegar.

Put tomatoes, onions, apples, garlic and raisins through mincer; add other ingredients (cloves in a bag), and boil 2 hours.

— E. Bird, "Inverary," Victor Harbor.

When making chutney or relish, boil the tomatoes for 20 minutes, and rub through a colander. This gets rid of the skins and saves peeling tomatoes.

TOMATO KETCHUP

Cut up 4 lb. of tomatoes and 1 lb. of onions. Bring slowly to the boil with 2 tablespoons of salt, 1 lb. of brown sugar, a saltspoon of cayenne, 2 oz. peppercorns, 12 cloves, ¼ lb. allspice, and one pint of best vinegar. Simmer for one hour. Stir to prevent sticking. Rub through a sieve while hot, then bottle. — C. Finn.

TOMATO SAUCE

Twelve lb. tomatoes, 3 lb. onions, 3 lb. apples, 2 cups sugar, 2 tablespoons salt, 3 oz. garlic, 2 oz. ground ginger, 1 oz. cayenne pepper, 1 oz. white pepper, 1 oz. cloves, 2 oz. ground allspice, 4 pints vinegar.

Boil tomatoes, apples, onions, garlic and cloves together, then strain through a colander. Add other spices, and boil for 2 hours. Bottle and cork while hot.

— E. Bird, "Inverary," Victor Harbor.

SAUCES

PLUM OR BETTY'S SAUCE

Three cups vinegar, one cup dark plum jam, one cup treacle, ½ oz. bruised ginger, ½ oz. allspice, chillies, cayenne pepper.

Boil together for two hours. Strain through a colander.

— Mrs. S. Roberts, Kadina.

EGG PLUM SAUCE

Six pounds plums, one pound sugar, six pints vinegar, two tablespoons salt, one teaspoon each of cloves, allspice and mace.

Crush the spice well and add pepper to taste and a little cayenne. Boil together till fruit leaves the stone. Strain and boil till a nice dark colour. — Miss M. A. Adams, Port Elliot.

PLUM SAUCE

Six pounds plums, 3 lb. sugar, three pints vinegar, one handful bruised ginger, one teaspoon cayenne pepper, one teaspoon salt, ½ oz. allspice, ½ oz. cloves.

Boil all together till the stones separate. Strain through a colander and bottle. — Mrs. A. V. Morris.

— M. Thiem.

— B. L. Rowley.

Six pounds plums, 1¼ lb. sugar, three pints vinegar, six teaspoons salt, one teaspoon cayenne pepper, one tablespoon black pepper (ground), one handful cloves (ground), one handful whole ginger (bruised).

Boil plums and ginger to a pulp, then add other ingredients. Boil for two hours or till thick. Strain through colander and bottle. — Miss Niehuus, King's Park.

WORCESTER SAUCE

Six cups vinegar, one cup treacle, one cup plum jam, 1 oz. garlic, ½ oz. ground ginger, ½ oz. cloves, ½ oz. chillies, one tablespoon pepper, one tablespoon salt.

Boil all gently for two and a half hours, strain, and bring to boil again.

TOMATO SAUCE

Boil 12 lb. tomatoes and 2 lb. cooking apples, 2 tablespoons salt, 2 oz. garlic, 4 oz. pepper, ½ oz. chillies, ½ oz. cloves, ½ oz. allspice, ½ oz. ginger, ½ oz. mace, three pints vinegar three hours, and then strain and bottle. — M. A. Ferrier.

Twelve pounds of ripe tomatoes, 1 tablespoon of salt, ½ oz. mace, ½ oz. chillies, ½ oz. of cloves (whole), ½ oz. whole ginger, ½ oz. cayenne pepper, 1 lb. sugar, 1 lb. apples, ½ oz. white pepper, 4 oz. garlic, 4 oz. shallots, ½ oz. whole allspice.

Boil tomatoes and apples and salt until the skins curl. Pound the spices and other ingredients, add three bottles vinegar. Boil five hours, strain through a colander. When cool bottle and cork tightly and seal.

— Mr. W. H. Chard, Mitcham.

Twelve pounds tomatoes cut into slices, 1 lb. sugar, 1 teaspoon salt, a pint and a half of vinegar, ½ oz. of cloves, ½ oz. chillies, 1 oz. white pepper, 1 oz. ginger, ½ oz. allspice, 2 oz. shallots, 1 oz. garlic, and a little cayenne pepper.

Boil together three hours. Strain through sieve, then boil for one hour. — Mrs. Stan Miller, Port Pirie.

TOMATO SAUCE

One and a half cups tomatoes (canned ones may be used), ¼ pint water, 1 clove, 1 bay leaf, 1 onion, salt and pepper, 1 oz. butter.

Cook together slowly for half an hour; strain and thicken with 1 oz. flour mixed to a thin, smooth paste.

TOMATO SAUCE (Mild)

Eighteen pounds tomatoes, four large onions, 1 lb. sugar, 1 tablespoon salt, ¼ oz. cloves, ¼ oz. mace, ½ oz. ground ginger.

Boil all together, excepting sugar, about two hours. Then strain through sieve or colander and boil again with sugar and two pints vinegar until thick enough. When nearly done add half a tea-spoon cayenne pepper. —A. Evans, Kenilworth.

PICKLES

APPLE AND ONION PICKLE

Four pounds apples, 4 lbs. onions, ½ oz. chillies, ½ oz. allspice, ½ oz. cloves (in bag), 1 oz. tumeric, 6 oz. mustard, 2 lb. sugar.

Cut up apples and onions. Cut apples into six or eight pieces, moonshape, then in three. Cut onions finely. Put over two small handfuls salt, and let stand all night. In morning drain off liquid. Put apples and onions into preserving pan. Put plate on top and keep hand on top of plate to keep apples, etc., down. Pour on vinegar until it comes to edge of plate. Boil all ingredients (except mustard and tumeric) for 15 minutes. Mix mustard and tumeric with vinegar, and add. Let all just boil up once. Bottle and seal. — Miss O. Mawby, St. Peters.

CAULIFLOWER PICCALILLI

One pickling cauliflower, break in small pieces, sprinkle with salt, and let stand all night. Put three bottles vinegar in a pan. Bring to boil and thicken with following:—Four tablespoons flour, four tablespoons mustard, one tablespoon curry powder, one tablespoon tumeric, half teaspoon cayenne, one cup sugar, half cup golden syrup. Make these into a batter with water and pour into boiling vinegar. Add cauliflower, and boil for half an hour.

— Mrs. H. R. Adamson, Malvern.

CAULIFLOWER PICCALILLI

Cut large cauliflower into small pieces, sprinkle salt on, and then drain on towel. Two bottles vinegar, bring to boil. Mix two tablespoons plain flour, four of mustard, one of sugar, one dessertspoon tumeric, quarter teaspoon cayenne pepper, and enough water to make smooth paste. Then add to boiling vinegar. Put in cauliflower, and boil till tender—about half an hour.

— Miss A. Stinson, Clarence Park.

CAULIFLOWER PICKLE

Two cauliflowers, 2 oz. mustard, three-quarters cup sugar, three pints vinegar, 2 lb. onions, two large tablespoons flour, one spoonful tumeric, two handfuls salt.

Method.—Break cauliflower into small pieces. Cut up onions and cover with brine. Let stand overnight. Next day bring to a boil and boil gently till tender. Strain off brine. Place vinegar and sugar on fire, and when boiling add mustard, flour and tumeric mixed to a smooth paste, and boil for two minutes, stirring all the time. Then pour over cauliflower and just warm through. Then bottle. — Mrs. Rea, Adelaide.

CUCUMBER PICKLE

Cut up 4 lb. green tomatoes, 4 lb. cucumbers, 4 lb. onions. N.B.—Do not peel cucumbers. Pour over brine made of four quarts cold water, 1 lb. salt. Stand all night, put on to boil. Boil for five minutes. Lift off and strain well.

Boil one gallon vinegar with two teaspoons ground allspice. When it boils stir in the following ingredients well mixed:—Five cups sugar, two cups plain flour or cornflour, one and a half tablespoons tumeric, two teaspoons white pepper, two tablespoons curry powder, two tablespoons mustard. Mix all these to a paste with three cups cold water. Stir well into vinegar, bring to a boil, put in the pickles. Leave until nearly cold. Bottle and cork well. — Miss O. Mawby, St. Peters.

GRAPE PICKLES

To one quart vinegar add 1 lb. sugar, half teaspoon salt, one teaspoon cinnamon, cloves, allspice, pepper, and a little ginger bruised. Boil all together and pour hot over grapes (about half a dozen lb. large black ones), which have been cut with scissors from the bunches, leaving small piece of stem attached. Let them stand for a week. Boil vinegar, etc., again. Pour hot over grapes as before. Then ready to seal down.

— Miss E. Hill, Black Forest.

GREEN TOMATO PICKLE

Six pounds green tomatoes, 6 lb. onions and cucumbers (any other green vegetables may be used). Cut up the vegetables, make brine with four quarts of water and one pint of salt, pour it over the vegetables and let them stand for 24 hours. Put on the fire and heat just enough to scald them, tip into a colander and let them drain.

Put two quarts vinegar on the fire and add one cup sugar to it. Mix six tablespoons flour, six tablespoons of mustard, one tablespoon of tumeric with enough water to form a smooth paste. Add to the vinegar when boiling, stirring all the time till it thickens. Add vegetables and cook till heated through.

— Mrs. Alfred Anderson, Blythwood.

Six pounds green tomatoes, two large onions, two large cooking apples, 1 lb. sugar, one pint vinegar, put half teaspoon cloves and peppercorns in a bag, little salt to taste.

Boil slowly for an hour after it comes to the boil.

— M. Sharples, Kadina.

MELON AND ONION PICKLES

Four pounds piemelon, four pounds onion. Cut small and sprinkle one cup salt. Let stand all night. Pour off water, put half gallon of light vinegar over pickles, and boil together for three-quarters of an hour. Mix one ounce tumeric, four tablespoons mustard and one small teacup of cornflour, one small cup of sugar into smooth paste mixed with water. Boil together for half an hour. — Mrs. S. Roberts, Kadina.

MUSTARD PICKLES

Cut cauliflower and one pound onions up overnight, and let stand till morning. Then drain well.

Second.—Put cauliflower into pot and nearly cover with vinegar, and let boil ten to fifteen minutes, then add thickening.

Paste.—One small cup flour, two or three cups sugar, two tablespoons mustard, one teaspoon tumeric, one teaspoon cayenne pepper.

Mix into smooth paste with cold vinegar. After adding thickening, let boil for about five minutes to cook it.

Cucumbers instead of cauliflower, done the same way, are also very nice. Cut cucumbers and onions into small squares, and proceed as above. — Miss K. B. Shannon, Encounter Bay.

PICKLED FIGS

Soak as many firm unripe figs as you can cover with a gallon of vinegar for three days, then pour off the vinegar and add to it 2 oz. of sugar or treacle, one-quarter teaspoon of cayenne pepper, 2 tablespoons salt, 2 oz. allspice, 2 oz. ground cloves, and 2 oz. ground ginger and boil for a quarter of an hour. Pour over the figs while boiling and cover the jars.

— E. S. Rutt.

Four quarts vinegar, 2 lb. loaf sugar, 4 oz. salt, 2 oz. allspice, 2 oz. cloves, 2 oz. whole ginger, ½ oz. peppercorns

Soak the figs in these ingredients for three days, then put them into a bigger jar or bottles. Boil the ingredients for 10 minutes and pour hot over the figs. Cover when cold. Figs must only be about half ripe, and have stalks on.

— Mrs. E. R. Ingham, Highgate.

Use 1 lb. loaf sugar and half teaspoon cayenne instead of peppercorns.

— M. Wilks.

PICKLED CUCUMBERS OR GHERKINS

Cucumbers or gherkins carefully picked and as near the same size as possible, brine strong enough to float an egg. For every two quarts of white vinegar add $\frac{1}{4}$ oz. cloves, 1 oz. white ginger (bruised), $\frac{1}{2}$ oz. mustard seeds, $\frac{1}{4}$ oz. mace. Boil the brine and pour it over the cucumbers in an earthenware basin and leave overnight (they must be well covered), then drain them quite dry. Put all the spices and vinegar into an enamelled stew-pan and bring to the boil for a few minutes. Pack the cucumbers into a jar and strain the vinegar over them and let them stand 24 hours. Then put all back into the stew-pan and simmer until the cucumbers are green, taking care they do not boil. Put in jars or bottles and cork and seal at once.

If you prefer a sweet pickle add a breakfast cupful of sugar to the pickle.

PICKLED ONIONS

Twelve pounds onions, 1 lb. white sugar, 2 tablespoons salt, 1 oz. whole allspice, 1 oz. whole ginger, 1 oz. cloves, 1 oz. pepper and mix with the salt and bruised spices and add sugar. Peel the onions and put in a jar with a sprinkling of the mixture between each layer of onions and fill up with good cold vinegar and cork down. Fit to use in a month and will keep for a year.

Peel skins off and put into salt and water and let stand 24 hours. Drain and rinse well. Put into jar with half a gallon vinegar, 1 lb. sugar, 2 tablespoons salt, teaspoon peppercorns, teaspoon whole ginger, teaspoon whole spice, and two teaspoons cloves. Cork tightly and let stand two weeks before using. (Do not boil vinegar or spices.)

— Mrs. Alfred Anderson, Blythwood.

Put the onions into a dish of strong salt and water and let stand 24 hours. Next day skin the onions and drain dry. Put them into perfectly dry jars and cover with lukewarm vinegar and spices. To half a gallon of vinegar use $\frac{1}{2}$ oz. allspice, $\frac{1}{2}$ oz. peppercorns, eight cloves, two or three pieces mace. This quantity of vinegar is sufficient for 8 lbs. onions. The vinegar and spices should just be allowed to come to the boil.

— Vida A. Lushey.

Use small, hard onions, pour boiling water over them, remove skins quickly, sprinkle with salt and let stand until next day. Fill glass jars three-quarters full of onions, boil some vinegar with a little broken ginger and 1 oz. of whole pepper and a few cloves to a quart of vinegar. Let cool and pour over onions.

— E. G. Gill.

PICKLED ONIONS

The following recipe for pickled onions keeps the onions from going dark. Choose fair-sized onions, make a strong solution of salt and water, and put in the onions without paring. Change this daily for three days, and save the last brine. Take off the outside skin, and put into a saucepan capable of holding all. Take equal parts of milk and the last lot of brine, and two large spoonfuls of salt; put in the onions, and watch and stir carefully. If it is allowed to boil the pickle is spoiled. Then have ready a colander and drain the onions, covering them with a cloth to keep in the steam. Next day they will be yellow and shrivelled. Take off the skin, and they will be perfectly white. Make half a gallon of vinegar, 1 oz. bruised ginger, quarter teaspoon of cayenne, 1 oz. allspice, 1 oz. black pepper, a quarter of an ounce of whole nutmeg bruised, six cloves, and a quarter of an ounce of mace, into a pickle by bringing it to the boil and simmering for a quarter of an hour. Pour hot on the onions in a pan, cover closely to keep in the steam, let stand till next day. Pack into jars with a tablespoon of good olive oil on top. Tie down with bladder. They will be ready in six weeks, and should be beautifully white and crisp. White wine vinegar will help to keep the colour.

PICKLED WALNUTS

Gather before shells begin to form. Wipe them and prick with a needle or fork to allow flavourings to penetrate. Put in a crock or basin and cover with brine. (Allow ¼ lb. salt to each quart of boiling water; allow to cool before pouring over walnuts.) Leave in brine for a fortnight. Stir occasionally, and change the brine twice. Drain the walnuts, spread on trays in single layers and place in the sun until they turn black (from 12 to 24 hours). Three parts fill bottles with walnuts, fill up with prepared vinegar, cover tightly, and store one month before using.

Green almonds may be done the same way.

PREPARED VINEGAR

To one quart of best vinegar allow ½ oz. each of black peppercorns, allspice and bruised ginger, half teaspoon salt, a little grated horseradish. (A little garlic may be added.) Boil for 10 to 15 minutes and use at once.

SPICED PEACHES

Take 12 fine peaches, wipe off the down. To 8 lb. sugar take water sufficient to dampen to a very thick syrup, 2 oz. fresh ginger (sliced), ½ oz. mace, 2 oz. cloves, ½ oz. white peppercorns. Simmer slowly till a straw will enter the fruit, then take out carefully and add to the syrup a breakfast cup of vinegar. Boil for ten minutes, and pour over peaches when cool.

—Mrs. David Williams.

TOMATO RELISH

Three pounds ripe tomatoes, four large onions cut in slices, put in a dish and sprinkle with handful of salt, let stand all night. In morning drain off liquid and put in pan and barely cover with vinegar, boil five minutes, then mix one tablespoon dry mustard, one tablespoon curry powder, three-quarter cup of sugar, one-quarter teaspoon cayenne pepper with little vinegar. Put in pan with other ingredients and boil half an hour.

—Miss R. Burke, Maitland.

RIPE TOMATO RELISH

Twelve pounds firm, but ripe tomatoes, 4 lb. onions, 3 lb. sugar, four level tablespoons curry, six level tablespoons dry mustard, one level teaspoon cayenne pepper, two hands salt, sufficient vinegar to cover.

Cut tomatoes in medium sized pieces, place in dish and sprinkle with one handful salt. Slice onions on separate dish and sprinkle with the other handful salt. Let both stand for 12 hours then drain off liquid. Put onions and tomatoes in stew-pan, add sugar, almost cover with vinegar, put on fire and boil for five minutes. Then add curry, mustard, cayenne pepper which has been mixed while still hot. —Mrs. James Hurst, Paracombe.

Six pounds tomatoes, two large onions, one cup treacle, 1½ bottles vinegar, ¼ oz. cloves, 2 oz. whole ginger bruised, one small teaspoon cayenne.

Peel and slice tomatoes and onions and put in an enamel dish, sprinkle with plenty of salt and leave overnight. Pour off liquid and place all the ingredients in a stew-pan and boil for one hour. Tie ginger and cloves in a bag.

To skin tomatoes easily dip in boiling water or rub well with the back of a knife.

—Mrs. H. Arbon.
—Miss E. Cooper, Farrell's Flat.
—M. Wilks.

For tomato pickle, use green tomatoes in the above recipe.

—M. Wilks.

GREEN TOMATO PICKLES

One gallon green tomatoes cut in slices and sprinkled with salt; leave 12 hours, then strain off the liquor, and mix together 2 quarts vinegar, 1 pint treacle, 1 teaspoon powdered cloves, 1 teaspoon salt, 2 teaspoons mustard. Heat to boiling point; put in tomatoes, three large onions, a few chillies. Thicken with 2 dessertspoons cornflour, and boil 1 hour.

— Mrs. Appleby, Port Pirie.

PICKLED CUCUMBERS

One gallon vinegar, 4 oz. salt, 2 oz. cloves, 2 oz. cinnamon, 1 oz. allspice, 1 oz. whole ginger, 1 oz. mustard, 1 oz. celery seed, small piece of alum.

Scald all together. Wash cucumbers and dry them. Put into vinegar when it is cold.

GREEN TOMATO PICKLES

Slice 1 gallon green tomatoes (16 lb.). Sprinkle one handful salt between layers. Stand all night, and then draw off liquid. Add 5 sliced onions. Boil ½ gall. vinegar, ½ lb. sugar, ¼ teaspoon cayenne pepper, 1 teaspoon ground allspice, 1 teaspoon black pepper, 1 teaspoon tumeric, 8 cloves, for half an hour. Add tomatoes and onions. Mix 4 tablespoons mustard with little vinegar. Stir in with rest. Boil for 20 minutes.

— Mrs. G. A. Noble, Brighton.

CONFECTIONERY

CONFECTIONERY

ALMOND TOFFEE

One quarter pound butter, ½ lb. brown sugar, ½ lb. golden syrup. Melt butter in a saucepan, then add syrup and sugar and boil 10 minutes, then try in cold water. Stir with a knife continually. Pour on a buttered plate and add almonds.

CARAMEL TOFFEE

Ingredients.—One cup sugar, three tablespoons honey, one teaspoon vanilla, 3 oz. butter.

Method.—Boil for 10 minutes. Test by putting a little in cold water, and pour on buttered tins. — (Mrs.) L. A. Barbour.

CHOCOLATE CARAMELS

Half pound sugar, 2 oz. grated chocolate, half teacup good cream, one teaspoon butter.

Boil gently and stir till it begins to leave the sides of the pan. Add vanilla. Pour into a buttered square tin. Cut into squares when cold. — Mrs. A. V. Morris.

CHOCOLATE FUDGE

Two and a half cups sugar, quarter pound butter, two teaspoons cocoa, half cup milk, vanilla.

Method.—Put milk and sugar on together in an enamelled saucepan. When the sugar is dissolved add the butter and cocoa. Cook gently for half an hour, then take off the fire. Add essence and beat it until it becomes thick. Have a buttered plate handy, pour the fudge on and leave until set. Then cut into little blocks.

— Miss O. Mawby, St. Peters.

Put two cups of sugar into saucepan with half a cup of milk and a small piece of butter. Add a tablespoon cocoa. Let boil for a quarter of an hour (with gas turned down low). Add cake crumbs and chopped up almonds—about three-quarters of a cup altogether. Bring to boil again and then take off and stir till fudge begins to thicken. Turn into buttered dish.

— Shirley Morris, Unley Park.

CHOCOLATE ROUGHS

Make a chocolate dip by breaking up ½ lb. of chocolate. Add to it 2 oz. cocoa butter and ¼ lb. icing sugar, and mix well. Put into a basin, stand in a saucepan of boiling water, and stir well, being careful it does not boil. To make the roughs, use the warm chocolate dip, adding enough desiccated coconut to make it quite stiff. Take a fork and lift the rough pieces on waxed paper.

CHOCOLATE CANDY

One lb. sugar, 2 tablespoons butter or margarine, a pinch salt, 2 tablespoons cocoa, a cup of milk, vanilla.

Place sugar, butter, cocoa, milk and salt in a saucepan. Stir over a low heat till the sugar is dissolved, then bring to the boil. Cook gently to soft ball stage (240° F.). When bubbles cease, add vanilla; cool slightly, then beat with a wooden spoon till thick and creamy. Pour into a well-buttered sandwich pan, and when cold mark in squares.

CREAM TOFFEE

Take equal quantities of cream and sugar. Boil together, adding a little essence of vanilla.

When it begins to thicken drop a little into cold water and feel whether it is hard, but not as hard as sugar toffee; if so, pour into flat buttered dish and cut when cool.

Take 1 lb. brown sugar, 1 oz. butter, half cup treacle, one gill cream, the white of one egg, one teaspoon vanilla. Butter an enamelled pan thickly over the inside, and put into it the brown sugar and treacle. Let them melt. Add the cream and the white of egg, whisked to a very stiff froth. Stir constantly, and let it boil as fast as it can for 20 minutes. Take the pan off the fire, add the vanilla, and turn all into a buttered dish to set. Some sugars need a little more boiling; so it is better to try the toffee before taking it off the fire. Put just a little drop into a cup of cold water; if it sets, it is done, but if it is still sticky it needs to be boiled for a few more minutes.

CREAM CARAMELS

One tin condensed milk, 4 oz. sugar, 2 oz. butter, one teaspoon vanilla.

Put sugar, butter and milk together. Boil 15 minutes, and stir in a double saucepan. Add vanilla when cooked. Pour on buttered plates. —Dorothy Sibley, Angaston.

COCONUT ICE

Take two cups of white sugar, half cup of milk, three-quarters of a cup of desiccated coconut.

Boil sugar and milk for five minutes, stirring all the time. Add coconut and boil one minute more. Remove from fire. Beat while cooling till it creams, then pour quickly into wet dish. Make a second layer and colour it with cochineal.

Three cups sugar, three-quarters cup milk, 4 oz. coconut.

Boil sugar and milk five minutes, stirring all the time. Remove from fire. Add coconut and a little more milk. Bring to the boil. Remove from fire, stir until white and thick. Pour half into buttered dish. Colour the remainder with cochineal.

—Mrs. F. J. Farrow, Tea Tree Gully.

FONDANT

One pound sugar, one small cup water, pinch of cream of tartar.

Method.—Boil sugar, water and cream of tartar for five to 20 minutes. Test by dropping small quantity into cold water. If it can be taken up in a soft ball, it is done. Pour into a bowl and leave until cool. Then beat briskly till it begins to thicken and turn white. Any flavouring may be used. — R. Forss.

Two cups sugar, a heaped tablespoon glucose, and a cup boiling water.

Method.—Boil sugar, glucose and water until done. Test by dropping small quantity into cold water. If it can be taken up in a soft ball it is done. Pour into bowl and leave until luke-warm, then stir thoroughly until thick and white. Knead like bread with the hands. Use any colouring and flavouring.

— R. Forss.

FRENCH JELLY

Soak two ounces of sheet gelatine in two cups of cold water for two or three hours. Put in a saucepan with two pounds of white sugar and half a cup of boiling water. Boil for five minutes, stirring all the time. Remove from fire and add two teaspoons of citric acid and two teaspoons of essence of lemon, and colour with cochineal. Pour in a buttered tin and let it stand for 24 hours. Cut with a wet knife. Must not boil after acid goes in.

— N. Newman. Wayville.

FRENCH JELLIES

One oz. gelatine, ½ pint cold water, 1 lb. sugar, flavouring.

Put half of water on gelatine and soak for ½ hour; put rest of water on sugar and soak for ½ hour. Then put together in pan and boil for 5 minutes; add flavouring and colour. Pour into wet dishes and leave until firm, cut into squares and roll in icing sugar. — T. E. Abbott.

FUDGE

One cup brown sugar, 1 cup white sugar, ½ cup milk, 2 table-spoons golden syrup, 1 dessertspoon butter, vanilla.

Melt the butter, add the syrup, sugar and milk. Stir over a slow heat until the sugars have dissolved. Then bring to the boil and boil to the soft ball stage (240° F.). Remove from the heat and when bubbling has ceased, add vanilla; beat until thick and creamy.

Pour into well buttered sandwich pan; cut into squares when cold.

GELATINE JUBES

Two ounces gelatine, two pounds white sugar, two teaspoons citric acid.

Soak gelatine in two and a half cups of water for one hour. Bring to boil, and boil for five minutes, stirring all the time. Take off fire and add citric acid and lemon essence. Colour half. Pour on slightly-buttered dish.

HONEY CANDY

Ingredients.—One cup honey, one cup sugar, one cup water, three dessertspoons powdered gelatine.

Method.—Put water and all ingredients in a saucepan and boil quarter of an hour, then pour into dishes that have been dipped in cold water, and when set cut into squares and roll in icing sugar. — (Miss) Queenie Bowering, Barker Street, Prospect.

MARSHMALLOWS

One level teacup sugar, one level tablespoon gelatine, few drops vanilla, barely three-quarters of a cup of hot water, pinch of salt. After the gelatine has soaked for five minutes in half the hot water, place the remaining water with the cup of sugar over the fire, and boil to 238 degrees or until a soft ball can be made in cold water. Add the gelatine and water, and leave till about cold. Beat after adding flavouring and salt till the mixture is thick and white, and pour into tin thickly dusted with icing sugar. When set, turn out and cut into cubes, rolling each piece in sifted icing sugar. If preferred, can be coloured pink and chopped nuts or dates can be added. Also makes a delicious filling and icing for sandwich cakes. — Miss B. Colliver.

MARSHMALLOWS

Four dessertspoons gelatine, 1 lb. sugar, 3 cups hot water, 2 teaspoons lemon juice. Soak the gelatine in 1½ cups water, boil the sugar in the remaining water for 10 minutes. Add the gelatine and boil for 20 minutes. Cool a little and flavour with lemon juice, turn into a bowl and beat until thick. Turn into flat dish and set. Cut into squares and roll in coconut.

— T. E. Abbott.

"THE GOOD LITTLE NORMEY"

Mix equal quantities of sultanas, currants and seeded lexias. Put through a mincer; roll into little balls and coat with desiccated coconut.

RUSSIAN TOFFEE

Three ounces butter, one cup sugar, two tablespoons golden syrup, one tin condensed milk, one teaspoon essence vanilla.

Melt butter. Add sugar and golden syrup. Stir till it boils, or about three minutes. Add milk and three tablespoons of ground nuts and boil about 15 minutes or till thick. Add vanilla and turn into a dish. When cool cut up in squares. You can roll them in paper if wished. — L. C. Weber.

A pound and a half sugar, one tin condensed milk, one cup milk, two ounces butter, vanilla and almonds.

Method.—Boil until it thickens, and stir well all the time from three-quarters of an hour to one hour and ten minutes. Chop almonds and add just before turning out.

— Miss O. Mawby, St. Peters.

TURKISH DELIGHT

One large cup boiling water, two large cups sugar, 1 oz. powdered gelatine, one saltspoon citric acid, cochineal for colouring and vanilla for flavouring.

Boil gelatine, sugar, acid and water together for 15 to 20 minutes, stirring well. Divide mixture and colour half with cochineal and flavour with vanilla. The other half keep white and flavour with essence of lemon. Grease flat dishes and pour on, using one dish for red and one for white. When cold, cut in squares and roll in icing sugar.

— (Miss) Queenie Bowering, Barker Street, Prospect.

Two ounces gelatine, two pounds sugar, colouring, one teaspoon citric acid, three or four drops essence lemon.

Soak two ounces gelatine in one cup of water for one hour. Place in a saucepan with two pounds sugar and one and a half cups boiling water. Boil for five minutes and stir in one teaspoon of citric acid, and boil briskly for a few seconds. Then place in dishes which have previously been filled with cold water. Add colouring as desired to each dish of mixture.

— B. D. Roberts, Keyneton.
— E. O. Sharman.

TOFFEE

Eight dessertspoons sugar, one dessertspoon of water and vinegar, half teaspoon butter.

Stir over the fire until brown. Pour into buttered patties.

— Elsie Anderson.

Two cups sugar, half cup water, one teaspoon cream of tartar.

Stir well, then boil quickly without stirring about 10 to 15 minutes. (Try it in water.) Put in blanched almonds about two minutes before removing from fire. Pour into well-greased tins. For fruit toffee any desired fruit may be put in the tins before pouring out the toffee. Currants, sultanas and ginger are very good. — Mrs. Harry Arbon, Clarence Park.

One pound white sugar, quarter teaspoon cream of tartar, 2 oz. almonds or nuts, quarter pint of water.

Method.—Warm it till sugar is dissolved (stir). When boiling add cream of tartar (dissolved in two teaspoons of cold water). Boil for five minutes with lid on. Take lid off. Boil till sugar has become a pale gold (about 20 minutes). Test a little in cold water. Butter saucepan before using. Turn into buttered plates or pastry tins. — V. G. Schultz.

Two pounds sugar, two tablespoons vinegar, ¼ lb. butter, four tablespoons golden syrup, four tablespoons cream, ¼ lb. almonds.

Boil for 15 minutes or half an hour. Stir all the time.

— Mrs. W. Dickson.

WALNUT OR ALMOND CREAMS

Two cups of sugar, half cup of milk, few drops essence of vanilla.

Method.—Boil milk and sugar in an enamel saucepan from four to six minutes, stirring all the time. (Count time from when it commenced to boil.) Take off the fire, add the essence, and beat well. Form into little balls the size of the nut. Blanch and dry the nuts, then press them well into the cream. Set them near an open window to dry. The cream may be coloured with carmine if liked. — Dulcie Besanko, Clarence Park.

PEANUT BRITTLE

Two pounds loaf sugar, half teaspoon cream of tartar, half pint of cold water.

Method.—Boil all together about a quarter of an hour or more, until it just turns slightly yellow (don't stir). Then add half a pound of split peanuts. Boil until pale brown. Turn out on greased tins to cool and harden. — R. Forss.

INVALID COOKERY

INVALID COOKERY

BARLEY WATER

Into a pint and a half of fast boiling water put one pinch of salt and three tablespoons of barley kernels. Boil rapidly for four minutes. Strain and flavour with sugar and lemon.

Note.—Barley kernels do not require to be washed or blanched.

CUP OF CORNFLOUR OR ARROWROOT

Half pint milk, one pinch salt, one teaspoon sugar, one dessert-spoon arrowroot or cornflour.

Blend the arrowroot or cornflour with a little of the milk, and put rest of milk on to boil. Add the blended arrowroot off the fire. Boil three minutes, add the sugar. Serve in a small bowl or cup and sprinkle nutmeg over the top.

CUP OF GRUEL

One tablespoon oatmeal, quarter teaspoon salt, half pint milk, one teaspoon sugar, one teaspoon butter.

Soak the oatmeal and milk for half an hour, and strain. Put milk in a saucepan, stir till it boils, simmer 10 minutes. Add the sugar, butter and nutmeg if allowed.

STANDARD BEEF TEA

Half pound lean juicy beef, half pint water, salt if allowed.

Wipe the meat with a damp cloth. Remove skin, gristle and fat. Shred with a knife against the grain. Put into a jar or double boiler saucepan with salt and water. Cover, and let stand for half an hour to draw out juices. Place jar in a saucepan of cold water and bring slowly to the boil. Simmer for two or three hours. Stir and squeeze well. Strain through a coarse strainer and remove fat.

QUICKLY-MADE BEEF TEA

Half pound lean juicy meat, half pint water, salt if allowed.

Prepare meat as for Standard Beef Tea. Place in a saucepan with salt and water, and allow to stand half an hour. Squeeze and stir well. Heat over a slow fire till a pale brown colour, stirring and pressing well with the back of a wooden spoon. Strain through a coarse strainer.

TREACLE POSSET (For a Cold)

Half pint milk, two tablespoons treacle.

Put milk on to boil, stir in treacle, and continue stirring till milk curdles. Strain through muslin, and serve the liquid very hot. Should be taken in bed.

RAW BEEF TEA

Half gill water, 2 oz. meat.

Prepare meat as for Standard Beef Tea. Add the water and let stand for an hour. Squeeze well and strain.

BEEF TEA CUSTARD

One gill beef tea, one egg, salt and pepper if allowed.

Beat egg and add beef tea and flavouring. Pour into a greased cup or mould, cover with greased paper. Steam gently till set—15 to 20 minutes.

BOILED SAGO

One dessertspoon sago, half pint milk, one teaspoon sugar.

Wash sago in three waters. Cover with water and leave for half an hour. Cook in the milk till sago is clear. Add sugar, and serve hot.

CHICKEN BROTH

One chicken, one quart water, salt and pepper.

Cut chicken into pieces and put in a saucepan with water, salt and pepper. Simmer for three or four hours; strain and remove fat. If liked, a little rice may be added to broth when reheating.

DRINK FOR INVALIDS

Three ounces rice, 1 oz. sugar, one tablespoon of raspberry or other flavouring.

Wash rice. Boil in three pints of water till reduced to one quart. Strain off, sweeten and flavour with essence.

MILK JELLY

Half pint milk, 1 level dessertspoon powdered gelatine, 2-3 teaspoons sugar; a piece of thinly peeled lemon rind.

Put the milk, gelatine, sugar and lemon rind in a saucepan. Heat gently until the gelatine is dissolved, stirring all the time. Strain into a basin and stir occasionally so that the cream is mixed in. When cold put into small moulds which have been rinsed in cold water. When set, turn out and decorate.

— A. L. Sharman, Black Forest.

FRICASSEED BRAINS

One set brains, 2 teaspoons butter, ½ oz. flour, a pinch salt, ¼ pint milk.

Put the brains into cold water, leave soaking in cold, salted water for 1 hour. Blanch by putting them into cold water and bringing to the boil. Strain, then cook in boiling water with a little salt for 7-10 minutes. Drain and cut into small pieces. Melt the butter in a saucepan, remove from the stove, add the flour, and stir with a wooden spoon till smooth. Add all the milk. Stir over a slow heat till boiling. Boil 3 minutes, add salt and a little pepper (if allowed). Add the brains, cook a few minutes longer to make thoroughly hot.

Serve on a round of toast, dry or buttered, and sprinkle with finely chopped parsley. — A. L. Sharman, Black Forest

FRICASSEED BRAINS

One set brains, one teaspoon butter, one teaspoon flour, one-eighth teaspoon salt, a gill and a half milk.

Remove skin from brains and soak in salted water for half an hour. Blanch by putting into cold water and bringing to the boil. Melt the butter in a saucepan, stir in the flour, and when smooth add gradually the milk. Boil three minutes. Cut the brains in neat pieces and heat in the sauce. Add chopped parsley. Serve on a hot plate with snippets of toast.

EGG FLIP

One fresh egg, one teaspoon sugar, one gill milk, flavouring.

Separate the white from the yolk, and beat stiffly. Add milk, sugar and flavouring to the yolk, and beat well. Add the stiffly-beaten white and mix well before serving.

LEMONADE

One lemon, 1 oz. loaf sugar, one pint boiling water.

Wash the lemon and peel thinly; rub rind with sugar. Put in a jug and pour on the pint of boiling water and the strained lemon juice. Cover and strain when cold.

LIGHT BREAD PUDDING

Half pint milk, one egg, one tablespoon bread crumbs, one dessertspoon sugar.

Put bread crumbs in a basin, pour on the hot milk. Add sugar and yolk of egg. Beat white of egg stiffly and fold in lightly. Pour into a greased pie-dish. Bake in a slow oven till set—10 to 15 minutes.

In an Electric Cooker bake at 450°.

MUTTON BROTH

Half pound leg chops, one pint cold water, half teaspoon salt, one dessertspoon rice or pearl barley.

Wipe the meat, remove fat, put in a saucepan with the salt and water. Simmer for two or three hours. Strain, return to saucepan, add the washed rice or barley and boil for 20 minutes. Remove fat.

STEAMED CUSTARD

One egg, one teaspoon sugar, quarter pint of milk, flavouring.

Beat the egg well and other ingredients. Pour into greased cups or moulds, cover with greased paper. Steam for 15 to 20 minutes.

STEAMED FISH

Fillet and skin a whiting, wash and dry. Rub over with lemon juice and sprinkle lightly with salt. Place between two buttered plates and steam over a saucepan of boiling water till done—15 to 20 minutes. Serve on a hot plate, and pour over any liquid.

CULINARY HINTS

1. To remove scale from citrus fruit skins, rub with a nylon mit. Rinse well.

2. For frying without fat, place meat in a pan in which a teaspoon of salt has been heated.

3. Wrap different foods in aluminium foil when cooking in an electric frypan, to prevent interchange of flavours.

4. To prevent sponge cakes from sticking, grease or oil the tin and dust with equal parts of cornflour and castor sugar.

5. When chopping sticky ingredients (e.g. suet or raisins), sprinkle with some of the measured flour. They will not then "clog."

6. If cheese is too fresh for fine grating, either vitamize or rub through a sieve, using a wooden spoon.

7. **Egg-cooking hints**

   (i) When hard-boiling eggs roll them round with a wooden spoon in water deep enough to cover, until boiling, to keep the yolk in the centre. Immerse in cold water immediately to prevent dark ring forming around yolk. Egg rings can be used for garnishing, or segments on a mixed salad or savoury platters.

   (ii) Salt in the water helps eggs to set more quickly when boiling or poaching.

   (iii) Vinegar added to water (1 dessertspoon per egg) prevents aluminium saucepans from discolouring. It also helps eggs to set when poaching.

   (iv) Egg spoons will lose dark stains if placed in the hot water in which the eggs were boiled.

   (v) If eggs are stored in the refrigerator, remove some time before using.

8. **Salad-making hints**

   (i) Lettuces should be bought crisp and stored in a crisper dish in the refrigerator. To separate leaves, remove the centre stalk and hold under running water.

   (ii) Tear lettuce leaves for tossed salads.

(iii) Lemon juice sprinkled over "white" fruits (e.g. apples, pears, bananas) will prevent discolouration.

(iv) To curl salad vegetables, slice and place in iced water an hour before use. Celery and radishes open up in iced water.

(v) Tomatoes can be peeled more readily if first dropped in boiling water.

9. Roast potatoes may be boiled for a few minutes and then placed in hot fat.

10. Marinade meats for better flavour. Equal parts of oil and wine or vinegar, with chopped herbs and spices, and a little chopped onion or garlic if liked—makes a good marinade. Meat for grills, kebabs, and cold-meat dishes benefit.

11. If a saucepan is burnt, pour in a thin film of full strength detergent. After soaking for a short time, wash as usual.

LAUNDRY AND DRY CLEANING HINTS

STAIN REMOVAL

Treat stains promptly, try mild measures first and rinse thoroughly to remove reagents.

1. **Ball-Point Pen Ink.**—Pour a little methylated spirits over the stain, stretching the material over a bowl. If the dye is not fast, the methylated spirits may remove the colour.
2. **Blood.**—Put a teaspoon of salt in cold water and soak the stained material. A piece of damp starch rubbed on the spot will remove any stain remaining.
3. **Chocolate.**—Put a little borax in warm water and sponge the spot. Then sponge with carbon tetrachloride.
4. **Coffee.**—Put a little borax in warm water and sponge the stain.
5. **Dye.**—Mix equal parts of household ammonia and methylated spirits, and in it wash the material. This can only be applied to white and fast dye materials.
6. **Fruit Stains.**—Treat as soon as possible. Once dry they are hard to remove. Boiling water (if the material will stand it) or even warm water will remove most fresh fruit stains. Do not use soap as this tends to set the stain. White cottons and linens can be bleached if any stain remains.
7. **Grass.**—Sponge the mark with methylated spirits.

   On silks and woollens, sponge the stain with warm water, then apply glycerine, rub between hands and leave for one hour. Apply a few drops of vinegar, leave for a few minutes and rinse well in warm water.
8. **Grease.**—A grease solvent such as carbon tetrachloride is effective, so also is petrol.
9. **Ice Cream.**—Use warm water, and then sponge with carbon tetrachloride.
10. **Ink.**—If fresh wash out with cold water. **Blue ink:** sponge or dip stain in equal quantities of methylated spirits and household ammonia (test on coloured fabrics first). Rinse in warm water. Remove any remaining mark by dipping in bleach and rinsing well afterwards.

    Red Ink: Usually washes out quite well if it is rinsed in cold water first and then washed in the usual way.

11. **Iodine.**—(i) Wet stain with a solution of 1 oz. Hypo (obtainable from chemist) dissolved in half a cup of water. Stain should disappear at once. (ii) Iodine stains will disappear by the morning if the article is left in water in which has been stirred common mustard. Repeat the process if the stain is an old one.

12. **Jam.**—Sponge the stain with warm water.

13. **Lipstick.**—Sponge the mark with carbon tetrachloride.

14. **Milk.**—First sponge with warm water, and follow this treatment with a grease solvent.

15. **Paint.**—Soften the paint by soaking in turpentine, and then rub the spot with a cloth that has been dampened with cloudy ammonia. So called plastic paints, when fresh, wash out with cold water. If allowed to set are virtually impossible to remove.

16. **Perspiration.**—Use warm water to sponge the stain, and then follow with methylated spirits. Unwashable garments—apply a paste of 1 tablespoon cream of tartar, 3 crushed aspirins and warm water. Leave for twenty minutes. Rinse well in warm water. Repeat if necessary. Follow this with vinegar and water to restore the colour if necessary.

17. **Rainspots.**—Steam the article over boiling water, and while it is still damp press with a warm iron.

18. **Rust.**—To remove the stain from white material rub with juice of a lemon and some salt, then place article in sunlight. If rust has not disappeared, repeat. It may be necessary to rinse out the lemon and salt between each application. This method is much cheaper than salts of lemon and quite as effective. Commercial bleaches may be used.

19. **Scorch.**—Light scorch marks on any fabric (test colours first) may be treated by sponging with dilute hydrogen peroxide to which a few drops of household ammonia have been added. Rinse well in warm water.

20. **Tea.**—Treat as for coffee. If old or obstinate stain on white cottons or linen use a commercial bleach.

21. **Water.**—Same treatment as rainspots.

22. **Wine.**—Wash in cold water and ammonia.

Metric Conversion Table

Note: The conversions given below are rounded to the nearest whole figure for ease of use. Whichever system you choose, the important thing to remember is to be consistent and keep the balance the same between the ingredients within the recipe. If you convert all the ingredients in the recipe using these tables you will end up with the same proportions as you would if you followed the recipe using the imperial measurements.
For oven temperature conversions see page 54A.

DRY MEASURES

16 ounces (oz.) = 1 pound (lb.)

1,000 grams (g.) = 1 kilogram (kg.)

OZ.	GRAMS
1	30
2	60
3	90
4	120
5	150
6	180
7	210
8 (½ lb.)	240
9	270
10	300
11	330
12	360
13	390
14	420
15	450
16 (1 lb.)	480

LIQUID MEASURES

1 cup = 8 fluid ounces (fl. oz.)
or 227 millilitres (ml.)

CUPS	FL. OZ.	ML.
¼	2	60
⅓	3	90
½	4	120
⅔	5	150
¾	6	180
1	8	240
1½ (½ pint)	10	300
3 (1 pint)	20	600
6 (1 quart)	40	1200

USEFUL CONVERSIONS

¼ teaspoon	1.25 ml.
½ teaspoon	2.5 ml.
1 teaspoon	5 ml.
1 dessertspoon	12.5 ml.
1 tablespoon	20 ml. (4 teaspoons)
1 UK/US tablespoon	15 ml. (3 teaspoons)

Butter/Shortening		
1 tablespoon	½ oz.	15 g.
1½ tablespoon	¾ oz.	20 g.
2 tablespoons	1 oz.	30 g.
3 tablespoons	1½ oz.	50 g.

First compiled 1923

First published in this format 1960
Forty-first impression 1985
Reprinted 1987, 1989, 1990, 1991, 1993, 1994, 1995, 1996, 1997
by Landsdowne Publishing Pty Ltd

75th Anniversary Edition 1999
Reprinted by New Holland Publishers

100th Anniversary Edition 2024
Reprinted by New Holland Publishers

A CIP record of this title is available from the National Library of Australia.

ISBN 9781864367164 (PB)
ISBN 9781742573748 (HB)

Managing Director: Fiona Schultz
General Manager/Publisher: Olga Dementiev
Production Director: Arlene Gippert
Printed in China

Keep up with New Holland Publishers:

NewHollandPublishers
@newhollandpublishers